D0122460

CHOOSING A COUNSELLING OR PSYCHOTHERAPY TRAINING

A practical guide

sylvie k. schapira

London and New York

First published 2000
by Routledge
11 New Fetter Lane, London EC4P 4EE

Simultaneously published in the USA and Canada
by Routledge
29 West 35th Street, New York, NY 10001

Routledge is an imprint of the Taylor & Francis Group

© 2000 sylvie k. schapira

Typeset in Times by Keystroke, Jacaranda Lodge, Wolverhampton
Printed and bound in Great Britain by MPG Books Ltd, Bodmin

British Library Cataloguing in Publication Data
A catalogue record for this book is available from the British Library

Library of Congress Cataloguing in Publication Data
A catalogue record for this book has been requested

ISBN 0–415–20846–7

TO THE MEMORY OF MY
BROTHER TONY

To go in search for knowledge and learning is to search for one's self.

CONTENTS

CONTENTS

ACKNOWLEDGEMENTS

I would like to acknowledge and thank some special people: Doreen White, Andy Jarvie and Dr Harry Schapira for their time and efforts in reading the manuscript, and for their valuable comments. My thanks also to Katherine Byrne for the checking she did, and to Lynda Graham. I should like to thank my children, Maya and Anton, for their well-timed contributions, and to my husband Daniel for his patience, loving support and computer expertise.

The idea for this book came from the experiences of my own training and working with trainees on courses and supervisees over the years.

INTRODUCTION

The Second World War changed our society, our beliefs and moral values; and the changes have accelerated over the past three decades. As a consequence, attitudes towards religion, men and women, marriage and the family, have been severely jolted and forced to shift.

RELIGION

Religion was the traditional containment for people's spiritual and existential pain. A place of healing. The impact of the effects of a world war on so many people has caused us to question the role of religion. There have not been any answers, but there has been disenchantment with Judaeo-Christian teaching.

As people have turned away from religion, so counselling and psychotherapy have become a replacement: an inner searching. The need for spiritual healing has not decreased, but for many people going to a spiritual leader seems no longer a choice. The idea that God will resolve human pain has lost its potency. Trying to make meaning of life and suffering is seen by many as an inner, personal journey, a part of a cultural revolution that has become disconnected from religion.

CHANGING ROLES OF MEN AND WOMEN

The feminist movement has been instrumental in making society look questioningly at the traditional roles for men and women. These roles, together with our expectations of ourselves, have changed radically. Role models and messages that have been passed on to us are being redefined and adapted to the fast-changing world we live in. Nowhere is

1

this more apparent than in the therapy room. We need to be flexible to cope with changes in the ways that we relate, live and work. Flexibility is a healthy response to living.

FAMILIES

Many young people are rejecting marriage and redefining the ways of living together. The family has redefined itself, and the nuclear-style family is just one of a number of definitions. The concept of a family has expanded to include lesbian and gay families, single-parent families, stepfamilies and multi-layered stepfamilies. There are waves of changes in the ways in which we choose to live and interact within these different family groups and communally.

Science is taking over from nature with fertility treatment that leads to multiple births. Women are choosing to have children in their mid-forties and older; challenging the traditional ages of parenting and grandparenting.

DEATH

People are living longer, raising the question of whether one has the right to choose one's own time of death. Through the acceleration of technology we are faced with moral dilemmas about euthanasia and abortion, and feel unsure and perplexed about our decisions.

WHY PEOPLE TURN TO COUNSELLING AND PSYCHOTHERAPY

Any changes, like any revolution, bring about difficulties before there is an acceptance or a status quo. The process of change is also the process of transition and adjustment. For many people this uncomfortable period is just the time when they may seek outside help for themselves.

How does counselling and psychotherapy fit into this great kaleido-scope of values and roles?

The essence of counselling and psychotherapy is to try to get to some middle ground. Moderation or balance resonates with this understand-ing. There is some common-sense idea about this, when we consider that neuroses and mental illness are gradients along a continuum and that therapy is a healing of psychic pain so that we can regain equilibrium in our lives.

The problem is that humans are in a state of constant paradox or dilemma. One part of ourselves seeks to grow towards health, is robust and spontaneous, whilst the other part pulls us back to our safety zone or familiar ways of doing things when we feel hurt. Usually those familiar ways are reactions or defences of armour-plated protectiveness. When we realise that we can see no way out, it is then that we usually seek help. Looking for support is usually the first step towards helping ourselves.

If counselling and psychotherapy are about healing human despair, then the advent of counselling and the availability of psychotherapy to a growing number of people reflects the changes in society.

Counselling and psychotherapy have replaced the cushioning of the extended family and the solace of religion. We turn to trained people for help with our relationship difficulties. We also turn to these professions in ever greater numbers for the difficulties of being with ourselves.

INTOLERANCE TO DIFFERENCES

We have still not learnt one of the most important lessons of the last war: to understand where prejudice and racism can lead. Homosexuals are still vilified, just for their sexuality; foreigners are still killed for being foreign. We still have problems with tolerating the differences of others. Perhaps counselling and psychotherapy can be seen as society's safety valves: a place for working through our own personal injuries, so that we can learn not to project our inner pain onto others. In the process, we can learn to tolerate the 'otherness' in ourselves. Counselling and psychotherapy offer the human tools of learning how to accept and integrate the intolerance within ourselves.

Those tools are acquired patiently, through learning, experience and self-development. These are the ingredients of training courses.

WHAT THIS BOOK IS ABOUT

The intention of this book is that it should be a valuable guide to individuals who are thinking about training in either counselling or psychotherapy but do not know where to begin. Like so many people coming to a crossroad on a journey, it is difficult to know which path to take when you don't have much idea of where you are going, or what the place is like until you get there.

The jargon and mystique involved in both professions are bewildering, as is the volume of information available. Clarification is needed for those new to the world of counselling and therapy. The purpose of this book is to assist that process.

The book is also intended to be beneficial to organisations wishing to send staff onto training courses, to learn skills that will enhance their employees' existing work. Counselling skills are of enormous importance in improving communications and relationships.

The book is a valuable resource for libraries, careers advisory services and higher education centres. The feedback that is offered in this book to training centres is intended to help with the effectiveness of their training. This in turn will benefit everyone: the trainees, the tutors and the courses, eventually affecting clients, who are the people who turn to counsellors and psychotherapists.

For trainees who are already studying on a short course or at certificate level, the information in this book may save much agonising over which training to pursue next, and whether it will help in the kind of work or study setting wanted. Trainees may not know the kind of setting which attracts them, but reading this book is also intended to assist along that path.

Counselling and psychotherapy are constantly evolving and developing. More rigorous standards and policies are being implemented by organisations such as the British Association for Counselling (BAC) to ensure that training institutions will improve the quality of their courses. The aims of such organisations are to ensure that trainees become competent practitioners. Because quality must be the aim, this often means increasing training fees and the length of courses to deepen or broaden the training.

Changes in training also need to reflect the demands of the public, who are becoming more knowledgeable about the services that are offered, and their rights as the recipients of health care. As the public gain more information so they become more discriminating. Service providers have to adapt to these changes, which will affect what they offer.

There is a swing towards time-limited counselling and psychotherapy being offered by the National Health Service, and in many organisations in industry and commerce, for reasons of limited resources and cost efficiency. Yet courses in general do not yet offer this training. The training is very specific and institutions need to be aware of what is demanded in the public arena.

The information in this book outlines the kind of courses available and what they offer. There is some practical advice on the questions that can be raised in assessment interviews before applying for courses.

The book is not intended to identify or evaluate any particular training institute. Where training institutes are mentioned by name it is because I am indicating, within the context of the chapter, specialised courses that they offer.

The formal type of counselling training in this country generally aims to equip a counsellor with specific skills, amongst which are the ability to listen to a client, not to judge or give advice, to respect and empathise with a client. Depending on the model of counselling, counsellors see the client as the 'expert' in their own life and not the counsellor. Training in counselling is more than a set of skills, however, it is understanding a process over time.

COUNSELLING AND PSYCHOTHERAPY

It was Carl Rogers who described counselling as the 'new' psychotherapy. Whether there is a difference between counselling and psychotherapy is an ongoing debate within the profession, which I discuss in Chapter 1.

There is no doubt that counselling has a mixed reputation in the media. What has tended to bring counselling into controversy are the people who call themselves counsellors but who are ill-trained and do not practise to any code of ethics, thus bringing the profession into disrepute. The same can be said for training courses that spring up without reputable accreditation and turn out trainees who are incompetent and barely skilled.

As a trainer, I believe in improving the standards of training in order to produce competent practitioners. As a counsellor and psychotherapist I know how important good training is to my own competence. I hope that this book will contribute towards an understanding of the need for high standards of training in both counselling and psychotherapy.

UNIFYING TERMS FOR CLARITY

In spite of the continuing debate over the word 'therapist' – whether it refers to a psychotherapist and to none other – I have mainly chosen to use the term 'practitioner' in the book. Where I have also used the word 'therapist', I mean either a counsellor or a psychotherapist. I use the word 'therapy' for what takes place in counselling and psychotherapy sessions. I refer to 'trainee' rather than 'student' as the individual on a counselling or psychotherapy course. When talking about someone on a master's degree training, I refer to 'student'.

It becomes more difficult to keep continuity when speaking of 'patient' or 'client', and I have opted for 'patient' when referring to people who are in psychoanalytic psychotherapy, and 'client' for people who are in other forms of therapy.

I have chosen to use the word 'she' when referring to a practitioner, rather than the inelegant 'he/she'. For the person who comes for therapy, I write 'he' to keep clarity. I refer to tutors as 'she' and trainees as 'he' when speaking about them collectively, but if I am speaking about trainees in general, I have used 'she'. These gender terms are in no way meant to represent any bias other than to retain clarity by unifying the pronouns.

THE CHAPTER CONTENTS

Chapter 1, 'An Overview to the Field', offers brief explanations of some of the many professional and non-professional roles that have some relation to counselling and psychotherapy. A definition of counselling and psychotherapy, the similarities and differences between counselling and psychotherapy, confidentiality, and supervision are included.

Chapters 2, 'Theoretical Approaches: Background and Description', 3, 'Towards Humanistic Therapy', and 4, 'Towards Cognitive-Behavioural Therapies', give some explanation of the theoretical approaches there are in the profession; it is beyond the scope of this book to list all the different approaches that exist at present as there are more than 400. Some explanation of the major approaches is offered to show the range and diversity.

I have chosen to outline the stories of some of the early pioneers who devoted their lives to their theories. The sketches of their theories cannot give more than a flavour of such monumental works, but I hope that they will whet your appetite to want to read more. Whilst these chapters set out to show the structures of differing theories, it is well to remember that they all have a common purpose: they are all models or ways of approaching the question of human suffering.

Consideration about the nature and particular theory is important to each person before they embark on training. Having some understanding of the differences between, for example, psychoanalysis and humanistic therapy, is a place to begin.

Reflecting on your own personality and the attraction of the approaches described will help you to decide which approach may suit you. Taking a short introduction in the course you feel may be right for you will then either confirm your decision or help you to reconsider.

Chapter 5, 'Thinking of Becoming a Counsellor or Psychotherapist?' helps you to consider why you want to train. There is a lengthy critique of counselling and psychotherapy from within and outside the professions. This is all aimed at raising your awareness of what is happening in the counselling and psychotherapy world. Having information will help you make more discerning choices. Included in this chapter is a flavour of what happens in two therapy sessions from two different therapeutic perspectives.

Chapter 6, 'Preparation for Starting a Course', considers how we learn and why it is important to make a shift from the way most of us learned as children. Being curious and asking questions are as fundamental to effective learning as to effective counselling and psychotherapy.

There is now an overwhelming number of courses (and the number is growing), and it can be difficult to understand the content of courses. Brochures help, but may not satisfy every individual's questions – especially if the reader is unfamiliar with the terminology or the profession. Apart from the information in a brochure, it may not always be a simple matter to appreciate the details of the training at the initial interview.

Some of the known grievances about courses will be mentioned throughout the book, to enable applicants to consider the questions that they may want to ask at an interview. The responses to those questions may help to assess suitability of a course.

In Chapter 7, 'What to Expect on a Course: Introduction, Certificate and Diploma', I set out the types and content of courses, including study and practice time involved. I refer to the hidden extra hours and costs that need to be checked out, such as weekend training that can be added to a course, external supervision, personal therapy and clinical practice placements.

Without an understanding of what a course entails, many people may be disappointed with the reality of the training and leave the course. I have heard course organisers call this fall-out 'natural self-selection'. It may be, however, that the individual was ill-suited to the course at the beginning, *or the other way round*. It is also likely that applicants did not give enough consideration to their needs before the course, or did not have sufficient information to make an informed choice.

There is also the problem that interviewers did not assess the suitability of applicants appropriately. Inadequate assessments and competitive commercial pressures to enrol participants can cause mismatch of expectations and requirements between trainees and courses.

It is becoming more common for training centres that used to run a two-year diploma training to now increase it to three or four. This is a step towards a more thorough training for the profession. Three or four years (or more if one proceeds onto a master's level), may feel like a long-term investment. If someone is not satisfied with the training, it could be three or four years too long.

There are courses that have an excellent reputation and integrity, with trained and experienced tutors providing adequate support and high standards of theoretical and practical experiences, and there are other courses. How is a prospective trainee to know the difference between those courses that are reputable and those that are not? Regrettably, there are many courses that do not give satisfaction. How is someone to know how to avoid those courses that are badly managed, provide inadequate training, and do not fulfil their responsibilities as effective learning centres? How can someone avoid those courses that do not reflect the ethos and philosophy of counselling and psychotherapy?

Reading this book is intended to reduce the negative possibilities. Using the list of suggested questions that you will find in the book should help you to gain the information that you need. From reading each chapter, you may think of other questions that you could ask. The important thing is to ask. Having as much information as possible will help you before you commit to a lengthy period of study and a large investment of time and money.

It is important to know at the outset that your investment will not end with training: the training is ongoing in terms of reading current, relevant journals and books, participating in workshops, conferences and seminars, maintaining regular consultancy or supervision, and being in personal therapy.

Chapter 8, 'Qualifications, Registration, Accreditation and Research', gives an explanation of what the qualifications are and their meaning. An explanation, reasons and requirements for accreditation and registration are discussed. In particular the British Association of Counselling accreditation and the United Kingdom Council of Psychotherapists' procedures for registration are given.

Readers are advised that some courses advertise in their brochures that they are applying for accreditation, which is highly suspect because they may not actually manage to get it by the time the trainee has completed the course.

Research is relevant to the profession of counselling and psycho-therapy. Some of the mystique about research is explained in this chapter. The gains to the professional are outlined, pointing out the academic path that can be taken and why this is helpful.

Assessing the tutor and supervisor support is fundamental to all trainees. Knowing the accessibility and support of the staff is important at all levels of study, and becomes even more essential when studying at a master's level, which can be a lonely period of study.

Chapter 9 deals with 'Other Forms of Therapy and Specialised Training'. The specific subjects considered are integrative therapy, group, family, couple, psychosexual, intercultural, bereavement and post-traumatic stress disorder training.

I urge that training courses include intercultural counselling as a relevant aspect of any general training. There is also a need for specialised training in this subject as well as in the others listed.

Chapter 10 looks at 'Careers in Therapy'. It is useful to consider the kinds of jobs that are available and to see which therapeutic approaches might be a requirement of the job. Certain psychotherapy practice in hospital units, for example, may require a cognitive-behavioural or psychodynamic approach. There are posts that require particular approaches and experience. Having some idea of these requirements may help you to choose the type of training you need.

Suggestions are made as to where to look for work. The pros and cons of private practice are discussed.

FURTHER READING LIST

At the end of most chapters is a suggested further reading list. The further reading list gives an indication of the kinds of books that are available to help you have more understanding before you decide on your chosen approach.

I would recommend that you look for the books in libraries or second-hand bookshops first, unless you are unconcerned about the financial aspect. Courses generally give out long reading lists, and many of the theoretical textbooks are expensive. There are a number of bookshops now buying graduates' books and reselling relatively cheaply to trainees, which is a practical solution. The costs involved in the training are high and continuous for some years.

At the end of the book there is a 'List of Resources'. This list contains some of the training institutions. There is a list of some organisations and associations that you may wish to join. There is also a list of relevant journals and magazines. Some journals start up but fall by the wayside. If I have entered the details of such journals, it is regrettable but inevitable.

There is a glossary of commonly used terms in the profession, as therapy tends to be full of terminology. An attempt has been made to keep the specific vocabulary to a minimum within the book itself.

In the Appendices are my own contracts that I give to clients and to supervisees (therapists in supervision).

AND FINALLY . . .

Counselling and psychotherapy are very special professions. They are amongst the highest of the human services, since they offer the potential and possibility of so much healing, support and care to individuals who are suffering.

People who are drawn to this work are generally compassionate people who have the deep desire to work with others in this way. Very often, however, the same individuals who are so good at giving to others are not so good at giving to themselves. Being in personal therapy is the greatest self-learning. Self-learning is ongoing and continuous throughout all the stages of life, and it is right that courses require trainees to undergo their own therapy.

The theory and practical learning on a training course can be a rewarding and deeply satisfying experience. Unexpected experiences occurring on a course are often the most potent. It is all part of self-discovery. In the writing of this book I too have discovered that the most valuable learning was the unexpected.

After reading this book you should have a better understanding of the field before making a commitment to a course. Counselling and psychotherapy are all about commitment, both for clients and practitioners. This level of commitment maintains and develops the efficacy and competence of the practitioner. I hope that this book will aid you on your journey of self-discovery.

FURTHER READING

Rogers, C. (1942) *Counselling and Psychotherapy*, Boston, Mass.: Houghton Mifflin.

1

AN OVERVIEW TO THE FIELD

If counselling and psychotherapy are new fields to you, there may be a number of questions that you have regarding the different aspects of counselling, psychotherapy and other related domains. Even if the subjects are not new to you, you may wonder about the differences between psychology and psychiatry, for example, and how they compare with counselling and psychotherapy. The next few pages will introduce you to the variety of roles related to counselling and psychotherapy.

Fundamental to counselling and psychotherapy practice is the use of specific communication skills, details of which follow.

COUNSELLING SKILLS

Counselling skills are techniques and strategies in communications that are useful in virtually all human interactions, and can be acquired by almost everyone. People in many professions, such as debt advisers, those in education, social work, management, nursing, teaching, personnel and welfare, the police, the clergy, the medical profession, the voluntary caring services, etc., may automatically employ some of the skills, often without being consciously aware that they are using them. There may be several million people who use counselling skills within their existing jobs. *The Sunday Times* (26.9.93) estimated the figure to be 2.5 million.

People in management and the personnel departments of industry and business, who are trained specifically, find that counselling skills enhance their interactions and relationships with others. The skills that they are trained in may be labelled 'effective communication skills', 'how to deal with difficult people' or 'communications enhancement', but it is the same thing when it comes to improving interaction between people. In short, human relationships can benefit from training in these skills.

VOLUNTARY COUNSELLING

There is a strong tradition in Britain of voluntary work, which has become part of the national web of support and aid. There are very many people in this country who give their time generously to the support and care of others who are vulnerable and in need. An estimated 270,000 voluntary counsellors are employed in a variety of organisations. Voluntary counsellors are usually trained by the organisation where they are working. As awareness and expectations of counselling have grown and developed, so too have training standards.

Voluntary agencies offer free or low-paid counselling to an ever-wider public. Like paid agencies, they are increasingly being evaluated for effectiveness. Rigorous assessments are frequently required to become a volunteer with some agencies, and ongoing training and super-vision is offered to improve standards. These standards are required to work with young people in voluntary agencies, Relate (marital and relationship difficulties), Drop-In agencies (time-limited counselling, as well as youth counselling), CRUSE (bereavement counselling), Rape Crises, and MIND (working with mental health). These are all examples of charitable organisations that have enlisted the help of volunteers, whilst doing their best to ensure that the volunteers receive training according to the resources of the organisation.

Training and working in a volunteer capacity can help you see whether you like working in this way with people, and would want to proceed to a more formal, lengthy and disciplined training in counselling. You could choose to learn some counselling skills first, through an Adult Education Centre or a short introductory course.

BEFRIENDING

Befriending is informal and voluntary. Boundaries of time, setting or relationship are not defined as in the more formal setting of counselling. There is no contract to do a piece of counselling work. Befrienders (sometimes called Buddies) may take out their 'friends', or both may visit each other's homes. The Befrienders may spend 10 minutes or a whole day with the friend. The Befriender may invite the friend to dinner, do their shopping or drive them to an appointment; in short, support them in a number of different ways. Befrienders need to have empathy for the people they are helping, and learn some counselling skills to enable them to listen, without rescuing or plying the friend with well-intentioned advice.

The Befriending service is seen as an important and valuable part of a support network that surrounds those who are vulnerable. There are many people who benefit from being befriended: people with HIV and AIDS, people who are bed-ridden, the elderly, the disabled, young people in hostels or living on their own, those who are mentally ill, people who are bereaved and alone. The list and the needs are endless.

TELEPHONE COUNSELLING

Telephone helplines have mushroomed and many provide training to ensure safety of the public and the volunteers. ChildLine and The Samaritans are examples of telephone voluntary counselling where training of skills are employed.

Listening to someone who is distressed on a telephone is not easy, and has a different quality to being with someone in the room. Vital visual clues are missing and the volunteer has to rely heavily on listening to what is being said or *not* being said.

If you are thinking of becoming involved in this type of voluntary counselling, it is important to find out whether the trainers of the service are qualified to do the training, or at least are experienced in the needs of the service. Volunteer agencies have mainly volunteer workers providing the service. In many of the larger volunteer agencies this attention to quality and credibility is in place; when it is not, the volunteers themselves may be left unsupported and floundering.

A recommendation for training is for 4 days minimum, with follow-up training at regular intervals, with group supervision as part of the learning. Techniques of listening skills need to be a part of the training: helping volunteers to listen for the meaning behind the words, learning how to deal with the silences and with crises on the phone.

CO-COUNSELLING

This is a form of egalitarian counselling that is practised by two people who agree to take turns in being counsellor and counselled. It is a reciprocal agreement; a form of dyadic self-help. It is often a practical way for trainees to practise their skills and to get constructive feedback from their colleagues during training. Whilst it is an economical way of receiving counselling in terms of cost, there are limitations for trainees from the lack of experience and skills. Another difficulty is the boundaries of the relationship. If two colleagues who agree to co-counsel are together on a course, their personal relationship may interfere with the co-counselling work.

SOCIAL WORK

Social workers use counselling skills in their work and counsel people, but they are not counsellors. The concerns of social work are rooted in legislature. Social workers study economics, relevant aspects of law, political philosophy, public administration and some psychology. This is a caring profession that works supportively with families, individuals and children in difficulties.

Social workers are employed by local authorities in the prison service, probation service, mental health settings, and drug and alcohol units amongst other settings. Their obligation is to meet statutory requirements. Placing vulnerable children on an 'at risk register' is an example of social work; monitoring families with whom such children live, and removing them to a place of safety (a children's home or foster parents), where necessary.

With the withdrawing or stretching of funds in all areas, many social workers find that they are unable to offer the time that they would like to give to clients for counselling. Some of the counselling that would have been done by social workers previously is now dealt with by purchasing counselling services or by the voluntary sector.

PSYCHOLOGY

The term is not new. The ancient Greeks used the word *psyche* to mean the very essence of life, and association with philosophy. At the end of the nineteenth century, psychology became differentiated from philosophy into the field we know today. Psychology is an experimentally based observation and analysis of human behaviour.

Compared to psychotherapy, psychology rigorously applies a scientific experimental model of inquiry. Behaviour is observed, hypotheses are put forward to explain the observations, and then tests or experiments are devised to try to refute or confirm the hypotheses.

The experimental rigour has led to a predominant view that behaviour is collectively inherited, modelled and develops as a result of stimuli being followed by reward or punishment. Behaviour develops that favours acceptance and survival. Although the truth of this is evident for many things, it can be viewed as an abstraction that does not fully explain the subtle complexities of emotions and behaviour.

The nature of psychologists' work can be very different from that of counsellors and psychotherapists. For example, occupational psychologists may help design work environments to minimise stress or boredom. Educational psychologists are concerned with children's learning and development, working primarily in schools, enabling teachers to become aware of the social factors affecting teaching and learning.

Clinical psychologists apply their knowledge of psychology to people with health problems or severe learning difficulties. Counselling psychologists apply systematic research-based approaches, including assessment and testing, to help people understand their problems and to develop solutions to them. They are able to apply counselling skills from their own perspective.

There is a beneficial crossover of ideas between counselling and psychology. Whilst there is a growing awareness amongst psychologists that a helping relationship is a useful way of working with people, counsellors can benefit from the greater scientific objectivity of psychologists to inform their practice.

All psychologists have a degree in psychology. Postgraduate experience and specialist training is necessary for registration as a chartered psychologist with the British Psychological Society. The BPS offer a diploma in Counselling Psychology. Application is open to graduates with a psychology degree or equivalent.

PSYCHIATRY

Psychiatrists are medically qualified doctors who have undergone postgraduate specialist training in psychological illness.

Until this century madness was inexplicable, so a variety of ill-founded explanations and superstitions arose in the absence of any reliable information. In the latter half of the twentieth century the medical profession made progress by explaining the causes of some mental illness in physical terms. It is a popular misconception that doctors regard all mental illness as arising from a biochemical imbalance that can be corrected by drugs alone. There are, however, some mental illnesses that are a direct result of infections, metabolic, hormonal or biochemical disturbance. Antibiotics, hormone replacement therapy or other simple measures can now dramatically abolish the psychological symptoms of these illnesses.

Doctors and psychiatrists are the only professionals legally empowered to prescribe drugs for the treatment of psychological illness. Without necessarily believing that drugs are the total answer, they often prescribe anti-depressants, anxiolytics or sleeping pills as a partial or temporary fix. Whilst some critics will accuse them of reckless over-prescribing, there are occasions when pharmacological intervention is the only option. For example, the sedation of schizophrenics is sometimes necessary for their own safety or the safety of others. Schizophrenics may hear voices in their head telling them that they can stop a train just by standing in front of it, or they may believe they have to kill someone who is an agent of the devil.

An NHS psychiatrist will usually be responsible for a number of in-patients and also see people referred by their GP for specialist psychological help. These days psychiatrists work closely with other specialists such as community psychiatric nurses, psychologists and social workers, both for the assessment and management of those people referred by GPs.

Together with social workers and doctors, psychiatrists are responsible for implementing the legislation that permits the involuntary detention of suicidal or dangerous people in mental hospitals.

PSYCHOANALYSIS

Psychoanalysis is the original Freudian treatment that is practised by psychoanalysts. Their numbers are small, partly because their training is lengthy and costly, and partly because patients, or *analysands* (the preferred term), are committed to four or five times a week treatment for prolonged periods. Anything up to ten years is not considered extreme. The numbers of people are small who can afford either the time or the money to engage with this treatment.

This classic approach utilises the couch and focuses on the analysand's unconscious thoughts and feelings. Freud considered these the repressed infantile sexual desires that caused neurosis and needed to be paid attention to. The analyst remains neutral, resistant to gratification of the analysand's wishes for her to become an approving, all-loving, or critical, rejecting parent. Without these wishes being granted the analysand comes to understand how he has repressed his own needs in order to try to win his parents' approval. He must search deeper and deeper into his unconscious to understand what his own wishes and needs are.

By fully understanding the repressed desires, and having choices about them, the analysand gains mastery of himself. The goal of the treatment is to remove neurosis caused by the conflicting desires.

This form of treatment is not considered suitable for someone who is psychotic. It remains suited to the treatment of neuroses. The individual has to be articulate, have a capacity to tolerate the frustration of the treatment, the analyst's neutral approach, and be patient with the time it takes.

PSYCHOANALYTIC PSYCHOTHERAPY

This is a modified form of analysis. The person who presents for treatment is called a patient, and the couch may be dispensed with altogether. Having the patient facing the therapist is a very different experience for both people. Treatment is usually twice a week for periods of two years or more. The purpose is not purely to focus on the repressed material buried deep within the analysand's unconscious. Other problems are explored, such as the concerns of daily living.

COUNSELLING OR PSYCHOTHERAPY?

There is a great deal of overlap between counselling and psychotherapy and there are some differences. You will be able to make more informed choices for your training if you are aware of the similarities and the differences between them.

Both counselling and psychotherapy work at developing a client's psychological awareness so that a client can make sense of the things that trouble him. With the practitioner's help, a client's emotional resilience and resources are developed and maintained. Both counsellors and psychotherapists use skills to facilitate changes that help clients deal more effectively with problems in their lives. Ultimately, this enables clients to live more satisfying lives.

Counselling is not an inferior discipline to psychotherapy, although there are many people – counsellors and psychotherapists alike – who subscribe to this notion. This has resulted in confusion rather than clarity. There are counsellors calling themselves psychotherapists either to increase their perceived status, or for some other reason. There are also psychotherapists who call themselves counsellors because of the stigma that is attached to psychotherapy as a treatment for mental illness.

DEFINITIONS

Counselling

In writing this section on counselling I have tried to define the word, but the more I have explored it the more difficult I have found it. The term has come to mean many things to so many people.

It seems easier to say what it is not. Counselling is not befriending, though the elements of support are strong in both befriending and counselling. Counselling is not a friendship. There are qualities of the sharing in friendship within the counselling relationship, but it is very one-sided. The counsellor does not share her problems or bring her needs into the relationship. There must be trust in the relationship, as there has to be in friendship.

There are those who would argue that counselling is not a profession, as it is used by so many disciplines in so many spheres (Feltham 1995).

Many people use techniques and strategies of guidance, coaching, common sense, task-setting, 'permission' giving, persuasion, information and practical advice in their work. These techniques and strategies may not be considered counselling or counselling skills amongst many counsellors. They are, nevertheless, elements used in formal counselling and psychotherapy, whether consciously or unconsciously intended.

Counselling has been described as:

> A principled relationship characterised by the application of one or more psychological theories and a recognised set of communication skills, modified by experience, intuition and other interpersonal factors, to clients' intimate concerns, problems or aspirations. Its predominant ethos is one of facilitation rather than of advice-giving or coercion.
>
> (Feltham 1995: 8)

The BAC says quite simply, that

> Counselling is an activity with clear boundaries and the client will identify the helper as their counsellor . . . an interaction in which the counsellor offers another person the time, attention and respect necessary to explore, discover and clarify ways of living more resourcefully, and to his or her greater well-being.
>
> (BAC 1999: v)

Counselling is also described as a marriage between religion and science; an acceptable response to the individual's perceived problems;

as well as an important component of the caring professions (Bolger 1982).

Whilst many professionals are able to offer counselling to the people that they are trying to help, it is important for them to recognise their limitations of training. People can become confused, or even harmed, if those who are counselling are inadequately trained, or have a conflict of roles between counsellor and teacher or counsellor and manager, for example (McLeod 1993: 3). This is discussed further in the section on therapeutic relationship boundaries (pp. 25–27).

Counsellors (and psychotherapists) have formalised boundaries, which distinguish them from the informal use of counselling skills. Boundaries are the rules, or parameters, which are clearly defined within the therapeutic work to make the relationship safe. These rules cover confidentiality, time limits, payments, the prohibition of physical contact between the counsellor and client and other ethical principles.

Counselling is frequently described as an 'enabling and facilitating' approach. This means that a trained person gives skilled help to another person, to make it easier for them to explore their own options and find their own solutions.

To give advice is generally considered in counselling to take something away from the client's own potential for solving his own problems. Advising creates a dependency on the counsellor and undermines the client's capacity for decision-making and autonomy. Giving advice can also prove to be a grave mistake, as you will know if you have ever given advice to someone who then finds that it was the wrong advice, and is furious with you for your pains.

The counselling focus is usually in the present, and relates to the current issues that a client brings.

Clients who are suitable for counselling need to have a capacity for developing insight and can learn to take responsibility for their emotions and behaviour.

The range of issues that counsellors see is expansive, anything from a desire for self-awareness, relationship difficulties, depression, substance abuse, effects of physical and sexual abuse, self-harming, birth-control, adoption, parenting, anxiety and suicidal feelings, to work-related issues, career change, vocational assessing, assertiveness programmes, etc.

There are counsellors who work in a wide range of settings: industries, business, personnel departments, youth service, education, welfare and support teams, pastoral, hospital, hospices and GP practice settings.

Psychotherapy

Psychotherapy shares the above descriptions with counselling. A psychotherapist engages in a dialogue with the client just as in counselling. Psychotherapy is seen as a 'talking treatment', as opposed to a pharmacological treatment, which is the treatment of drugs.

A difference between counselling and psychotherapy is that some psychotherapists may be medically trained and can administer drugs. They are usually psychoanalytic psychotherapists or psychiatrists who practise psychotherapy as a part of their work. Some psychotherapy approaches have more proximity to the medical model in the way that psychotherapists take family and history details, make assessments and diagnose and formulate treatment for a 'patient'.

In spite of the parallels to the medical model, psychotherapy emphasises intervention of a non-medical kind.

Psychotherapy training is generally longer than counselling training. Many psychotherapy training courses require trainees to be in their own therapy two or three times a week. This may be for the duration of the course, but a trainee may have to be in therapy before commencing a course. Counselling trainees are invariably required to have once a week therapy, usually for the duration of their training.

Many counselling approaches emphasise a supportive relationship for the client. Psychotherapy emphasises relationship and development within a firm theoretical structure. A question that is often asked is whether psychotherapy is a theoretical structure or a mode of relating. Maybe it is more than that. This structure encompasses a theory of development and the stages that an individual needs to experience for healthy psychological maturation. Psychotherapy training covers these stages, and provides an understanding of the consequences of events that can be detrimental to the individual's development. Psychotherapists use this understanding as part of their work to help clients make changes and eliminate neuroses.

Psychotherapists use many counselling skills but take a more active approach in diagnosing clients and offering therapeutic interventions. A psychotherapist may work entirely from one of many different theoretical approaches or may integrate several theoretical approaches.

Psychotherapy has been described as a place and *relationship* that allows the patient to regress, or feel more dependent and childlike, whilst freeing him from the requirements of needing to take care of the therapist (Colman 1993: 96). Like counselling, the therapy sessions are a reparative relationship for the client that does not depend on reciprocation.

Psychotherapists work in the NHS and in private practice, but less often in industry and the diverse settings that counsellors work in. Although they are capable of dealing with clients who are more severely disturbed, they usually work with the same range of emotional problems that counsellors do.

ORIGINS

Counselling

As counselling in this country has evolved from the human potential movement of the late 1950s and 1960s, it is very much a white middle-class, western cultural model. The emphasis is on the individual to become a separate, autonomous person, taking responsibility for his own choices and ultimately his life.

At one time, counselling was seen more in a voluntary, caring role. Advice for careers was associated with counselling. Today, counselling has evolved and is about relieving and resolving human distress, in a supportive setting. The counsellor is trained to use very particular skills, non-judgemental acceptance, her own intuition and life-experiences to help the other person.

Psychotherapy

Many of the psychotherapies have their roots in psychoanalysis that originated with Freud. There are different schools or approaches that have broken away and evolved. The last decade has seen an explosion of a great variety of both counselling and psychotherapy approaches. This is discussed further in the following chapters.

DEVELOPMENT

The counselling process

The counselling focus is usually on the here and now situation; the current issues that a client is bringing. Nevertheless, a counsellor of any approach may explore something of a client's past. This is done in order to link the way a client learnt to respond to problems in the past as a vulnerable and helpless child, with the way he does so in the present as an adult. How much time the counsellor spends in the client's past usually depends on the counselling approach. Some of the humanistic schools, like Gestalt or person-centred approaches, would not dig around much in the client's past, for example, believing that all the material that is necessary is presented in the present.

Because approaches and counsellors' styles vary, it is impossible to say exactly how all counsellors practice.

Some counsellors, for example, may suggest reading material to support the work that they are doing with the client. Some of the books that they recommend may be of a self-help kind. Other counsellors may feel that reading keeps a client at an intellectual level and that they are deprived of having an immediate experience of understanding in the session. There is a difference between an experiential understanding and an intellectual one.

Some counsellors see that elements of assertiveness training, practical advice giving – or suggesting options – are all possibilities that are workable. They adapt their approach to an individual client rather than the other way around.

The majority of counselling approaches in this country (apart from psychodynamic) are usually non-interpretative. This means that the counsellor is not the expert. Unlike many psychotherapies, interpretations of the client's issues are not the rule. The counsellor's role is to help the client find the interpretation that has meaning for him.

The psychotherapeutic process

Counselling does not usually use such terms as 'treatment', and would rarely consider the client as a sick person in need of treatment or cure. Psychotherapists are more likely to use the term 'patient' and 'not client'. (See my comments in the Introduction.)

Psychotherapy may focus on in-depth work of a client's childhood difficulties. This is to understand the mechanisms that were erected as a defence against psychic pain and emotional injury. Depending on the approach, counsellors can also work at in-depth past-related issues of disturbance.

Reworking through early emotional experiences allows a client to reconnect to that part of themselves that was closed down in protection against psychic pain. In this process, a client is offered a different experience with someone he comes to depend on and trusts not to re-injure him. In some psychotherapeutic orientations this experience is called a 'corrective emotional experience'.

According to the particular approach, psychotherapists may take a 'neutral' approach towards their clients. In psychodynamic psychotherapy this is to encourage transference from a client. The transference is the feelings, thoughts and attitudes that the client has experienced towards parents or other significant figures from childhood and which are transferred onto the therapist. This is an important aspect of the work as it enables the client to work through the transferential feelings in a different way with the therapist. The therapist also has feelings that arise from the client or their work together. Countertransference refers to all the therapist's feelings and thoughts and is valuable to the work of therapy. These reactions are central to psychodynamic psychotherapy, but are recognised as important in many other approaches.

Many psychotherapists sit on a chair facing the client who also sits on a chair, just as counsellors do with their clients. This is so that the client and therapist can see and observe each other. The therapist's gaze is an important element of the work.

Some therapists still use the couch, usually those who favour a more orthodox approach. The couch precludes eye contact or other clues that the client or therapist may search for from each other's faces. This forgoing of (what may be seen as) vital clues to some therapists, is seen by others as maintaining the 'neutral' stance, which is so important to the transference in psychoanalytic and psychodynamic psychotherapy.

Setting

Psychotherapists in the National Health Service are likely to be practising psychodynamic psychotherapy, brief therapy, systemic, integrative, cognitive-behavioural or cognitive-analytic psychotherapy (see descriptions in following chapters). Patients are usually referred to the units via the family General Practitioner. There are long waiting lists and the demand is very heavy.

Suitable clients

Clients who are motivated and committed, are reasonably articulate and have some capacity for personal insight, are considered suitable for psychotherapy and counselling.

Clients who see psychotherapists may have personality disorders. They may be at risk of breakdowns or mental illness. They are contained by the frequency of sessions, which can be several times a week. The psychotherapist should have access to a consultant psychiatrist, a GP as well as her supervisor. This form of back-up support is advisable for counsellors as well.

Frequency and depth of work

Because a great deal of counselling tends to be supportive, and the counsellor will work at the pace and depth that the client can tolerate, counselling may be considered to be less challenging than psychotherapy. This is a general observation. There are practitioners from both fields who will be more or less challenging according to their own style.

Whilst it is more common for counsellors to see clients once a week, psychotherapists will frequently see people once, twice or more times a week, though not usually the five times a week that an analyst practises.

The frequency of therapy sessions makes a difference to the depth, breadth and intensity of the work and the detail with which patterns of behaviour can be observed and worked with. There is a process in psychotherapy where the practitioner must consider a client's capacity for tolerating interventions and challenges.

The practitioner also monitors her own countertransference and impact on the client. This monitoring is done with the support of the supervisor.

Equally important is knowing one's limitations, as it is not possible to work effectively with every individual. Knowing how to refer people on to more appropriate forms of support is vital for the well-being of the client and the practitioner, and is a mark of competence in a practitioner. If a practitioner cannot work with a client, but persists, there may be a failure of empathy for the client, which if persistent can be unhelpful at best and damaging at worst for the client. This usually leads to a failure of therapy.

THE SPECIAL RELATIONSHIP

The relationship between the client and the therapist is considered to be very important by all psychotherapists and counsellors. It is the quality of the relationship between the therapist and the client that creates the dynamic for change and is central to therapeutic work. This quality develops when there is trust between the two people working together, and the therapist has empathy for the client.

Empathy is the prime quality that a therapist or counsellor needs to work with another person. Empathy means an ability to identify sufficiently with the other person and to view the other person's world as they see and experience it. Empathy conveys understanding and compassion without having to act on it. This feeling is not sympathy. Sympathy is to feel pity for someone, which is a feeling *for* the other rather than trying to understand what the other is feeling for himself.

Psychotherapists and counsellors alike need to have the capacity for empathy with a wide range of different types of people, and to have worked through many of their own unresolved difficulties in their own therapies, during training. Unresolved issues can still arise for the therapist or counsellor when working with a particular person, and when this occurs therapists need further periods in their own therapy. Counselling courses used not to insist on a trainee undergoing personal therapy, but this is changing. Therapy is considered a journey of self-discovery, and the individual needs to have the support of someone who has been on, at least, a good part of the journey herself. A therapist can only help someone to the point where she has been.

Listening to the client respectfully, not telling him what to do, and enabling the client to make his own choices, are all central to counselling. Psychotherapists listen empathically and may use interpretation as a central skill.

The communication that takes place between the two people, the practitioner and the client, whether this is spoken or unspoken, is of the greatest importance. There is an interaction that happens between the practitioner and the client that may not happen in any other relationships. It is the primary purpose. The practitioner is there for the client; the client's welfare, needs and process take priority.

BOUNDARIES

Counsellors and psychotherapists have formalised 'boundaries'. These are like parameters and containers. Boundaries define what is different from informal counselling. This word needs some explanation. The therapy session has to be a safe, containing and private place for a client in order for therapy to work. The boundaries set the context of the therapeutic work.

For some clients who have not had clear boundaries in their upbringing, experiencing them in the therapeutic relationship is a new opportunity.

The very first boundary that needs to be in place once therapy has been agreed between practitioner and client, is one of *confidentiality*. The practitioner should explain to the client in which ways their sessions together are confidential. There are issues that arise from this subject that are discussed further on.

The second boundary is likely to be the *time* boundary, where, for example, the practitioner says to the client; 'Your session is always Thursdays at 2.30 p.m.'. The client then knows exactly where he is. This is nobody else's appointment, of that he can be sure. Equally, it is his responsibility to get himself there for that time. At the end of the session time the practitioner tells the client that the session is ended. For many clients this is difficult. They may feel they have been cut off, that they had just got going, or that they were just about to get to something important. For others, the time may have felt too long.

In practical terms, the practitioner would find it difficult to arrange appointments if she ran over by long periods and kept others waiting. Clients who were kept waiting would have every right to feel neglected. Treating clients in this way would not be respectful of them and their time. Clients with issues about not wanting the session to end, or who come early or late, or who miss sessions have an opportunity to deal with this through the time boundary being in place. They are reminded of their issue each session.

There may be boundaries of *touch*. In an intimate and private setting of two people with one sharing deep and personal feelings, the subject of touching must be seriously considered by the practitioner. In some orientations touching the client is regarded as totally inappropriate or interfering with the process, and would not need to be considered as it would not arise. There are practitioners whose theoretical approach does not adhere to non-touching, but they themselves feel uncomfortable with touching. There are other practitioners who disagree with this, believing that human touch is essential, and will hold a client's hand or hug the client when he is sorely distressed.

Touching the client could be the need to be needed by the practitioner, and could therefore be harmful to the client, as it is a manipulation by the practitioner for her own gratification. Clients may misunderstand the practitioner's touch or construct thoughts and fantasies that have nothing to do with a gesture of comfort.

Various counselling and psychotherapy organisations are quite clear in their Codes of Ethics and Practice about sexual relationships between client and practitioners. Any form of sexual activity between practitioners and their clients is considered exploitation and is prohibited for the safety and welfare of clients.

Caution about touch is therefore a boundary that trainees have to explore and reflect upon, and practitioners who do touch their clients need to continue to reflect on. Touching is not the only way to hold a client, as the client can feel held and close to the practitioner without any physical touching taking place at all.

The therapeutic relationship boundaries are put in place so that the relationship between the practitioner and client is clear. If the practitioner is a friend or known personally to the client, she will find it very difficult to be the therapist to the same person. This is not the same relationship as two good friends who share their problems and give each other advice on how to deal with them.

This relationship is about one person being there for the other, but if they are both friends already, then the boundaries become blurred. Thoughts can come up for both people. What is expected of me/her/him now that only one of us is in this situation? Will the prior knowledge of the person affect what is presented now? Will unexpected memories, resentments, envy, mistrust, inhibitions or any other feelings get in the way? How does the relationship switch smoothly from one to the other?

This can present dilemmas for people who work in settings where they are expected to have more than one professional role; someone may be a teacher and student counsellor, for example. Wherever possible, the relationship should have firm and clear boundaries. Any other relationship that is desired should not be entered into until considerable time has lapsed after the termination of the therapy. Even then, caution is needed. Entering into a friendship with an ex-client means that the client cannot return, if they so wished, to the previous therapeutic relationship. They are then deprived of that relationship. Would the new friendship be equal? And, what would the expectations be of both people?

Containing boundaries. This refers to the client's strong feelings that can be expressed safely within the therapy room and the practitioner's own capacities at tolerating a client's strong emotions.

It can refer to the practitioner containing the painful issues for a client, because the client is not able to express the feelings at first. This idea is like the practitioner holding something very heavy or difficult for a client that the client finds too much to hold on his own at this particular time.

Containment can also refer to the space for reflection that is offered through the privacy of a therapy session.

Personal boundaries. The practitioner should not react in a way that would be detrimental or harmful to a client. This work for the practitioner is entered into in training, supervision and personal therapy and is continuous.

CONFIDENTIALITY

The subject of confidentiality raises many issues and difficulties, and must be explored in depth on training courses. Dilemmas are likely to arise throughout the working life of a practitioner.

Confidentiality is vital to the relationship in both counselling and psychotherapy. Keeping confidentiality engenders trust. Without trust the relationship will not feel safe. If the client does not feel safe with the therapist he will not be able to speak of those things that may be difficult. He will not render himself vulnerable in any way if he believes that the counsellor or psychotherapist will tell someone else.

If information needs to be passed to anyone else, such as a client's doctor, or as a legal requirement for insurance or court hearings, then the client's consent must be sought first. Clear understanding must be made of what is to be disclosed, and under what circumstances. The consequences can be discussed in the session.

It is the practitioner's responsibility to disclose to the client what aspect of their work will be shared and with whom. As all practitioners should be in supervision, then they are sharing aspects of their work with their supervisor. This needs to be put to the client with the assurance that care is taken to hide the client's identity. Using a first name only when referring to a client in supervision is done to protect the client's identity. As the point of supervision is to monitor the practitioner and her work, the supervisor is equally sensitive to the confidentiality issue.

There are work settings where a practitioner may be part of a team, where there are expectations of clients' details being shared to assist all the team in their work. If the practitioner does not share certain information, this may be seen as obstructing, or creating difficulties. Compared to therapy, for example, there are significant differences between what is expected to be shared in medical or legal requirements. How can a solicitor or doctor act on behalf of their client if they are not aware of as much information as possible? How can they take the responsibilities that are required of them?

The practitioner, on the other hand, respects clients' autonomy to withhold information about themselves. A validation of that respect is confidentiality. In such settings it is the practitioner's responsibility to assess the situation in open discussions, to clarify what the expectations are. To ascertain what information is required to assist clinical or legal requirements, the practitioner needs to explain the boundaries of confidentiality as required for therapy, and to negotiate a way through the difficulties.

The practitioner advises and discusses with her clients what she will have to disclose. The client can then be prepared for what will be disclosed and what will not, and has choices as to what he can safely share. Having an understanding of the limitations is less likely to affect the trust in the therapeutic relationship.

Where the practitioner believes that there is a serious risk of the client causing harm to himself or others, she should consult with her supervisor and try to get the client's co-operation and agreement to stop. Where this fails then confidentiality can be broken. The circumstances that permit a breach of confidentiality are stated in the Code of Ethics and Practice that a practitioner abides by. There is a breach of confidentiality clause in the copy of the Agreement that is in Appendix 1.

Suicidal clients raise an issue that counsellors and psychotherapists have to face during their practice. Any suggestion of suicide has to be taken seriously. Clients may speak of suicide and this needs to be carefully and sensitively discussed with the client first. If the client denies that they are suicidal, and the practitioner is worried, then she has to consult with her supervisor.

Discussing and assessing the risk of suicide, or where there is any ethical doubt or clinical problems, the practitioner turns to the supervisor. To understand what the supervisor's role is and how supervision works is the subject of the next part.

SUPERVISION

This first paragraph of the Introduction to *The Supervisory Encounter* (1995) states the importance of the supervisory role in the therapeutic process. The same importance applies to counselling.

> In the process of becoming a psychotherapist or psychoanalyst, the supervisory encounter is second in importance only to the clinical encounter itself.
>
> (Jacobs, David and Meyer 1995: 1)

Psychotherapists and counsellors alike need to have good, supportive, regular supervision from an experienced supervisor who is familiar with their theoretical approach. This ongoing support is an essential part of their work. Supervision and therapy are a combination of the practitioner's work.

So what exactly is supervision?

The regular use of supervision, or consultation, is a necessity for any form of counselling or psychotherapy. The word 'supervisor' is not an ideal word in this context, as it suggests that the supervisor 'oversees' the work. There is a lot more to therapy supervision than this; supervision is a form of consultation with another person who monitors the therapeutic progress, attends to the maintenance of ethical standards, boundaries, practitioner effectiveness, and ongoing education of the practitioner. These elements are essential for good practice and are major aspects of the supervisory role.

The practitioner or trainee is called a *supervisee* whilst engaged in a supervisory session.

> *The paramount point of supervision is the welfare of the client through monitoring the supervisee's work.*

For experienced therapists, the supervisory session is still a place for monitoring competence and enabling a therapist to be effective. Regular supervision should be continuous throughout a therapist's working life. Supervision is central to the personal and professional growth of a trainee and an experienced therapist. Supervisors themselves have supervision on their work.

A part of the process of supervision is the supervisee's ability to describe aspects of clinical work. The supervisor observes the supervisee's manner of telling the client's story and may ask the super- visee questions to facilitate exploration and gain understanding. The descriptions relate to the client's issues, the supervisee's interventions, the therapeutic relationship, the process and progress. The supervisor watches for what is impeding progress; she explores where the supervisee feels unsure or de-skilled. The supervisor enables the inexperienced supervisee to develop his skills.

The supervisor may ask how the supervisee arrived at a conclusion about a client, or how the supervisee felt during a particular part of the session with the client. This form of questioning is to enable the super- visor to gain a deeper picture of what is happening in the therapy session.

The supervisor is emotionally and physically removed from the client, and this distance enables more objectivity about the work. The supervisor's responses are informed by her own training and clinical experiences.

The supervisor acts as a guide to help the trainee or experienced professional to make sense of the complexities of the therapeutic process. When the trainee (or experienced practitioner) is confused or overwhelmed, it is difficult to have enough degree of objectivity, or even to mobilise thinking. The supervisee may feel stuck. The supervisor is the anchor in the chaos that helps refocus through offering another way of seeing the difficulty.

Supervision needs to be a safe place where supervisees can bring their anxieties and concerns to be explored without fear or judgement. A time and place for themselves where they can trust that the supervisor will support and encourage them and enable them to learn and progress. Supervision is a place that safeguards the client whilst the supervisee is supported to make their work more effective. A good supervisor also pays attention to the growth of the supervisee, supporting him to go on further training courses, read academic papers and books. Review of the supervisee's work should be regular.

The BAC recommends that a practitioner should have 1 hour's supervision to every 6 hours of therapy work. This is dependent on the experience of the supervisee and the difficulty of the work.

Therapy and counselling should never be practised without a supervisor

In a work setting, supervision may be part of a managerial role. An independent practitioner chooses and sets up her own arrangement with a supervisor. It is necessary to make arrangements in the very beginning between supervisee and supervisor for having emergency access to the supervisor outside their agreed hours.

The supervisee's personal issues

Although some personal disclosure about the supervisee may occur during supervisory sessions, supervision is not the same as therapy. Personal disclosure could feel like exposure, and it may sometimes be difficult for the supervisee to know how much of their personal world they can share with their supervisor.

There may be a repetition of issues from the clinical work that the supervisee finds difficult. The client's feelings or difficulties may resonate with unresolved personal issues for the supervisee. The supervisor will help outline them and suggest that the supervisee raise them in personal therapy.

If the clinical work has stirred up strong feelings for the supervisee, then some space for ventilation may be required in the supervisory session. The supervisory relationship is a working relationship, and the supervisor's role is to keep the boundaries clear. But there are occasions when the supervisee can feel strong emotions from the clinical work, and these need to be explored in supervision. The supervisor helps the supervisee to distinguish which feelings are related to the client and which belong to the supervisee, what feelings to ventilate and what to take to personal therapy.

The supervisee's personal problems may also impinge on his work, and it is right that this is discussed with a supervisor. According to the severity of the supervisee's feelings, a supervisor may suggest that the supervisee takes time out from the work.

An experienced supervisor listens with compassion and without judging, and brings the focus back to the clinical work when it is appropriate.

Supervision is a working relationship with the goal of making sense and meaning of the client's material and process, and the supervisee's responses to it. Keeping the boundary between supervision and personal therapy is important for the supervisory relationship. Personal therapy should take place outside supervision.

Just as many practitioners now work with a written contract, or agreement with their clients, it is also important to consider a written contract between a supervisor and supervisee. Each person can sign and exchange their copy with the other. A contract can give all the information regarding the details mentioned in this section. A copy of this contract is in Appendix 2.

FURTHER READING

BAC (1999) *The Training in Counselling & Psychotherapy Directory 1999*, Rugby: BAC.

Bolger, A.W. (ed.) (1982) *Counselling in Britain. A Reader*, London: Batsford Academic and Educational Ltd.

Brown, D. and Pedder, J. (1979) *Introduction to Psychotherapy*, London: Routledge.

Casement, P. (1985) *On Learning From The Patient*, London: Tavistock Publications.

Colman, W. (1993) 'Marriage as a psychological container', in S. Ruszczynski (ed.) *Psychotherapy with Couples*, London: Karnac.

Dryden, W. and Thorne, B. (eds) (1993) *Training and Supervision for Counselling in Action*, London: Sage Publications.

Feltham, C. (1995) *What is Counselling?*, London: Sage Publications Inc.

Feltham, C. and Dryden, W. (1993) *Dictionary of Counselling*, London: Whurr Publishers.

Hunter, M. and Struve, J. (1997) *The Ethical Use of Touch in Psychotherapy*, London: Sage Publications.

Jacobs, D., David, P. and Meyer, D. J. (1995) *The Supervisory Encounter*, New Haven and London: Yale University Press.

McLeod, J. (1993) *An Introduction to Counselling*, Buckingham and Philadelphia: Open University Press.

Miller, G.A. (1962) *Psychology: The Science of Mental Life*, Harmondsworth, Middlesex: Penguin.

Storr, A. (1979) *The Art of Psychotherapy*, London: William Heinemann Medical Books.

Walrond-Skinner, S. (1986) *Dictionary of Psychotherapy*, London: Routledge and Kegan Paul.

2

THEORETICAL APPROACHES

Background and description

FROM PSYCHO-ANALYSIS

There are currently more than 400 counselling and psychotherapy approaches in practice (Karasu 1986). The vast range of choice can pose quite a problem for someone contemplating a counselling or psycho-therapy training. Some of the newer, alternative therapies may be creative and innovative, but may not have a sound theoretical basis. This may be unimportant to some people, but vitally important to others. In this book I am concentrating on those approaches where theory is relevant.

In this chapter I am looking at the three main types of theoretical approaches, which represent the better known therapies. I will offer my understanding of them and describe which emphasis they give that distinguishes their approach from one another.

By 'better known' I mean those approaches that have been practised in this country for long enough to have stood some testing of time and have gained recognition as a result. The approaches that will be named have mainly evolved from psychoanalysis. Whilst many have branched completely away from it, they still owe some debt to it. There are approaches that have introduced eastern philosophies, spirituality and other teachings, and have no allegiance to psycho-analysis.

It is beyond the scope of this book, however, to attempt to name all the approaches that are currently practised. Having read this chapter, you may have a better idea of the ones that interest you.

Referring to the List of Resources (pp. 203–24) will give you the names and details of training institutes, journals and magazines that are of interest for a particular theoretical approach.

There are three main categories of therapeutic approach:

- psychoanalytic/psychodynamic;
- humanistic;
- cognitive behavioural.

Each presents a theory of human behaviour. In essence:

- the psychoanalytic and psychodynamic approaches are *reconstructive*, where the focus is on the patient gaining insight in order to make changes;
- the humanistic approach is *supportive*, where the focus is on freedom of choice and self-responsibility;
- the cognitive and behavioural approaches are *re-educative*, where the focus is on management and change of behaviour.

These three main core approaches represent the fundamentally different ways of seeing human beings and their emotional and behavioural problems (Mahrer 1989).

Within each of these categories there are numerous schools, or offshoots. They have all broken away from mainstream psychoanalysis. These collective breakaway schools represent the evolution of therapies in the struggle to understand the complexities and intricacies of the human mind, feelings and behaviour. Understanding, however, is only a part of the process or treatment. The fundamental questions that underlie the particular approach to therapeutic treatment are:

- In psychoanalysis/psychodynamic therapy. How to reduce neurosis (and psychosis) and resolve or repair the individual's psychic suffering.
- In humanistic therapy. How to develop potential and enable the individual to resolve or heal their own suffering.
- In cognitive-behavioural therapy. How to change the individual's faulty thinking, beliefs and behaviour.

The answers depend on the approach used.

The changes involved may be through an understanding of the way we unconsciously bury or repress our authentic feelings and thoughts, as in the psychodynamic approach.

In the humanistic approach we are supported to understand that our defences are purposeful and served us at an earlier part of our lives, but are probably counter-productive or destructive to us now. Having an understanding of this process enables us to explore other choices of how we may want to live.

There may be faults in perception, beliefs, thoughts (cognition) and behaviour that can be corrected, through practice, according to the cognitive-behavioural[1] approaches.

Before exploring each of these forces for change in more detail I would like to retrace the path to the origins of the therapeutic evolution.

HOW THERAPY EVOLVED

Our history is littered with a perpetual search to resolve human unhappiness. Even before recorded history there are signs and clues about a human need to diminish emotional pain. Stone gods were worshipped for protection, animals sacrificed to appease gods, amulets and other symbols to drive away the evil eye and evil spirits. These practices continue today.

The need to make meaning of our existence has inspired people to great scholastic deeds, such as deciphering the mystical meaning of numbers and letters in the Old Testament to explain God's words.

There is also a history of fear and torture in the pursuit of ridding the human condition of misery. The mental anguish of madness was feared within the human form and was seen by the Church, for centuries, as a battle to be won over evil – the 'exorcising of devils' and 'evil spirits'. The rituals of terror and purges were the attempt to drive out the evil, and thus the unhappiness that was the result.

There is an opposite view that has been and still is held in other societies, where the psychotic are attributed with special gifts of insight that the rest of us lack.

People used fetishes, potions, card reading, elixirs and superstitions by 'wise' members of a community, and still do today. Witches have been both needed and feared. Vast numbers of people have always consulted shamans and magicians for their cures; and there is a wide belief in astrology for deciding the individual's fate.

The reflections and 'thoughts of the soul' of the seventeenth century, and later European philosophers, have all added to the evolution of practice in the treatment of the human condition. In every society we can find the longing for what all humans desire – an explanation and meaning to the mystery of the problems of life.

Probably the most powerful form of therapy has been religion. People turned to the priest, rabbi or shaman for guidance in righting the 'sickness of the soul'. Fearing the evil eye, people wore or hung objects in their homes that would have the power to keep away the evil that could overwhelm them if they were not alert to it. Religion taught guiding principles, atonement and repentance for the 'evil' we manifest if we do not follow the righteous path. Self-punishment, or guilt, can be a consequence of much of this doctrine.

Rollo May, an existential psychotherapist, has named psychotherapy as psycho-religious therapy. Seeing therapies as ideologies or the new religion is a common observation.

A difference between the new and the old is the way that suffering is viewed. In some traditional religions the core teaching is that there is meaning in suffering, without exhorting the individual to change. In today's therapies, the primary task is to reduce or heal the suffering, but it is the individual that has to change in order to achieve their own healing. This shifts the responsibility for mental health largely away from an external source to an internal or personal responsibility. The bad news being that there is no one out there to do it for us, but the good news is that we do, at least, have some control over how we can live our lives.

Nineteenth-century Vienna was the beginning of a New World away from religious healing, chance remedies and superstitions. The leap was into respectability of scientific methods of treatment that formed the beginnings of the psychology that we understand today. Psychology is the science of mental life. There were numerous doctors in Europe involved in trying to understand the reasons for human mental ill health. Sigmund Freud is the most renowned, and to him is attributed the founding of psychoanalysis, from which most other therapies have sprung.

Therapy that is practised today is still a very young science. It is mainly comprised of a western approach to attitudes, thinking and view of the world. Contemporary therapies tend to reflect this society, which is individualistic and not communal based. A flaw in some therapeutic approaches is that the social environment, the community, world events and their impact on the individual, can be disregarded.

In essence, therapy considers:

- Philosophy, values, ideology, principles and theory of an approach.
- Political and social implications on the individual.
- The study of human stages of development.
- The observation of human thought, feelings and behaviour.
- The processes of evolutionary and revolutionary change for the individual.
- Resolution, integration and healing.
- The use of strategies, interventions and techniques.

With this set of tools it is not difficult to see that individuals will impose their own convictions and ideas in an endeavour to find the 'cure' for neuroses and psychic illness. This cure for human ills is a natural search for that which continually eludes us. No one school or approach has the answer, but this does not prevent us from working at improving on what we already have, constantly testing, researching and developing. Thus, we have arrived at a kind of therapeutic explosion with 400 different approaches.

What do they all mean?

The 'approach' is a term for a particular theory, the philosophy behind it, and its application to clinical practice. It may also be called 'orientation', 'model', 'school' or 'movement'.

A great many of the current approaches have been named after a person who expanded and evolved a concept or theory that distinguished it from Freudian psychoanalysis.

Different approaches frequently hold differing beliefs and concepts about the stages of human development. Those concepts may conflict with or vary from other approaches. This can be bewildering at first. The more knowledgeable you become, the more theories or aspects of theories will resonate with your own way of thinking and the ways in which you want to practise. Having information about the three fundamental approaches may help you to see which theoretical approaches you are drawn to.

THE PIONEERS

From the brief sketches of a few of the early pioneers' backgrounds that I have selected, it is plain that so many of them suffered from painful rejection, illness and losses. An example is Melanie Klein. She seems to have used her multiple bereavements as creative efforts to resolve her own suffering, and human suffering in general. Her losses included the tragic death of her son, and her own depressions which affected her children.

Klein, like Freud and a large number of the pioneers of the late nineteenth century and early twentieth, were also Jewish. The Nazis, amongst others, labelled psychoanalysis as the 'Jewish Science'. As a social, political and cultural context, a great many of the pioneers lived in Europe and were alive in an era where virulent anti-Semitism was never far from the surface. The Jewish pioneers who lived in that era took for granted that their education, careers and their lives could often be restricted, threatened and tenuous.

Perhaps one hypothesis to explain the Jewish interest in psychology was that there was a need to understand the hatred that was projected onto the Jewish people.

Psychoanalysis has been criticised as having negative views of human impulses. The critics point to the constant psycho-archaeological digging for childhood traumas and its depressed view of the world.

Some of the complaints have suggested that as so many of the early pioneers were Jewish, it is the collective Jewish persecutory experience that has helped to shape those pessimistic views of human behaviour. The concept of analytical interpretation and insights does have its parallel in biblical, traditional Jewish study, with its emphasis on exploration and interpretation. But here the comparison ends. An understanding of Talmudic[2] study is that the more one gives to the study of the Talmud, the more joy one can receive.

PSYCHOANALYSIS

Freud (1856–1939) was a neurologist and practising doctor who viewed human beings as biologically determined, motivated primarily by sexual and aggressive drives. He wrote prolifically, his collected works amounting to 24 volumes. His work resulted in the theories of personality and treatment of psychotherapy that have been handed down today.

There is little doubt that had Freud lived longer he would have reviewed and developed his theories as he did throughout his career. Whilst some of his concepts have fallen out of grace in our present society, it is important to remind ourselves that his contributions were a major force towards our own understanding of the psyche. Freud was very much a person of his own time and European place in the nineteenth and twentieth centuries of Vienna, and before him there was scant formulated understanding and little humane treatment of neurosis and psychosis.

The tenet of infantile sexuality or the Oedipal complex was Freud's theory that arose out of his own self-analysis through his dreams; his acknowledgement that he loved his adoring mother and was jealous of his authoritarian father. It was during the end of the nineteenth century, when Freud himself was suffering from depression, fears of dying, and anxiety attacks, that he carried out his most original work and developed his psychosexual theories. He challenged his sexual drive theories following the terrible neuroses that was experienced by soldiers in the First World War. After this period, Freud developed total personality theories, which included the concept of repression of aggressive and sexual impulses.

He introduced the couch for his patients to lie on because *he* did not like to be stared at for hours at a time every day. He also believed that the patient could free-associate (say whatever came into their minds) more readily when there were no visual obstructions.

In 1923 he was diagnosed as having cancer of the jaw, not helped by the twenty cigars that he smoked every day. In spite of thirty-three operations on his jaw, he suffered from pain for the rest of his life. In 1938 when the Nazis occupied Austria, Freud fled Vienna to come to London. He died in London in 1939.

Theory

At the beginning is the classical form of Freudian psychoanalysis. This therapy attempts to uncover the more frightening and more deeply hidden desires, thoughts, fantasies and dreams of the unconscious mind. These buried, or repressed thoughts are believed to cause us the conflicts that can often paralyse us. The concept of conflicts that influence people's thinking and cause neurotic disorders is central to this therapeutic view.

The method of treatment is to encourage the patient to say whatever comes to his mind: a free association of random thoughts that the analyst interprets or explains the meaning of. This method of free association means that the patient can bring the hidden conflicts into his consciousness and gain insights and understanding of them through the analyst's interpretations.

The patient usually lies on a couch with the analyst out of view. Because seeing the analyst does not distract him, the patient experiences the analyst as 'neutral'. This means that the patient does not know anything about the analyst. When we 'don't know something' that we want to know, we are likely to fantasise to fill in the gaps.

The patient fantasises things about the analyst and *transfers* onto her his feelings that he felt about the early significant figures in his life. Those figures were usually his parents, or other people who had an impact on him. The analyst fosters this transference. It helps her to give interpretations of the way that she sees the patient experience situations and react to them. This is a central concept of psychoanalysis.

Interpretations are the analyst's hypotheses, or understanding from the information received. They are the insights that are used to explore, analyse and link the patient's past problems to the present. A part of the patient wants very much to accept the interpretations, in order to change and feel happier, but the conflicting parts of himself resist any change. Working through the patient's resistance is seen as fundamental to the process.

The commitment for this kind of treatment is very great for both the analyst and the patient. Therapy can be as much as four or five times a week, for many years. With this length of time involved, the goal is a reconstruction of the patient's personality.

Psychoanalysts are sometimes medical doctors or hold a second or third degree in a related field.

Psychoanalysis gave rise to the contemporary form of psychodynamic counselling and psychotherapy that focuses on the process of change and development.

One of the earliest analysts to break away from Freud was his colleague and one-time friend, Carl Jung.

ANALYTICAL PSYCHOLOGY

Carl Gustav Jung (1875–1961) was born in Switzerland. His father was an Evangelical minister. Jung was surrounded by religion, as eight of his uncles were clergymen. Jung experienced his mother as unpredictable, with seemingly different personalities. These factors seem to have had a major impact in the therapy he went on to formulate.

As a child, Jung felt torn in his loyalties to his parents who were unhappily married, the impact of which was to affect his attitudes and writings. His mother was hospitalised when he was four and he felt, in adulthood, that this separation made him view women as unreliable. Until he was nine he had no brothers or sisters. This may account for his rich, fantasy inner world. He was a lonely and melancholy child, who had strange, vivid dreams, some that he remembered and wrote about when he was much older.

He spent most of his life studying his own and his patients' dreams and visions and evolving his theory. Through a dispute or jealousies, Jung became Freud's biggest rival.

Theory

Jung emphasised the spiritual aspects in therapy, and the archetypal phenomena; that is, archaic images and symbols that he named as differing aspects of the mind. The archetypal image is seen clearly in the 'wise old man' or when people have made scapegoats of others, blaming them for their own inadequacies and fears, and seeing them as demonic. Archetypes appear in dreams and myths. He saw that the myth-creating level of the mind is what gives life and the individual meaning and significance.

Jung was preoccupied with the reconciliation of the opposites within people. He saw this as a process of individuation, which was the central concept of his psychology. He believed that everyone has a number of personalities. He viewed all humans as divided selves, and that the personal unconscious, as well as the collective unconscious (that which we inherit from our family, culture, ancestors and mythology), consists of an indefinite number of complexes or fragmentary personalities.

He had a broad depth of interest in religion, telepathy and spiritualism. He developed the spiritual dimension of his theories in complete opposition to Freud, who ignored it. Transpersonal therapy has risen from Jung's spiritual and self-transcending concepts.

Jung's Analytical Psychology suggested that his patients' neuroses stemmed, in part, from the state of the world as much as from their personal disorders. Freud believed that his patients were arrested in the present by their inability to work through their unresolved past, whereas Jung considered that a regression to past fixations was due to something blocking them in the present. He considered that each person had a secret which was vital to uncover. He also strongly believed that the patient's neglected spiritual issues added to their unhappiness.

Jung's classification of people into extroverts and introverts is probably the most widely known of his psychological theories.

INDIVIDUAL PSYCHOLOGY

Alfred Adler (1870–1937) was a peer of Freud and Jung. He placed the emphasis upon the individual's own security and supremacy, looking at the effects of the child's perception of their place in the family group. As a child, he had felt inferior to an older brother, and suffered from the effects of the same sibling rivalry by being compared unfavourably to Freud and Jung.

He was constantly sick as a child and that created relationship difficulties within the family, particularly with his mother. He was a poor student; his father was told that he would probably be best suited as a cobbler. He struggled to achieve academically, finally studying medicine at the University of Vienna, specialising in psychiatry and neurology. He was always particularly interested in incurable childhood diseases.

He wrote and spoke in simple language, which understated his depth of academic prowess. He was one of the first to give live demonstrations to large audiences of professionals. These demonstrations were of him working with parents and children in the numerous child-guidance clinics that he founded.

Theory

Adler's view, different from that of Freud, was that it is not the biological and impulse drives that determine how we behave, but the social urges. Adler maintained that the individual is social-psychologically motivated. He did not believe in viewing the person in isolation but in their social context. Life goals provide the basis of achievement and satisfaction to overcome inferiority. It is the *conscious* not the *unconscious* that is central to Adler's concepts.

After having spent many years in close collaboration, Freud denounced him as a heretic when Adler rejected his views.

Through his thinking, he has indirectly influenced family therapy and many other therapies that do give acknowledgement to Adler. His Individual Psychology is an interpersonal psychology. This places an emphasis on the interaction with others and the struggle to find meaning within relationships. As a Jew, he took the simplest, and possibly the greatest, Jewish teaching of living as a fundamental tenet for his psychological principle: 'Love your neighbour as yourself'. His application of this principle was the acceptance of the self in order to accept the other.

Adler also rejected Freud's reductionism in favour of holism; that is, the study of the whole person and their progress throughout life. Through these views, he has been recognised as one of the early humanistic psychologists.

Adler maintained that there are challenges that life presents and that the person is confronted with them constantly. A person can either choose from constructive alternatives, or protect the self through the belief that they are inferior. Inferiority can result in the individual striving for personal superiority through over-compensation, like perfectionism and power.

Whereas Freud considered that neuroses have a sexual aetiology, Adler believed that neurosis is a failure from learnt distorted perceptions. Adlerian therapists will therefore ask how individuals use their bodies and their minds in the pursuit of their goals.

The world of internal images may be called archetypes by Jungians, distorted perceptions by Adlerians, or internal objects by Kleinians.

OBJECT RELATIONS

Melanie Klein (1882–1960) was an analyst of children, whose under-standings of human beings' difficulties trace the source to the earliest phase of life, with the infant at the breast.

Klein, born in Vienna, was the youngest child of an orthodox Jewish father who was a great deal older than his second wife. Klein felt unwanted by her father in particular. Two of her siblings died, one in childhood. Klein was not breast-fed and this may have influenced her studies of child development, stressing the powerful infantile feelings that she observed the child feels towards the mother's breast.

In adulthood she became depressed during her second pregnancy, and following her family's culture she travelled a great deal to relieve the depression. Her own mother took charge of her family during her absence. Klein and her mother had a complicated, rivalrous relationship that allowed for no separation between them until her mother's death.

Klein entered analysis during the First World War. Her analyst, Sandor Ferenczi, was impressed with her special talents and interest in observing and understanding children. He appointed her as his clinical assistant at the Association of Child Research. The informality then of promoting his patient to be his assistant is especially interesting to us today, where such practices would be unheard of. Klein became one of the few women in a profession that was 'naturally expected' to be male dominated.

After divorcing her husband and moving to Berlin in 1921 she was again encouraged by her new analyst to treat children.

The early 1920s brought a great wealth of psychoanalytic under-standing, and Melanie Klein's special contribution was to break new ground in childhood psychoanalysis through the technique of play. In her time her ideas were not easily acceptable, partly because she was a woman and partly because she expounded theories of aggression in young children, when children were not really seen at all, or at best seen as innocents.

Klein was invited to London in 1926 and helped to found the British object-relations school of psychoanalysis. Under her leadership, the English school of psychoanalysis evolved and emerged.

Theory

Klein emphasised the importance of primitive fantasies of loss and the feelings of persecution for the infant. These occur during the earliest stages of emotional development of the child. These stages separate images of the mother into entirely 'good' or entirely 'bad', an image of the all bountiful goddess or the wicked witch. Observing children at play, Klein considered that the child uses play to recreate real world objects and situations. The predicaments and problems in real life are thus learnt about in play.

Klein's theoretical concept contributions were of two particular positions or stages. The first she called the *paranoid-schizoid* position that she saw as a constellation of anxieties and defences similar to those of earliest infancy. Splitting, projecting and blaming form a part of this regressive state.

The second stage she called the *depressive* position that she viewed as a development in a later infant stage, but the process of working through the depressive position continues throughout life and is never completed. During critical events and stressful times, there may be regression to the paranoid-schizoid position.

Whereas Freud maintained that instinctual gratification was the fundamental need, Klein and Ronald Fairbairn (an English analyst), believed that a satisfying object relationship is more basic. The word 'object' refers to people. The primary motivation in human beings, they believe, is the need to seek satisfying relationships with others. Since the 1930s object relations theory has continued to develop in this country, and is not only concerned with the actual relationship between two people but also considers the internalised relations that the person (the subject) has with another person (the object).

The development of object relations, that is the need to relate to another, has made a shift in our understanding of human need and behaviour. Bion, Balint and Winnicott made other important contributions to this understanding of conscious and unconscious interaction. Winnicott emphasised the importance of the maternal 'holding' for the baby, meaning a psychological holding as well as the physical. He also referred to the importance of the space between the mother and child, where play and communication could be created. Bion also emphasised this relationship between two people when he referred to the analyst and the patient.

Bion contributed much to an understanding of the containment of the individual, as well as the group, in his concepts of group dynamics.

Both Michael Balint and his wife Enid were instrumental in bringing psychotherapeutic practice to doctors through seminars which they led at the Tavistock Clinic, and through their writing. They encouraged doctors to pay attention to patient-centred medicine; listening to what was behind the patient's presenting complaint. They also emphasised the relationship that developed between the doctor and the patient.

Other important analysts who have shaped theoretical changes in classical analytic thinking are, notably, Karen Horney, who drew attention to the social and cultural factors that impact on individuals; Erich Fromm and Harry Stack Sullivan, who emphasised the inter-personal, cultural and feminist attitudes that later developed; and John Bowlby, whose ideas on attachment and separation effect from the mother or primary caretaker have been so influential. These concepts are all viewed as important factors in understanding later difficulties in a person's life.

NOTES

1   'Cognitive' refers to thoughts and belief.
2   Biblical law.

FURTHER READING

Bateman, A. and Holmes, J. (1995) *Introduction to Psychoanalysis*, London: Routledge.

Beginners Series, *Freud for Beginners,* Cambridge: Icon Books Ltd.

—— *Klein for Beginners,* Cambridge: Icon Books Ltd.

—— *Jung for Beginners*, Cambridge: Icon Books Ltd.

Coltart, N. (1993) *How to Survive as a Psychotherapist*, London: Sheldon Press, SPCK.

Herman, N. (1987) *Why Psychotherapy?*, London: Free Association Books.

Jacobs, M. (1988) *Psychodynamic Counselling in Action*, London: Sage Publications.

Karasu, T.B. (1986) The specificity against nonspecificity dilemma: toward identifying therapeutic change agents, *American Journal of Psychiatry* 143: 687–95.

Mahrer, A. (1989) *The Integration of Psychotherapies: A Guide for Practicing Therapists*, New York: Human Sciences Press.

3

TOWARDS HUMANISTIC
THERAPY

SELF-PSYCHOLOGY

This therapy could be seen as a bridge that spans psychoanalysis and humanistic therapy in treating disorders of the self. In particular, narcissistic personality disorder.

Self-psychology has its roots in Freudian psychoanalysis and the British object relations school, which were the precursors of Heinz Kohut's theories. Kohut formulated the concept of drive *experiences* as opposed to the drive *impulses* of traditional Freudian thinking. These theories are still being expanded and developed today after Kohut's death.

Theory

The *self* in this psychology is the *I*, the centre of the personality. It is the experience of the self or the relationship to the self that is the concept.

The infant needs to have received adequate amounts of mirroring, empathic-responsive and prizing from the mother to have any sense of and confidence in a *self*. The infant also needs to have an empathic environment to be in tune with his psychological needs, to be able to go from dependency to autonomy and from narcissism to object love. Kohut felt that 'man can no more survive psychologically in a psychological milieu that does not respond empathically to him, than he can survive physically in an atmosphere that contains no oxygen' (Kohut 1977: 253).

One of the important aspects of the early stage of human development in self-psychology is that the infant needs to merge with the mother. This merging produces the psychological tension-regulating structures that he needs later on to deal with anxiety. A fragmented self is a person who has not had this opportunity, or has been confronted with a depressive or unresponsive mother.

Mirroring, idealising and twinning are the stages considered for the development of the self. The client who was deprived of them in childhood needs to experience them within the therapeutic relationship. The first stage of mirroring is the empathic stage. The second stage is where the client needs to idealise or take in the good part of the therapist – just as the child needed to idealise the parents. The third is where the client feels more of an equal with the therapist, seeing the real person of the therapist. This final stage is similar to adolescence and early adulthood, where optimal frustration or disappointment with the therapist is a part of the client's own need to be independent, separate and different from the therapist.

Kohut believed that people needed to learn optimal frustration at an early stage of childhood. The foundations for the way that we deal with the disappointments and frustrations that are an inevitable part of life are laid down by being given the appropriate amount of frustration to deal with, at the appropriate stage of development. People who have been faced with too many dilemmas too soon – or those who have been overly protected and dealt with too little – will have great difficulties in later life.

Kohut urged that psychoanalysts should not hide behind the theory of professional neutrality, which was in effect a deprivation for the client. He maintained that the psychoanalytic therapist's need for distance amounted to a narcissistic tendency within the therapist to value the therapeutic activity but not the client. He emphasised that therapists behave humanely, warmly and with appropriate empathic responsiveness to their clients.

Mollon has expanded these concepts to show that an aspect of selfhood is the capacity to reflect on oneself. This means that there is a knowing that there is an *I*. The capacity to do this can take in the self in relationship to others and allows for a perspective on self and others. He suggests that the presence of the father is crucial in facilitating the differentiation of child from mother (Mollon 1993: 110). It is the father who provides this capacity to maintain a perspective. Without this triangular relationship of the mother and child and the father, the person may be restricted in their capacity to reflect on the self.

Mollon has explored and deepened our understanding of the experiences of shame, embarrassment, self-consciousness and humiliation. These are the injuries and wounding caused to the self which need to be understood if we are to understand the concept of self and the application of empathy by the therapist.

These factors bring self-psychology closer to the humanistic understanding of human need.

MIND–BODY THERAPIES:
BIOENERGETIC THERAPY

Wilhelm Reich was the first to explore and identify emotional disturbances through muscular tensions, a concept that gave way to new ideas about how repression is held in the body. Known as *character armouring*, it is originally used by the child to protect itself against physical or emotional pain. In adulthood, the armouring becomes a 'shell' of self-protection against further wounding. From these ideas Alexander Lowen developed a whole new movement of therapy in the 1950s, focusing on the disorders of the body as the mirror of emotional disorders. Muscles are seen to hold back impulses as restricted movement.

Theory

Bioenergetic therapy was developed to encourage somatic, expressive movement to combat stresses, anxieties and defences. By increasing the motility of the organism and developing its natural aggression, strength is created at both the physical and psychic levels. The belief is in the growth of the person, not in a cure. The emphasis is on the body as well as the mind.

Lowen integrated Freudian and Reichian principles with his formulations of:

1 *Character analysis*: the fundamental observation and knowledge within the visual physical shape and posture of the client.
2 *Grounding*: the person's own realisation that to be standing on their own two feet in contact with the ground they will not fall, which is a deep-rooted human fear.
3 *Breathing*: observing the manner in which a person breathes can tell the therapist what is happening for the client. Holding the breath reduces the person's emotional experience of anxiety or pain and tightens the muscles. This creates a loss of contact with the person's felt experiences.
4 *Energy*: lacking energy produces a feeling of hardly being alive. Energy that is locked into the body cannot flow freely and restricts movement and feeling. Focusing on breathing and grounding releases the energy that is necessary to feel alive.

These principles combine to make the basis of the therapy.

Observing the shape and stance of the body gives information to the therapist. The therapist uses this information to aid the person's conscious awareness of the harmony of their mind with the energy of their body. The therapeutic emphasis is on the energy. This energy should not be used to maintain tensions and defences, but to create the well-being of vitality.

Lowen looked for ways of allowing people to learn to live with their problems in their present, without the Freudian belief in the psychological digging of their past. He concentrated on a person breathing deeply, moving freely, feeling fully and expanding the body's life through self-expression. When people did not pay attention to these things he believed that the life of a person's body was restricted and limited.

Lowen had an optimistic belief that people had the capacity to overcome their distresses and enjoy their lives; to move beyond the distress of the past through the psychological health that is to be found in the harmony of the body. This psychological attitude towards the health of the person, rather than the illness, is the humanistic element of this therapy.

HUMANISTIC THERAPY

Many of the humanistic pioneers were originally psychoanalysts and must have been influenced in some measure by their original training, even if they were in such disagreement with Freudian theories that they went on to develop their own.

The base of the humanistic approaches stem from the works of Martin Buber, Viktor Frankl, Abraham Maslow, Fritz Perls, Carl Rogers, and Jacob Moreno, with Eric Berne between the humanistic and a more structured theoretical system.

A weakness in humanistic therapy is the ignoring of the unconscious processes of the client. Although there are humanistic practitioners who pay great attention to their own countertransference (their own attitudes, feelings and thoughts towards the client), the role of transference does not have the importance it warrants in psychodynamic therapy.

One of the core beliefs in humanistic psychotherapy is a search for growth and awareness through self-responsibility. In the humanistic approach, the client is held to be the expert on his own decisions, feelings and attitudes, not the therapist. The client is helped to discover and develop his rich potential and resources through the exploration of his choices. He is also helped to be aware of what the blocks and obstacles are to those choices. The therapist's role is to support the client to explore his choices creatively, and make the realistic changes he wishes to make.

There is a consistent development of the relationship with the therapist through the therapist revealing her own authentic feelings. There is an emphasis on a deeply significant, real relationship that is a potentially profoundly healing force. This relational approach builds trust for the client to experience himself authentically within the relationship.

It is important in humanistic therapy to see the client's *modus vivendi* as purposeful and to be understood, not as a pathological aberration of the client. There can also be a spiritual dimension within many of the humanistic therapies.

> Orthodox, western psychology has dealt very poorly with the spiritual side of our nature, choosing either to ignore its existence or to label it pathological. Yet much of the agony of our time stems from a spiritual vacuum. Our culture, our psychology, has ruled out our spiritual nature, but the cost of this attempted suppression is enormous. If we want to find ourselves, our spiritual side, it's imperative for us to look at the psychologies that deal with it.
>
> (Tart 1976: 5)

EXISTENTIALISM

The principles of humanistic therapy are related to existentialism. Existentialism considers the ways that we feel or experience our existence in the world. There is an emphasis on free will and individuality of choice and action.

Existentialism is based on the phenomenological method; that is, the person's immediate experience, rather than intellectualising or thinking about it. Existential phenomenologists focus on people's existence, their relations with others, their fears of dying, and their life problems as they experience them in terms of meaninglessness, isolation and freedom.

These concepts do not fit easily into any category of psychotherapy, where structures of theory are broken down into component parts. An example of this difficulty is depicted in a story told by Viktor Frankl:

> Two neighbours were arguing, one was accusing the other's cat of eating his butter. They asked the rabbi to intervene. The rabbi asked how much butter the cat had eaten, and he was told that the cat had consumed ten pounds. The rabbi weighed the cat and found that the cat weighed precisely ten pounds. 'So if this is the butter,' exclaimed the rabbi, 'where is the cat?'

The idea from this story – that man is greater than the sum of his parts – is one of the central tenets of humanistic theory.

Viktor Frankl is usually chosen from amongst many to represent the principles of existentialism because of the enormity of his personal experiences and how he used them in his life and work. His beliefs were tested to their limits when he was imprisoned in Nazi concentration camps, where his parents, brother and wife perished.

His belief that love is the highest goal to which humans can aspire was reinforced by what he witnessed in prisoners who helped each other, even in the appalling conditions of the camps. He believed that we search for meaning and purpose and that we have choices, however small, even in the most terrible situations.

He learned the most profound learning of all: that everything can be taken away from a person, except for one thing, which is the last of human freedoms – 'to choose one's attitude in any given set of circumstances, to choose one's own way' (Frankl 1963: 104). These are central to the humanistic/existentialist principles.

Martin Buber (1878–1965) was not a psychotherapist, yet his mark in humanistic psychotherapy is profound. He is the bridge between Jewish mystical thinking and Hasidism[1] on one side, and modern relational theory on the other (Yalom 1980: 364).

He was born in Vienna, the son of assimilated Jews. When Martin was three his mother left his father. Martin was brought up by his grandparents, who strongly influenced him. His grandfather was a philanthropist and scholar and his grandmother an advocate of the nineteenth-century Enlightenment movement among eastern European Jewry that sought to modernise Jewish culture.

The continual searching for his lost mother became the basis for his 'dialogical' thinking.

Buber studied art, poetry and philosophy. He was instrumental in Jewish adult education, retraining Jewish teachers in Nazi Germany when Jews were progressively excluded from the educational system. He studied Hasidism and favoured a spiritual renewal. After he was forbidden to lecture by the Nazis, he immigrated to Palestine when he was 60 years old. There he was influential and emphasised a non-legalistic prophetic religion.

His open dialogic approach appealed to Christians and Arabs alike. At his funeral in Jerusalem, a delegation of an Arab student organisation placed a wreath on 'the grave of one who strove mightily for peace between Israelis and Palestinians'. This was the affirmation of his work in dialogic relationships.

This dialogic relationship is a concept that he called *I–thou*. The

I–thou relationship is one where both are in a mutual or total relationship with the other. Neither uses the other as an object for self-interest.

> *It means to be truly listening to the other and allowing oneself to be shaped by the other's responses.*

The true dialogue where each is in a living mutual relationship between oneself and the other.

This thinking has contributed to the humanistic movement: the prizing of the individual, the well-being of community and the authenticity of dialogue in relationship.

The humanistic therapies that came from the existentialist philosophy are experiential (see Glossary) and relationship-oriented, rather than cognitive and intellectual. Person-centred therapy is an example of the experiential – spontaneously allowing a session to flow from the client's needs and direction, rather than from the therapist's planned direction, or hypotheses. The therapy is supportive.

PERSON-CENTRED THERAPY

Carl Rogers (1902–87) came from an agricultural and Protestant fundamentalist background where play was discouraged. As a consequence, he sought scholarly activities in childhood. His education spanned agriculture, history and religion, where he spent time questioning the religious dogma that he had been immersed in.

After he had rejected the theological seminary where he had begun his studies, he moved to clinical psychology. For twelve years he worked at a child-guidance centre in Rochester, New York. During this period, he became increasingly dissatisfied with the commonly held views of psychotherapy and began developing his own approach.

Theory

The presentation of his paper, 'Some Newer Concepts in Psychotherapy', in 1940, is the moment that is identified with the emergence of his client-centred therapy, as it was then called. The idea of empowering the client in the therapeutic relationship as the expert, rather than the therapist, went against the grain of traditional therapy. Roger's approach influenced other fields outside individual psychotherapy: in couples and families, in the development of personal-growth groups, in teaching for student-centred learning, and in intercultural groups. Rogers's belief was that people would take responsibility for their own lives if they were only given the appropriate setting and opportunity. He saw traditional psychotherapy as depriving people of such an opportunity.

The psychological aid of the therapist here is not to direct the person, but to convey a genuiness within the relationship and provide a non-judgemental setting for clients to understand themselves. The client experiences this idea of a non-judgemental approach as acceptance and respect for him. Rogers's perception was to adopt the client's perceptual field as the basis for genuine understanding, trying to see the client's world through his eyes in order to really understand him.

Rogers called his approach 'counselling' to differentiate it from the term 'psychotherapy' with all its connotations of diagnosis, treatment and insights on the part of the therapist. The word gained familiarity in Britain in the 1960s. This approach has been accepted as fundamental for humanistic counselling and used widely in counselling training courses in this country.

Probably the most fundamental concepts of what is now known as person-centred therapy are trust, empathy, congruence, genuine respect for the other, and unconditional regard for the client that includes a non-judgemental view of them. It is interesting that a non-judgemental approach is one of the core principles of person-centred therapy. Later in life, after the death of his parents, Rogers was to remark that his mother would most likely have made negative judgements about the work that he had contributed.

A part of the *trust* concept is to accept that a client has a natural tendency towards the realisation of their own potential, or a drive to their own health and self-development. The therapist trusts that the individual can strive for this realisation. It is the therapist's role to help individuals to discover their own potential for themselves, and resist the temptation to solve clients' problems for them. This may be one of the difficult aspects of the training in the person-centred approach.

There is a human tendency to want to rescue or save others (some-times for vicarious reasons, and sometimes because it may be a natural act of saving our own species). Rogers maintained that unless clients undergo the labour of self-discovery and realisation for themselves, they would not find their own resources to solving life problems.

Listening to clients without judgement or interpretation is therefore a prerequisite of being present and available to clients. This concept relies on the moment to moment experience in the relationship. The therapist facilitates clients' own meanings of their present inner experiences. In person-centred therapy, the transference onto the therapist is not considered a necessary part of a client's growth. The concern in this therapy is the attitude towards self and life change, rather than the structure of personality.

People's perception of themselves is their *self-structure*. When a person's self-structure is *congruent* (or in total accord) with his experience of the world, his feelings can flow outwards to others in relationships described by Buber, as an *I–thou* relationship. There are problems when the self-structure is incongruent with the individual's experiences.

GESTALT THERAPY

Fritz Perls (1893–1970) and his wife, Laura, founded a phenomenological-existential therapy known as Gestalt therapy in the 1940s. There is no exact translation of the German word *Gestalt*; the nearest in English is 'whole' or 'meaningful shape' to suggest a needed completion of something that is incomplete.

Perls was born in Berlin into a lower middle-class Jewish family. He had an unhappy childhood and was a rebellious and difficult child at home and school. Nevertheless, he managed to complete his education and graduate as a doctor and psychiatrist. He worked with Kurt Goldstein at his institute for brain damaged soldiers from the First World War. It was this experience, and later when he was analysed by Wilhelm Reich, that helped incorporate his views of body–mind therapy.

Fritz and Laura fled Nazi Germany and travelled to South Africa to found the first psychoanalytic institute. The couple finally settled in the States where some of Perls' memorable trainings took place at Esalen in California in the 1950s. Much has been written about Perls' confrontational and performance style of working, and the impact that had on Gestalt therapists who tried to imitate him. Today, Gestalt therapy has evolved and the powerful, original holistic theories are practised without the need to perform like Perls.

Theory

The theory of Gestalt therapy is based on a holistic view of the person, relating to their environment. The concept of this therapy is that problems occur when the person's natural, healthy growth is blocked.

There is a cycle of experiences that each of us has with others, which will start with a sensation, then an awareness, and, if not prohibited, will take in other stages such as intimacy, or drawing closer, ending with feeling satisfied and a letting go or withdrawing. The sexual act is an example of this cycle of experiences that needs to flow through the various stages in order to make a completed Gestalt.

When the person's natural flow or cycle of experiences is interrupted, through fear, anger or some other means, this leads to an incomplete Gestalt. Humans return continuously to an incomplete Gestalt that is the unconscious need to complete it.

The difficulty is when someone keeps doing the same thing, which is negative and unproductive. It is as if the person is trying their best to resolve the problem, but hasn't yet found another way to tackle it and so keeps knocking away with the same blunt tool that is inappropriate for the job anyway.

A simple, but nevertheless very common, example is when someone – (I'll call him A) – won't ask for what he needs but complains and blames B because B doesn't see A's need. In fact, B becomes *more* defensive from the continual, perceived attack and is even less likely to understand A's needs. The cycle of not getting the needs met, and feeling more and more rejected seeps into other areas of A's life.

Another example is when something very emotionally painful has happened, a person might block out the pain and feel 'nothing'. When similar situations take place in the person's life he is likely to repeat the blocking out or feeling nothing, which prevents him from knowing that he is experiencing pain. If he were aware that he felt pain, he could take some action to release it.

This storing up of tension and pain is called 'desensitisation' in Gestalt therapy. The Gestalt therapist helps the individual to release the blocked emotions by becoming aware that they are blocked in the first place. How the client blocks and how he releases them is the process of resolving the 'unfinished business' or the incomplete Gestalt. When this awareness takes place, the client is ready to do something different, something that changes the situation, thus completing the Gestalt. The completed Gestalt fades into the background, allowing for a new, pressing and incomplete Gestalt to come into the foreground. So the cycle continues.

The emphasis in Gestalt therapy is on therapists helping clients to become aware of their perceptions, behaviour, feelings and thoughts in the moment. Phenomenology is the observation of how someone perceives and experiences an event. The therapist enables the person to distinguish the difference between what is actually happening and felt in the present and what is left over from the past. Explanations and interpretations are not considered as potent as the experience of the feelings.

> *The only goal in Gestalt therapy is awareness for the client of what he does, how he does it, or how he blocks himself from doing something.*

Gestalt therapists use experiments in the therapy session in order that a client can experience their feelings, rather than talk about them. The relationship between the therapist and client is of special concern in Gestalt therapy, growing out of the contact between the two people.

Contact, or intimacy, is developed through genuine self-expression and the sharing of feelings and thoughts. Through authentic contact, the person's self-esteem and identity grows. Martin Buber's idea that the person (the 'I') only has meaning in relation to others accords with Gestalt therapy, where real dialogue takes precedence over therapeutic techniques. The therapist practises transparency of herself, revealing her own feelings when she considers it appropriate and productive to the client. There has to be some opacity or discrimination of this readiness to reveal herself, however, depending on the stage that the client and the therapeutic relationship has reached.

PSYCHOSYNTHESIS

This approach was developed as a therapy to encompass the trans-personal elements that fill the spiritual gap in psychotherapy, and was founded by an Italian psychiatrist, Roberto Assagioli (1888–1974), a Freudian analyst and contemporary of Jung and Freud.

Assagioli was influenced by spiritual, mystical and philosophical teachings from eastern and western cultures. Although Assagioli saw himself as a scientist, using a medical model for treating his patients, he encompassed the spiritual. His understanding of the individual was related to the fragmentation of the world. He felt that self-acceptance of the individual's own fragmentation released his potential.

Theory

Sub-personalities are considered important in this therapy, and are seen as the conflicts and dilemmas that we continuously struggle with. The therapist works creatively with different parts of the client's personality that are in conflict. The therapist's task is to bring clarity to the confusion. When there is conflict, energy is blocked. When there is a freeing of conflict, the energy is unblocked and a synsthesis of two or more parts of the personality occurs. The essence of psychosynthesis is the harmonious integration of all component parts around a unifying centre.

Discovering the 'I', or the true self, is to find one's centre – an inner liberation. This is not enough for harmonious integration. The needs for contact with others and belonging are given equal focus.

Self-knowledge is emphasised for change, and this is not sufficient without the 'will' to consolidate transformation. The will is seen as a cluster of phenomena that are basic to mental health. It is the capacity for choice, the ability to direct the self.

Psychosynthesis pays attention to a higher consciousness called the superconscious. The psyche is conceptualised as seven stages of consciousness, with the higher self as the divine human being with their potential. The therapist is the mirror for the client's choice of whether to change or not. The dialogic relationship, as described by Buber, is seen as the attainment of true relationship.

The therapist uses many tools to support the work. She may encourage a client to use narrative and may make use of a sandbox and objects for the client to tell his story. The client chooses and arranges the objects in the sand to represent something in his life. The therapist mirrors the client's story so that the client can see where he needs to make the changes and re-tell his story. Creative imagery is another technique that the therapist employs.

PSYCHODRAMA

The potential for healing is considered only as limited as the human imagination. Creativity, spontaneity, movement, self-expression are all elements of the humanistic schools, of which psychodrama is a good example. Psychodrama is frequently integrated into other therapeutic methods.

The origin of psychodrama is attributed to the psychiatrist and philosopher Jacob Moreno (1889–1974), who is also considered to be the father of group humanistic psychotherapy. The human potential movement and the encounter groups take their origins from Moreno's early work.

His contribution of *role-play* to encourage creative change is used in many settings, such as psychotherapy and counselling, family and couple work, with children, education, the military, industry and management. He carried out important work with people who stammered. He was also the innovator of self-help groups, and instrumental in the 1950s in the setting up of therapeutic communities.

Moreno worked with people to put them in a centrally responsible role in their own life drama by empowering them to do their own healing. In the group, scenes from the past are enacted in the present through a method of improvisation, with the client directing and taking several roles. It is in this creative activity that the individual can discover his creativity and develop confidence. Activity and the creativity that is engendered is seen as the opposite of passivity, with all its inherent feelings of helplessness, shame and guilt. New approaches to old problems can be tried and experienced. Fundamental to psychodrama is the freeing of psychic energy (catharsis – see Glossary) that releases vitality and expression.

NOTE

1 Jewish mystical movement of the eighteenth century in Eastern Europe.

FURTHER READING

Buber, M. (1958) *I and Thou*, trans. R.G. Smith, New York: Scribner and Sons. (Original work published 1923.)

Frankl, V. (1963) *Man's Search For Meaning*, New York: Washington Square Press.

Kahn, M. (1991) *Between Therapist and Client*, New York: W.H. Freeman and Company.

Kohut, H. (1977) *The Restoration of the Self*, Connecticut: International Universities Press, Inc.

Kohut, H. (1984) *How Does Analysis Cure?*, London: The University of Chicago Press.

Lowen, A. (1969) 'The betrayal of the body', in W. Dryden and J. Rowan (eds) (1988) *Innovative Therapy in Britain*, Milton Keynes: Open University Press.

Mollon, P. (1993) *The Fragile Self*, London: Whurr Publishers Ltd.

Rogers, C.R. (1967) *On Becoming a Person*, London: Constable and Company Ltd.

Rosenberg, J.L., Rand, M.L. and Asay, D. (1985) *Body, Self & Soul: Sustaining Integration*, Atlanta, Ga.: Humanics Ltd.

Tart, C. (ed.) (1976) *Transpersonal Psychologies*, New York: Harper and Row.

Yalom, I.D. (1980) *Existential Psychotherapy*, New York: Basic Books, Inc.

Yontef, G.M. (1993) *Awareness Dialogue & Process: Essays on Gestalt Therapy*, New York: The Gestalt Journal Press, Inc.

4

TOWARDS COGNITIVE-BEHAVIOURAL THERAPIES

TRANSACTIONAL ANALYSIS

Transactional analysis (TA) is often included in the humanistic category, but is probably somewhere between a humanistic approach and a highly structured system that offers answers and directions. TA does this through its theoretical concepts and systematic approach.

Eric Berne (1910–70) originated TA in the 1950s, and saw it as a systemic phenomenology. Berne was a shy, private man who seems to have had difficulties in expressing his playful nature unless he felt it was safe to do so. This made for restrictions in his relationships. He formulated a theory that people wrote life scripts about themselves, and because they were pre-written they would have to live their lives according to them. Commentators on Berne believe that he may have lived his original life script to die of a heart attack at the age of 60, just as his mother had done.

Berne was involved in the human potential movement at Esalen, California, where he met with Fritz Perls, Abraham Maslow and others. In the 1960s he wrote a best-seller entitled *Games People Play*. His ideas that people are involved in playing games, in order to satisfy their needs, instead of being honest and up front about them, opened up a new way of thinking about human relationships.

Theory

Like Adler, Berne was interested in a person's life goals. Scripts and therapeutic contracts are important in TA. TA's approach to the theory of personality is presented through three active, dynamic and observable ego states called 'the parent', 'the adult' and 'the child'. Each state operates in any individual at any time. Each individual, through their basic human need for recognition and acceptance, called *strokes* in TA, formulates a plan for themselves. This is their life script in early childhood that they have founded on faulty beliefs about themselves in their relationship to others.

These existential beliefs are reinforced by repetition of unproductive patterns of behaviour, called *games*, in an attempt to get the individual's needs satisfied. When a person changes their problematic behaviour, or games, the psychological energy balance of their life changes accordingly. TA encourages a client's intellectual understanding whilst supporting a client's emotional expressions.

The TA concepts are not only expressed verbally but have symbols to increase understanding. The TA therapist will demonstrate the symbols, such as bar graphs or egograms, to show where there is imbalance in a person's behaviour patterns. This is frequently reflected in the client's way of seeing life, and their reaction to others. An imbalance may be from having an adaptive child, or critical parent attitude, for example.

The language of TA is very specialised and is taught by the therapist to the client. For example, a *transaction* is used instead of 'communication'. There are two levels of transactions: the social overt level (what we say to others), and the psychological covert level (what we feel, but don't say to others).

PERSONAL CONSTRUCT

George Kelly thought about the person in terms of activity. He took the ideas of the philosopher Kant that the individual is an active agent, a person in constant motion. Kelly's concepts and theories of Personal Construct are rooted in a scientific approach, a problem-solving model with a difference. They are not based on fixed facts, but on supporting current hypotheses and theories about why certain things happen. The testing out of these theories to see whether they are reliable and validated is Personal Construct's scientific approach.

Theory

Kelly's ideas are that we view the world as we perceive it to be, not as it really is. This was something that the Greek philosopher Epictetus believed when he said that 'men are not disturbed by the thing itself, but by the attitude that they take of it'.

We are constantly making predictions about ourselves and events – construing in our minds. The client tries out alternative ways of thinking, acting and being within the safety of the therapy setting. There is an experimental view employed in Personal Construct therapy that if the client behaves 'as if' something were another way he can test out for himself the usefulness of the experience.

Reconstructing and experimenting are the central elements to this form of therapy. Using role-play or enactment for the client to try out other alternatives is the humanistic dimension of experiencing rather than talking 'about' feelings and thoughts. In this way, there is similarity to psychodrama and Gestalt experiments, and like Gestalt therapy Personal Construct takes a here-and-now stance.

Personal Construct therapy believes in the psychotherapist risking herself creatively in testing out new hypotheses to avoid therapeutic sterility. The tenet of this theory is in re-creating the self.

THREE-STAGE HELPING MODEL

Gerard Egan devised an integrated approach of the humanistic and behavioural cultures. Defined in problem management, with a focus on goals, Egan's emphasis is on the creativity of the practitioner within a structure of three stages.

The first stage is to understand the presenting problem that the client brings. The second stage is to explore a preferred scenario. The third stage is to explore and agree the action that is needed to reach the desired goals.

The emphasis is on the tasks and skills for action that the client needs to take to make changes. Egan's model subscribes to empathy and respect for the client. Challenging, when appropriate, and teaching assertiveness if necessary. He believes that the client needs more than listening by the practitioner to help him make the changes he needs. The focus is on action and changes. This model was very popular in the 1980s, and is often incorporated into a wider range of counselling methods.

There were two major schools that developed as a further radical departure from traditional psychoanalysis, and have become therapies in their own right. One focused on the behavioural aspects of an individual and did not regard cognition as important, whilst the other school focused on cognition first and then the behaviour.

COGNITIVE AND BEHAVIOUR THERAPIES

These therapies stress thinking, analysing, decision-making and doing. Cognitive and behavioural therapists are directive and give tasks to complete outside the session. Therapy tends to be brief.

The basis for these therapies is on the assumption that cognition, emotion and behaviour have a reciprocal cause and effect relationship. It is not the experience that counts but the cognitive creation, or interpretation, that produces psychological disturbance. In this respect there is a similarity to Personal Construct therapy.

Aaron Beck, Albert Ellis, Hans Eysenck, Joseph Wolpe, Albert Bandura and B.F. Skinner are leaders in the field of cognitive-behavioural therapies. They based their work on the learning and conditioning experiments of Ivan Pavlov in the 1920s. Whilst Ivan Petrovich Pavlov (1849–1936) was a physiologist, it is his extensive programme of research into experimentation on conditioned responses for which he is best known. He never referred to himself as a psychologist, but his contribution to psychology and to the treatment in cognitive-behavioural psychotherapy is fundamental.

In learned helplessness the individual perceives his own responses as inadequate and himself as a failure. Thus the individual's behaviour is an indicator of his beliefs and consequently the perception he has of the control over his life. Symptoms that the individual develops are seen as behaviour which has arisen through faulty learning and thinking.

The Maudsley hospital in London has played a significant role in advancing the behavioural therapies, especially in treating anxieties, panic attacks, phobias, eating disorders, sexual dysfunction and obsessive-compulsive disorders.

Many behavioural therapies themselves have undergone changes, where they have been modified and expanded to include cognition theories and approaches in their work.

Theory

Behavioural therapy is a problem-solving strategy that uses a scientific method, supported by continuous research, revision and empirical testing of concepts and procedures. In spite of its scientific approach and the directive and active stance of the therapist, it is not a non-human approach. Research shows that, whilst there may be less emphasis on the relationship in this approach, the relationship still has an importance to the outcome of therapeutic success.

The influence of behavioural therapy is felt in medicine, rehabilitation programmes, working with autistic and hyperactive children and stress management. Treatment is effective for eating and drinking disorders and to stop smoking. One of the popular outcomes of behavioural therapy is assertiveness training, which is an interpersonal skills training. Behavioural therapy regards such skills as fundamental, to be taught throughout the stages of life.

The goal of behavioural therapy is to change the behaviour; to interrupt the learnt negative reflexes. A person's life can often be so restricted as to handicap them. Altering the behaviour affects the quality of the person's life.

The aim is to put anxiety into a more realistic perspective by teaching the individual to confront the situations and events that lead to the anxiety. This is a method known as desensitisation, reducing the sensitivity to the situation by normalising it through repeated confrontation.

Crucial to the effectiveness of the treatment is that the patient and therapist work together co-operatively to define specific goals at the beginning of therapy and to agree tasks. It is the client's responsibility for choosing the changes he wishes to make.

Albert Ellis is regarded as the grandfather of cognitive-behavioural therapy. He developed a theory called rational-emotive therapy. Ellis was an anxious young person, who was terrified of speaking in public. He overcame his fears through the adoption of his own theories.

Rational-emotive therapy has been developed in this country largely by Windy Dryden at Goldsmiths College, London, and is now called rational-emotive behaviour therapy. One of the aims of the therapy is to address the faulty internalised thoughts and beliefs that clients have about themselves (but may be unaware of).

Cognitive therapy shares some features with some forms of behavioural therapy, and is different from others. Both forms of therapy are problem-oriented and focus on the present. Cognitive therapy recognises that humans hold a 'dialogue' with themselves, and that focusing on the dialogue is important. Metaphors may be used to enable someone to see another way of thinking about something. There is a common-sense approach that what people think and say about themselves is important to the way that they feel about themselves.

Hans Eysenck was born in 1916. He was an extraordinarily prolific writer and researcher, with wide interests. He, like so many of the pioneers, suffered from a difficult upbringing. Both his parents were actors and were frequently separated through work. His parents divorced when he was young, and Hans saw little of either of them. His experience of parenting was one of emotional and financial deprivation. He was brought up by his maternal grandmother, who gave little in the way of discipline but loved him very much. She struggled financially to provide for both of them.

During the war, Eysenck's father joined the Nazi party. Eysenck despised his father. Whether it was because of the strong feelings he had for his father, or his own strength of convictions, Hans was violently anti-Nazi. He was forced to flee to France with his grandmother and mother. When the Germans overran France, his grandmother, who was crippled, was transported to a concentration camp and died there. He blamed himself throughout his life for not having appreciated his grandmother's loyalty and love when she was alive.

Eysenck was rigorously attacked for his controversial views later in life, for his research and writing. Shortly after the war, when he was living in London, he founded the psychological department of the Institute of Psychiatry. He had a passion for truth, and scientific methods that frequently clashed with the field of psychiatry and psychoanalysis, which did not evaluate theories and treatment outcome.

His interests were wide and varied and included the study and assessment of personality and intelligence, introversion and extraversion, behavioural genetics, and behaviour therapy. He studied the prophylactic effects of behaviour therapy in cancer and heart disease. An example of this would be to study the effects of relaxation techniques to see whether they prevented people from getting cancer or heart disease.

He brought his scientific approach to other topics such as the social attitudes of sex, violence, and the media, crowd behaviour, smoking, criminality, suggestion and suggestibility. He was also very interested in parapsychology and astrology.

Aaron Beck researched depression in the 1960s. He rejected the traditional Freudian concept that depression is retroflected anger (anger turned back into the person themselves). What he observed was that patients had a negative bias in their cognitive processing. He went on to develop his theory of a cognitive model of depression. Beck's contribution to the understanding of suicide came from a longitudinal study of depressed, suicidal patients. He found that those patients who scored high in hopelessness went on to commit suicide. Assessment through the kind of scales that Beck produced is common in cognitive therapy. The Beck Depression Inventory is the most commonly known and used in clinical work.

Theory

'Guided discovery' is a strategy of cognitive therapy that explores the patient's misperceptions and beliefs in the present and links them to experiences of the past. The aim is continuously to test and evaluate the person's reality against a more neutral or balanced perception. The basic beliefs are tested for accuracy. When the patient discovers that they are not accurate they are encouraged to work with the therapist to construct other, more realistic beliefs as hypotheses, and to test them. The cognitive shifts that occur have been likened to a computer programme. The programme dictating the kind of data admitted decides the way that the data are integrated and determines the resultant behaviour (Beck and Weishaar 1989).

Cognitive therapy does not work with infantile repression or the unconscious. The concern is not with experiencing the emotions, or being aware of sensations, or expressing feelings. The therapist is directive and active and the collaborative arrangement with the patient is paramount. Cognitive therapy is highly structured and emphasises linking the conscious beliefs and current experiences that produce distorted interpretations. Therapy is short term (usually about 3 months), which is proving to be popular in many settings where cost-effectiveness and efficacy are essential. The NHS and the commercial world are prime examples of settings for this therapy.

There are therapies that have not been mentioned, such as hypnotherapy, or those that have Asian influence and are spiritually based, for example. It is not possible to cover all the therapies that are current, but I urge the reader to visit a library or bookshop. There is a wealth of reading material on all the approaches mentioned here, and others. There are several bookshops that specialise in counselling and psychotherapy and you will find some in the List of Resources (pp. 203–24).

The therapies that have been mentioned are all different, yet they all form a continuous evolutionary system for the same human well-being. All therapies have their strengths and their weaknesses. All are restricted in some way by the limitations of their own theories.

There is a wealth of understanding and a weight of theory behind the profession that is continuously under scrutiny, most notably from within the profession itself. Research into the effectiveness of different therapies continues to grow.

There is a push towards greater academic input into theory and process through research. In meta-analytic studies gathered over the last twenty years, there is evidence to show that all methodologies of the major psychotherapies worked effectively, and none were seriously deficient.

> *An important outcome of research is that no one therapeutic*
> *school is more effective than any other, and that it is the*
> *relationship between the therapist and the individual that has*
> *the most healing effect.*

All the therapies that have been described here show a variety of approaches that differ from each other. There are often differences in the meanings of the terms and language that are used, even when the same words are employed. Therapists also vary their practice according to their own personalities. Even the exact goal of one therapy may be different from another.

How is anyone to know which training they should undertake? Being informed is a good way to reach a decision. Read more about the approach or approaches that interest you. Speak to tutors on courses and ask them to explain, in straightforward terms, what their particular approach is. Taking your time to find out what approach interests you will benefit you in the end.

The next three chapters deal with training.

FURTHER READING

Beck, A.T. and Weishaar, M.E. (1989) 'Cognitive Therapy', in R.J. Corsini and D. Wedding (eds) *Current Psychotherapies*, Illinois: F.E. Peacock Publications, Inc. pp. 285–318.

Berne, E. (1964) *Games People Play*, New York: Grove Press.

Egan, G. (1986) *The Skilled Helper*, Mouterey, Calif.: Brooks/Cole Publishers.

Erikson, E.H. (1995) *Childhood and Society*, London: Vintage.

Fransella, F. (1995) *George Kelly*, London: Sage Publications.

Sheldon, B. (1995) *Cognitive-Behavioural Therapy*, London: Routledge.

Stewart, I. and Joines, V. (1987) *TA Today*, Nottingham: Lifespace.

Trower, P., Casey, A. and Dryden, W. (1988) *Cognitive-Behavioural Counselling in Action*, London: Sage Publications.

5

THINKING OF BECOMING A COUNSELLOR OR PSYCHOTHERAPIST?

The subject of human behaviour is fascinating: why we do what we do? Trying to understand this and the rich, inner life of human beings is challenging and rewarding.

Training is demanding. The sorts of demands that are required of trainees are outlined in this chapter and the next two.

In this chapter I am looking at:

- How I got to go on my first training.
- Why you want to go on a course.
- The criticisms directed at counselling and psychotherapy.
- The expectations of potential trainees.
- The personal qualities of a counsellor and psychotherapist.
- What happens in a counselling or therapy session.

HOW I GOT TO GO ON MY FIRST TRAINING

Sometimes the original reasons for wanting to do a particular training can change once you are on a course. I will give you my own experience as an example of how some people may make a decision about a training course.

In the early 1980s I was a teacher of English to foreign students. Many of the students I taught sought my advice relating to their problems of acculturation in their new country. Acculturation is the process of accepting a new culture into which a person has either chosen to live or has to accept to live in. This is a very difficult place (for some) to integrate the new culture with the one that the person was brought up with.

I was concerned that I could have been giving the students the wrong advice. Most of them came from an eastern culture and had difficulties not only with the language but also with the system: using the telephone, going to the doctors, finding work, and reading bus timetables, etc. Every small daily detail can be a problem that lowers self-confidence. What was expected of them was often a mystery to them. Manners were different and had different meanings to them, as theirs do to us. Shrugging the shoulders in one culture is an acceptable response. In another culture it is seen as disrespectful. If you don't have enough knowledge of the language to raise this seemingly minor point, how can it be checked out?

Many expressed to me in various ways that they felt they had been flung into a game where they did not know the rules. They were embarrassed or distressed by the mistakes that they would make in their speech or behaviour.

A colleague told me that I needed to go on a counselling course. Without wondering what it was about or whether there were any others to compare, I enrolled on the one he had heard about from someone else.

I was nervous that I would not be accepted on the course because I had no prior knowledge of counselling – even though I didn't know what counselling was, or that I could have already been practising some elements of it in my work.

I suspect that many people may feel this and do not check what courses are offering because they believe that they may not be accepted, particularly those who have not studied for many years. They may feel a lack of confidence about their abilities and worry more about that than what a course can actually offer *them*.

There were few courses around in the early 1980s when I did my original training, so my choice would have been limited anyway. But it was whilst undergoing the certificate year in counselling that I realised two things:

1   that counselling was not about giving advice, which was a great relief;
2   that I wanted to leave teaching and make counselling my career.

On the counselling training course I found something that I was really engaged with and was hungry to know more about. It was the beginning of a long road that I still travel.

I have some clearer ideas of who I am now and how I respond to my world, but I know that the learning is ongoing. The love of learning is as important to me as the work that I do. Writing this book is a facet of that learning.

Feeling concerned about giving advice was the trigger to undergo training that opened up layers of knowledge, understanding and awareness for me. The value of that training experience was immeasurable, and went way beyond learning about the difficulties of advice-giving.

WHY YOU WANT TO GO ON A COURSE

Have you considered carefully why you want to go on a training course for psychotherapy or counselling? Ask yourself the question, 'Why do I want to be a counsellor or psychotherapist?' Honest self-searching is vital.

It may help you to discuss this with someone else, or to write down everything that comes into your mind, without censoring any of your thoughts. If you don't judge your thoughts at this stage you will find that you can explore your motivations more deeply. There are many reasons why someone chooses a course of counselling or psychotherapy. Here are a few of the reasons that I have come across during my work as a trainer:

- You may be in a job where you feel that counselling skills would enhance your work.
- It may be that you have had some counselling or psychotherapy yourself, and found the experience so valuable, or the therapist or counsellor so helpful, that you want to do the same for someone else.
- You may be the kind of person to whom others are always bringing their problems.
- You believe that a training would offer you discipline and boundaries, as well as theory and structure.
- You may like helping or caring for others and are interested in their stories.
- You may want to find out more about yourself.
- You are fascinated by human behaviour.
- It may be that you want to train for a different career, and consider that you would make a good counsellor or psychotherapist.
- You may not recognise your own needs, vicariously helping others who are needy.

You may think of a combination of those points or some other reasons entirely. When applying for a course that is more than a short introduction, you will be asked for your reasons. You will also be asked what you consider that you can offer. It is as well to think about these questions very thoroughly for your own self-understanding. The questions may raise anxieties when you search more deeply, and you may not find the answers, but to raise them and reflect on them is important. Being reflective and searching are qualities for counselling and psychotherapy.

Hidden motives

There may be reasons that are hard to acknowledge. Those things we don't want to admit to can be 'hidden' motives. Helping others acknowledge the things that are difficult to speak about is an important part of counselling and psychotherapy work. We must begin with ourselves in order to understand any relevance for others.

Not wanting to speak about something is one aspect. Another aspect of a hidden motive is that it is something that we may not even be aware of. This makes it difficult of course. A way to test this out is to consider the reasons you don't think could apply to you. I usually find the things that I don't want to look at are the things that I need to look at!

An example of this is where someone may want to work on aspects of themselves that they find very difficult, but instead of entering therapy they choose to do this work through becoming a counsellor or psychotherapist. This is an example of vicarious therapy. Doing something for another that really belongs to the self. Trying to heal others instead of healing the self. This can happen unconsciously. If someone does this without knowing it, then they are using clients to work on their own process. This does not make for effective practice or for integrity. In therapy, a client may re-experience an early relationship with his mother or someone else significant, where he had been used for her emotional needs.

There are issues for clients that resonate for practitioners. However much therapy a person has had, there are residues that linger. Going into different stages of our lives we are faced with different issues. Being aware that this happens enables us to take our issues to personal therapy, rather than trying to work them through vicariously.

Another criticism that has been made about counsellors and psychotherapists is that many enter the profession because they are emotionally needy people, and get their needs met through working with people who need them. It is reasonable to say that it is human to want to be needed and valued. If those needs are not met humans can feel a range of things, from dissatisfaction to despair. However, if there are overriding needs of the counsellor or therapist that are not recognised, understood and worked on, then there will be problems within the therapeutic relationship.

One of the things that counsellors and therapists learn in their training is that they have to get their needs met outside the therapeutic relationship. It is during the training that the trainee understands and appreciates why an expectation that clients could satisfy those needs is unethical, and harmful to the client.

Practitioners of all approaches need to have a balanced life-style where their different needs can be satisfied.

There will be a great deal of emphasis concerning the 'needs of the client' on a course, and 'keeping your own needs outside the counselling or therapy relationship'. This is as it should be, for someone who comes into therapy is already vulnerable and is expecting to receive some clarity and help into their process. It is not helpful to them if the therapist brings in her own problems and needs of the moment.

You will probably realise that hidden motives have very particular meaning (which is often why they were hidden in the first place). This exploration is a way of understanding more about yourself. Bringing those motives out will not only help you in your self-understanding but will test the strength of your feelings about wanting to embark on a training path.

Positive and negative reasons

Once you have listed your reasons, you could then begin to explore how the demands of this kind of work might affect you emotionally and practically. When thinking about the demands, it is relevant to explore both the *for* and *against* of each of your reasons. Exploring the against, or negative side, is not intended to defeat yourself at the outset. It is a way to help you weigh up all the consequences and come to a decision for yourself.

A positive aspect for your wanting to train may be that you like working with people. You may enjoy the interaction and closeness, or the stimulation of working with other people. The intensity of focused work may have a strong appeal to you.

You may feel that an in-depth training is very appropriate for you at this time of your life; that this kind of training would enrich you in a particular way. You may want to develop your self-understanding and improve the way that you interact with others. You may feel that you have the time to devote to this training right now. You may feel that you have had a great many experiences and have gained relevant insights to bring to the work.

You may want to train because the work appeals to you. Developing a special and real relationship so that others can make the changes that they need may be important to you. You may be fascinated and curious about the complexities of the human psyche.

The negative side for you may be the time constraints of training. Even on a certificate course there will be texts to be read and essays to be written. Can you fit your studies in with your work, family and social commitments? Can you cope with the emotional demands of exploring and sharing feelings in a group?

It is relevant to think through to working in the field. Counselling and psychotherapy is about quietness, and (for many practitioners) the loneliness of working in this particular way may be difficult to cope with. Try to imagine spending hours each day working a set time with just one other person, focusing on the issues that they bring without any shared chatter with colleagues. You may miss the relief that is felt through social interaction with work colleagues that can lighten moods. Consider what the difficulties of working in this kind of isolation would be for you.

The confidentiality boundary precludes therapists from the liberation of off-loading (see Glossary) to others about their clients. Ethically, counsellors and psychotherapists cannot chat to friends about clients' issues that have been raised in sessions. Neither can they puzzle over clients' dilemmas with friends. (See Chapter 1 on confidentiality.)

If you are someone who enjoys giving and receiving feedback about your work from peers or colleagues, then you need to consider the constraints of this element of your working life in counselling and psychotherapy.

The intimacy of working in a one-to-one situation also prevents others outside the therapeutic relationship from gaining any direct, visible knowledge, understanding or appreciation of the work that you do. Not being able to see the way that other colleagues work also means that it is difficult for many practitioners to evaluate their own style and professional progress. This is one of the reasons for having regular supervision, which is discussed in Chapter 1.

Badly run training courses

There are still too many badly run or inadequate training courses, and the many points raised in this book are intended to highlight this. The reader, as an intended trainee, can contribute to improving training through being aware of the information given here. Your understanding will enable you to raise the questions that will help improve training courses. Having such information will also help you not to accept low standards.

A further point about training is that it is interesting that the majority of counselling and psychotherapy (diploma) courses are part-time, one day a week, for a period of three to four years. Compared to a social work course of two or three years' full-time training, this is indeed economic, brief and time-limited.

Counselling and psychotherapy are an acceptable and recognisable force of human service providers in many spheres of public welfare, spanning education, medical settings and community settings, industry and the private sector. There are a great number of voluntary counsellors. There are also people who use counselling as part of their existing jobs.

Training courses have a responsibility to educate people according to the needs of society and to equip their trainees appropriately to meet those needs.

THE CRITICISMS DIRECTED AT COUNSELLING AND PSYCHOTHERAPY

Furthering the exploration, I will consider the criticisms that are directed at counselling and psychotherapy from within the profession and outside.

There has been a great deal of criticism about counselling, in particular, over the years. As it has grown in popularity, so some individuals have set themselves up to practise without undergoing the necessary path of a thorough and responsible training. The public has a right to be protected from bogus or ill-trained counsellors and therapists: those who have little understanding of the complexities of working with the emotions and trust of people who seek alleviation of their troubles.

Outside the profession there are forms of criticism that negate therapeutic work: where people demean or dismiss the skills of coun- selling and psychotherapy. I have heard remarks about the therapist's participation as *only* sitting there and listening, which does sound non-demanding and something almost anyone could do; the reality, however, is far from that.

There is a great deal involved in training that it is important to have considered; psychotherapy and counselling are not the easy option that many people believe them to be. These disciplines are often stressful and difficult, demanding a great deal from the practitioner in terms of personal qualities, skills, knowledge, understanding, perception and resources, as I hope that this book will show.

It is a counselling axiom that the welfare of the person who enters into counselling must always be paramount. Equally, prospective trainees who genuinely wish to commit themselves to the rigours and demands of training in counselling (or psychotherapy), have the right to good standards of practice regarding the training available.

There are those who may view therapy as nothing more than a very particular relationship, where one person (the client) needs help from another (the practitioner) and can trust and feel supported at that particular time. This is a description that also fits for a good friend, or supportive partner; yet therapy is not a reciprocal relationship as the terms 'friendship' or 'partner' suggest.

There are critics who believe that therapy does not work at all, and is merely an obsession in the West of a self-indulgent society. Therapy has sometimes been associated in people's minds with the selfish society. The 'me first' concept, where an individual's personal needs and wants are paramount and encouraged at the expense of others and the community. If this is what therapy ultimately results in, then it has indeed failed.

These same critics say that people who have done things out of a sense of duty, or communal commitment, are being told by their therapists that they should put themselves first and ignore the needs of others.

Yet the opposite is in fact the case. There is a wise saying from the *Pirke Avot* (see Glossary) that could be ascribed to the positive use of counselling and psychotherapy in relation to self-indulgence.

If I am not for myself, who will be for me?
If I am only for myself what am I?
If not now, when?

Through therapy, an individual can come to realise that the things he has been doing for others out of a sense of duty were done, vicariously, in the (buried) hope of getting his own needs met. He learns that he has the right to ask for his needs directly, and whilst he may have responsibility to support other adults, he does not have responsibility for their lives. He also realises that he can contribute more positively to the community precisely because he has learnt how to get his own needs met honestly. He no longer needs to resort to manipulation of others, feel resentment, or subjugate himself – all of which led to his former unhappiness.

'Being for oneself' is vital to becoming an individuated (see Glossary) person, with separate and different ideas from others, and specific needs, wants, choices, responsibilities, likes and dislikes. It is who we are. There is a great deal of difference between taking care of the self honestly, and selfishly taking things away from others. This idea of someone autonomous and individuated is vital, but also not enough.

There is responsibility, on many levels, for others to be considered. The responsibility for others as well as ourselves is the way that couples, families, communities and societies can exist, and live in some harmony.

Therapy has made an enormous contribution to people's understanding of the difference between being for oneself and assuming responsibility for others. In this sense, therapy can make a major contribution towards the individual separating, individuating and giving willingly to society.

> *Counselling and psychotherapy are, hopefully, the very forum for clients who have got into difficulties, to work out how to be themselves and not only be for themselves. This is a paradox of life amongst the many paradoxes that we live.*

There are those who believe that therapy is a waste of time; that being involved in something worth while would take people's minds off their problems. On many levels this is true, as it is a human need to feel worth while and valued. Yet energy is needed in order to contribute. The very energy needed for motivation is often depleted through feeling worthless.

At best, critical voices suggest that if you believe something will work, then it probably will. So going to a therapist is a predetermined *fait accompli* – a sort of psychic placebo. There is nothing wrong in believing that something will work, or that therapy acts as a psychic placebo. Therapy can be the kick-start or affirmation that someone needs to get started on a particular course of action.

Critics may point to the deleterious effects that therapy has on an individual's family life. Therapy is often long term and expensive. This can be so. It is also a measure of what someone considers his life is worth. In practical terms, a commitment does have to be considered carefully.

A criticism suggests that therapy is intense and focused on details of the client's life, but cannot be considered in isolation (i.e. out of context). This is so. Individuals' lives are interrelated and are a part of family and socio-political environments, with all of the pressures that this entails. Changes from therapy will undoubtedly affect a client's relationships within his social setting. Other people in the client's social world may regard the effects as detrimental. The client may regard the changes as beneficial. The client's changes may act as a catalyst and encourage change in others. Change is a part of the evolution of living and cannot be avoided.

Counselling

Counselling has come under more critical attack than psychotherapy, probably because it is the more recent of the therapies. Regardless of all the external criticism that is hurled at counselling, its growth continues.

Structures and hierarchies are rapidly growing up around the counselling field: codes of ethics and good practice, complaints procedures, accrediting counsellors, and training. Research is carried out to evaluate the cost-effectiveness of counselling and counsellor competency. In spite of this, counsellors on the whole show no great urgency to evaluate and audit their work, and many ignore research by not reading about it. They apply themselves to the 'business in hand', that of the changes that clients want to make, and disregard the changes that are necessary for their work to be professional.

There are questions that are continuously raised but which counsellors themselves on the whole do not want to answer. Questions to do with the numbers of people currently choosing to become counsellors. Is this an unleashed appetite for self-awareness? Is counselling seen as an easy option for employment in a society that is changing rapidly, and is so competitive? Do people fear losing their identity in a techno-culture? Do they turn to training in counselling to find out who they are? And then there is the question concerning the number of training institutes and schools that are mushrooming, but may not achieve a good standard of training.

These are important and relevant questions. There may be as many reasons for training as there are counsellors. Reflecting on your own reasons for choosing counselling will be revealing to you and may add to an understanding of some of the changes taking place in society in relation to counselling.

Influence and abuse of power

Many people are more aware now that advice-giving is more applicable to debt-counselling and welfare work. The purpose of counselling and psychotherapy is not about giving advice; but it must be said that some approaches are more directive than others and counsellors and therapists may influence people in a number of ways.

It is sometimes suggested that therapy operates through coercion, seduction and other forms of manipulation and control over the client. These ideas would be rigorously refuted in the therapy world. Yet everything that the practitioner does and says models something to the client. There is, therefore, the potential for influencing the client consciously and unconsciously. This is a very good reason why therapists need:

- to be cautious about interventions;
- to be aware of the power they have;
- to be self-reflective about whose needs are being met in the moment;
- to be trained to take these possibilities into consideration.

Denying that the therapist has power is to misuse it or even abuse it.

There has been a great deal of controversy in the media surrounding counselling, in particular, regarding the way some practitioners have abused their power and their clients. Some of the criticisms have been justified as there are, unfortunately, a few unethical practitioners employing bad practice who bring the therapy world into disrepute. To redress this abuse in any profession it is necessary for practitioners to be members of organisations that have a complaints procedure and other rigorous safeguards in place for the public's protection, as well as for the reputation of the profession.

The fact that anyone can set herself up as a counsellor or psychotherapist without any prior training or accreditation, registration or licensing, has also been the subject of intense controversy and debate.

Criticism, on the whole, is constructively used as a major force in both counselling and psychotherapy. This has resulted in shaping more rigorous training, forming complaints procedures, and accreditation and registration for improving standards. Eventually, licensing to practise will be in place. These are all policies that are devised to protect clients and improve the standards of practice. The consequence of tighter rules and regulations eventually filters down through training courses to the individual practitioner.

Criticism from within

As well as the principles and ethics of counselling and psychotherapy, there is also wide ongoing debate and criticism from within the profession regarding the validity of different approaches. Members of the more traditional schools that have been around for longer, such as the psychoanalytic and psychodynamic schools, pass judgement on the newer, humanistic and alternative approaches as being 'without substance'. They complain about the lack of sound theoretical structure. They criticise the training for not being rigorous enough. They maintain that practitioners from such training backgrounds lack a deeper understanding of the complexities of human behaviour, and consequently do more harm than good.

Some criticism can even be stronger than that. It is as if there are those in the older, established schools who feel threatened by an avalanche.

The question they may be raising is. 'Who are these upstarts who think that they can take over our profession?' There is an implied hierarchy of absolute truth, with the traditional schools believing that they are at the top of the hierarchy.

Religion and therapy

I am reminded of the quarrelling amongst religious bodies, within the different gradations of the same religion, where the more orthodox form of a particular religion may feel that it holds the only truth. The reformed versions of a religion are considered wayward and somehow less than they should be.

There is also something of a generation gap about these criticisms. It is as if the psychoanalytic and psychodynamic therapists are the real professionals with the knowledge and experience, and the rest are immature and arrogant in their ignorance.

For their part, the humanistic and alternative therapists and counsellors who make up the members of other schools give back their criticisms just as vociferously. They consider the orthodox schools to be rigid and dogmatic. Therapists from these orthodox schools are presumed to make their clients fit the analyst's theory rather than the other way round.

Theories have developed and evolved, but the orthodox schools are seen to be stuck in approaches and attitudes that do not reflect the society that we now live in. The non-orthodox accuse the orthodox for seeing themselves as the 'experts' in a way that does not belong to a society that encourages self-directiveness and self-responsibility.

The non-orthodox practitioners argue that counsellors and therapists need different skills for different clients at different times of the process. The traditionalists are seen as unable to accommodate other cultures, necessary in a pluralistic society, and only able to work from a white, middle-class, western way of seeing the world that is outdated and unhelpful.

Envy and adolescence

Many orthodox therapists have, up to now, charged more fees and therefore earned more money than non-orthodox therapists and counsellors. Perhaps envy is also at work. Envy, it would seem, is on both sides.

The in-fighting is off-putting of course, and news of it may come as a deep disappointment to the reader, but it exists and I don't want to deny it does. It would be such a relief to be able to say that therapists, thank heaven, have grown beyond such squabbling. The truth is that they have not.

Perhaps the whole counselling and psychotherapy culture is at a very adolescent stage. The analytic, older siblings feeling envious and pushed out by the younger. And just as at adolescence, the different approaches are unsure of themselves, yet state with utter assuredness their own claim to being.

Perhaps a source of disagreement is not about whose approach is right, but more about intolerance of what (or who) is different. The intolerance of others who are different exists, sometimes even more strongly, in those very places where we would least expect it: in religion and therapy. This book is not the place to reflect on this point, but only by exploring and naming the flaws from within can we hope to make changes and progress.

What I have described here is chaos, and may also be reflected in training courses. Chaos is an inevitable part of evolution. It is a component in the process of change and is always uncomfortable. But order does follow chaos, eventually.

One way that therapy can help

It was the assertiveness of the feminist movement that gave rise, indirectly, to assertiveness training courses. This type of course has been criticised as encouraging women who do not accept their lot in life to be demanding and aggressive. The definition implied in assertiveness is to be neither demanding nor aggressive, but to stand for one's self, firmly, without imposing or violating the rights of the other. And, like the ethos of therapy, assertiveness helps women to take responsibility for their own lives rather than remain dependent on others to make choices and decisions for them.

Women are learning about their personal needs and true worth in therapy. So many centuries of accepting the way things are has hidden the real damage to women's identity and self-esteem. The oppression of women (amongst other groups) has been a deep-rooted part of human culture for so long that it is normalised and difficult to see it as such.

THE EXPECTATIONS OF POTENTIAL TRAINEES

Trainees' expectations are frequently unrealistic before beginning a course, so that disappointment and frustration may be an inevitable outcome. Expectations, anxieties, frustrations and disappointments, satisfactions and rewards, are all rites of passage for trainees to pass through.

I conducted a short survey of a small number of people who were thinking of going on a training course in counselling, to see what they wanted or expected. The expectations of the training were very high. From enhancement of people's lives, to changing their lives. There were few expectations or anxieties expressed about being assessed during a training course.

The style of teaching was important. People did not want to be 'preached' at. Many people had idealistic expectations of tutors.

Some did not have any idea of what would happen on a course. Some expected lectures, discussions and having to read books. Most thought that they would learn skills and have to practise them in the group. Few realised that they would be working with clients during their training.

Different people had images of themselves that ranged from knowing nothing to knowing a great deal about theory and practice. Nobody wondered whether others in the group would be at different stages from themselves.

Some were anxious that they would have to disclose things about themselves. Some thought that they would not have to disclose anything. Some viewed the training as a path to a career. Others felt that they would use the training for their work. A few wanted to do it just for themselves.

Once you have explored your reasons for wanting to pursue training and still feel committed, you need to be aware that your training will not end when you have finished your course. Ongoing training in various forms is considered essential for this profession. It is important continuously to update and monitor one's own effectiveness in a field that deals with the enormity and complexity of the range of human emotions and stages of development. Outside your personal counselling, or therapy and supervision, you will need to apportion time and money into going to lectures, seminars, workshops, conferences, reading journals and books, and you may want to go on and research or write about a particular interest.

Before discussing the personal qualities, I think that it is important to say that the counsellor's or therapist's good physical health is relevant. A therapist who is ill frequently or overtired cannot be emotionally available to her clients; neither is she likely to be reliable.

I am not suggesting that a person who is deaf, blind or physically disabled cannot become a practitioner. The use of signing in counselling is a valued skill in working with profoundly deaf clients, and clients who are blind or physically disabled may prefer to work with someone that they feel can understand their situation.

Age

The age of the practitioner is an interesting point. If we regard Erickson's stages of human development, we see that the *generative* phase is around 40–50 years. People at this stage are usually keen to give back something to society of their own personal life-experiences. They may well have children who are adult and are leaving or who have left the family home, which means that they have time and energy still to offer the considerable resources that they may have developed through attending to their own families.

For the most part, younger people are absorbed in finding their own identities and developing their careers, relationships and families, and are not at the stage of giving back what they have acquired in the way of wisdom. There may not be an ideal age, as such, but it is comforting to know that for many people who are becoming excluded from work in a youth-oriented society there is a field that encourages older people.

Gender

Counselling and psychotherapy are helping, caring professions, and they have generally attracted women. It is noticeable on training courses that women outnumber men. Men who come into the profession may be men who are comfortable with the nurturing sides of themselves, but I don't want to generalise or be simplistic about the gender number difference. There are many reasons for this.

What makes a good therapeutic outcome?

There has been a great deal of research carried out that has looked at what makes a good therapeutic outcome for any individual. What is the actual *mechanism* for a successful therapy outcome. The findings amongst all orientations are that it is the relationship between the client and the practitioner that is the most important for a successful outcome. The therapist's expertise and experience comes lower on the list. The cognitive and behavioural therapies stress less emphasis on the relationship, but still accept that it has an importance.

The relationship grows on a foundation of trust between client and therapist. Within this trusting relationship, the client's painful experiences in other relationships have the chance to be changed, resolved and healed. The benefits that the client gains from the thera-peutic relationship are similar to those in any loving relationship. There are, however, different parameters or boundaries to safeguard the client and the relationship. When this therapeutic alliance or relationship is in place, the client has the feeling that he has been heard and truly understood for who he really is. Sometimes it is a unique experience. Someone may never have felt this before. There is a deep feeling for the client of acceptance and validation by the therapist.

It is likely that the therapist transmits her own optimistic or positive beliefs indirectly to the client in the process of therapy that assists the client's changes. There are many different possibilities that have been suggested, but there is no agreement about the consistent mechanisms of change. What does seem to be agreed on, however, is that the client's emotional growth is possible because of this very special relationship.

It seems appropriate at this point to look at some of the qualities that make a counsellor or psychotherapist, before looking at what it is that they do.

THE PERSONAL QUALITIES OF A COUNSELLOR AND PSYCHOTHERAPIST

The knowledge of theory, the skills, the interventions and other strategies that someone can learn in training take second place to the personal qualities that the therapist has.

Many qualities that are considered essential are named, such as:

- atunement
- sensitivity
- non-possessive warmth
- openness
- calmness
- attentiveness
- intelligence
- genuineness
- compassion and empathy

Empathy

There is a difference between compassion and empathy to me. I understand compassion as feeling moved by another's plight; perhaps feeling so moved as to want to help them.

Empathy is not feeling pity, or sympathy, but trying to understand how the person is seeing their world and how this makes them feel. Empathy has a sense of being fully present with the person in that moment. Empathy is a way of trying to feel the other person's distress, without being disturbed by it because you are trying to understand how it feels for him.

It would be very difficult to work effectively without empathy. Without empathy, the therapist would be a sterile technician, lacking human understanding and warmth. Having empathy is a major ingredient for the trusting relationship that must be forged between the client and the practitioner. A sort of *empathic communion* can then take place from the practitioner to the client. This is the place where the client has a sense of knowing that he is really understood.

Genuineness

Another quality that is essential is to be genuine. Being genuine, or real as a person, means not to hide behind a professional mask or other defence. The word that is frequently used in humanistic therapy is *congruent*. This means that the person's words match their feelings; they are not feeling one thing whilst speaking as if they felt something else.

Through being genuine, a practitioner models to clients that this is how intimacy is formed and maintained. When the client experiences this aspect of human warmth and begins to trust the relationship, he is already participating in it.

These things are not always easy to do in reality, and have to be thought about and worked at.

Before we can know and help another, we must have formed a genuine relationship with ourselves, which means being honest and respecting of ourselves. Not wishing we were different and punishing or deceiving ourselves. Not accepting only the good parts or the parts of ourselves that we consider acceptable. If we can understand and deal with our own disappointments, sorrows and pleasures, then we are able to help others deal with theirs.

These are lofty qualities which practitioners may have to strive for, or develop, or may already have within them.

There are three main personal counsellor and therapist values that are emphasised by several organisations' codes of ethics and good practice. These are *integrity*, *impartiality* and *respect*.

Integrity

There is a concept of uprightness and honesty in integrity, but the word goes further, beyond moral principles yet relating to the core values that we hold about life, others and ourselves. I feel that integrity is something we all prize deeply within ourselves and want to believe that we have. I imagine that a person feels, unconsciously, that their integrity is at stake when they feel distressed and confused by the negative consequences of their own behaviour, in their relationships with others.

Impartiality

Impartiality means not to hold prejudices about others or make assumptions about them and their way of life. This is not so easy as we would like it to be. We all make assumptions a great deal of the time. This is part of the human condition.

You can test this out for yourself the next time you are sitting in a room and someone walks in. It is almost an instinct, as if we are trying to assess whether the person is friendly or not, so that we can protect ourselves if need be. We look for many clues to help us make such assessments: the person's dress, mannerisms, gestures, facial expressions – even before they begin to speak. In fact, the clues are often surface or insufficient in themselves, and do not tell the whole story about someone, yet we use them to make assumptions.

Respect

Respecting someone means you do not judge them, or demean them in any way for their values or behaviour, or tell them how to live their lives or impose your values onto them. Having respect for another is to listen to them. Respecting another is to acknowledge them and value them as a unique human being. When there is respect the other person feels it. Self-respect is a human need that can be confirmed or denied by others.

A responsibility of practitioners of counselling and psychotherapy is to learn to recognise and be aware when their attitudes, beliefs and values are negative towards others. It takes time to acknowledge our prejudices, but until we do we cannot challenge them. When we can start challenging them, we are on the way to preventing them from being destructive and harmful to others.

When we reflect on each of these qualities we can begin to see how we might work with another person therapeutically. When these qualities are practised, there is no forcing, coercion or imposing of values onto a client. These qualities are seen as fundamental for the client's capacity for self-determination.

There is no indication that such qualities are proven measures of therapeutic competence. Studies have nevertheless been carried out to show that there is a strong possibility between such personal qualities and the ability to form a strong therapeutic relationship, which may also have favourable outcome to the therapy (Gurman *et al.* 1986; Hunt 1985).

Therapy for counsellors and psychotherapists

Therapy is about helping people to reveal themselves to themselves with acceptance. Consequently to reveal themselves to others, without fear of reprisal or rejection. How could practitioners expect clients to travel this difficult road, if they themselves had not started out on their own journey?

Being in personal therapy gives the trainee the opportunity to experience the process of therapy that can only be understood at an intellectual level on the training course. Being at the receiving end of therapy or counselling is of double benefit for the trainee. The first is the obvious personal work that is beneficial, and the other is the experience of always remembering how a client will feel.

Practitioners need to have gone quite some way along their own personal journey of self-understanding to have reached the place where they are compassionate and empathic for their own life trials, and have learned some important things from them. They need to have self-respect and be honest with themselves, not judging and blaming either themselves or others. They know that they still have more learning to do as each new life stage is reached and new challenges await them, but they need to have done much to accept themselves. Because of this self-acceptance, practitioners should not need clients or others to reinforce their self-esteem.

Even the practice of skills in training is not felt at the same level as when experiencing personal therapy. But being in therapy without the training is not enough for a practitioner. It is relating the one to the other that integrates the learning with the experiencing.

Practitioners have to use themselves as instruments for their clients. It is their own persons – characters, sensitivities, philosophies, values, skills and resources – that they bring into relationships. The quality that practitioners have, combined with their own personal growth and maturity, can help them in this work.

Having a sense of humour is vital! Not taking yourself too seriously keeps a grounded perspective on life. An essential ingredient is to live life fully without fear of mistakes or hurt. Experienced practitioners know that they will experience both mistakes and hurt.

Practitioners who have these qualities can allow themselves to acknowledge when they make mistakes. This modelling is a vital experience for clients who have been brought up in a culture of perfectionism and fear of failure.

Skills and experience make practitioners more competent, but it is their own qualities that make them humanly effective.

The ability to hold the resultant anxiety and stress when a client is in crisis is a quality that the therapist may need to learn. It is important to be aware of our own stress and how we deal with it. When we are familiar and accepting of our own emotions and their effect, we are less likely to be frightened of clients' emotions.

An example of anger

A client who is angry with the therapist (or with someone else), and acts angrily but does not speak directly about it, may not be aware of the power of the unspoken emotion. If the therapist has not learned to understand and regulate her own anger, she may feel confused or frightened by the client's anger. There is then a danger that she may do some of the following:

- not speak of the client's feelings
- avoid the subject of anger
- act defensively
- feel angry with the client
- feel uncomfortable or anxious
- placate the client
- manipulate the client in another way
- diffuse the anger in another way.

You can reflect on how you deal with your own anger, perhaps with someone you are in a difficult relationship with. This will help you to have a better understanding of why it is important for practitioners to explore and work on their own anger. Understanding the patterns of behaviour that have been around for a lifetime is not enough to change them, however. This takes time to do in therapy, and is why training takes the time it does.

Bringing anger into therapy is just one issue that people present. They may want help with all sorts of other human troubles and worries: bereavement, anxieties, depression, loneliness, indecision, physical illness, relationships, obsessional behaviour, dependencies, addiction, sexual difficulties, lack of motivation, phobias. Think about your own life and the lives of your friends and loved ones, and you will be aware that the list is very long.

We may not have had all, or any, of the experiences in our own lives that clients are likely to bring. It is not the events that we share, but the range of human emotions that we can experience as a result of events. Exploring and working through these difficult emotional affects is the process that helps us empathise with another who is trying to do the same thing for themselves.

WHAT HAPPENS IN A COUNSELLING OR THERAPY SESSION

You may be wondering at this point what happens when clients are in therapy. What takes place? How does the therapeutic relationship happen? What does the practitioner do? All the therapies we are looking at come under the general heading of 'talking therapies', as opposed to the medical model of drug treatment. So we know that talking occurs in a session. At least, the client talks more and the practitioner pays attention and listens very carefully, weighing up when to speak and what to say that the client can use.

Yet I may disappoint you if I tell you that these are really very difficult questions to answer, because there are so many different counselling and therapy approaches that the process of a session would be different according to the theory. We would see how different if we were to be able to have a look at, say, a person-centred counselling approach and a Gestalt therapy session. The practitioner's style would also be different, not only from someone of another approach but from someone of the same approach.

I will, however, give a fly-on-the wall flavour of a small part of a Gestalt therapist's session, and then do the same with a client in a person-centred counsellor's session. These examples will be very purposely simplistic and stylised to demonstrate how the different models could be applied. The examples will demonstrate what the different approaches could focus on.

I will use the same client with the same issue, to show the contrast in approaches.

An imaginary session: Gestalt therapy

In this example, the aim for the Gestalt therapist in this session is to bring the client to an awareness of how he is blocking his anger. There are so many ways that the client does this blocking of his feelings that he has normalised them. He is not conscious that he does it until the therapist asks him to experiment, rather than just talk about what happens to him. The aim in Gestalt therapy is always to raise awareness.

It is useful to know that a Gestalt therapist focuses on a client's phenomenology – what the client does in the session, and how he does it; his physical movements; how he says things; whatever he is experiencing in the moment.

Let us imagine that the client has been coming to therapy for some time, perhaps a year, so that he is used to the way that the therapist works. When the therapist suggests that the client speaks to an object, or speaks as if he were the object, this does not seem odd or uncomfortable now to the client. This way of speaking to or for an object has a purpose. The client knows how the experience of doing something so different helps him to see something in a different way. This experience helps him to realise what he is really feeling in the moment. He is less likely to control or block feelings. Then he can become aware of how he stops himself from feeling his emotions fully around this particular subject – and others.

Gestalt experiments offer an experience that is often missing when someone reports an incident by talking about it. You may see what I mean by this example:

As the therapist opens the door to the client, the therapist observes the client's facial expression, and his body movements: how he enters; whether he marches in, moves slowly, looks at the therapist, etc. This observation continues throughout the session, and the therapist makes use of these observations from time to time when she feels that the client can use them to assist his awareness.

The client sighs. The therapist asks the client what he is feeling when he sighs. The client is slumped in the chair, head down, directing his speech to the carpet and not to the therapist. The therapist notices his body position, and she wonders aloud what this means for the client. Their dialogue goes like this:

Therapist: I notice how down you look, and how you are looking down at the carpet and speaking to it. I wonder what this means for you? (The therapist wants to keep the focus right where the client is, to maintain his feelings and not have him intellectualise.)

Client: I don't know. Perhaps I feel flat, down. Perhaps there's no point to speak to anyone about my feelings.

Therapist: (The therapist picks up on his words and maintains the focus.) The carpet is also flat and down. Perhaps you want to say your feelings to the carpet?

Client: (after a pause and another sigh, whilst looking at the carpet, he says softly) I want to say that I'm fed up with everything. (He sighs again, this time a little stronger.)

Therapist: (The therapist observes the client's feelings growing and wants to keep this awareness central for him, so she changes the 'talking to' the carpet, to 'being' the carpet.) Everything seems too much. (Pauses) If you were this carpet right now, what do you think you might be feeling?

Client: (Looks at the carpet more purposively.) I suppose that I feel that I am being walked on.

Therapist: (The therapist chooses the best moment for the client to express his real feelings when she sees that speaking for the carpet has given him the opportunity to get into contact with his feelings.) Do another sigh, and as you sigh out this time, be the carpet and tell whoever it is who is walking on you what you really think of them.

Client: (Does the sigh, and on the last letting out of breath speaks louder and stronger) I'm fed up with being walked on by you. You push me around and treat me like a doormat.

Therapist: (Notices that the client's face has coloured with emotion.) What are you feeling right now?

Client: I am angry.

Therapist: *Now* I can hear that you are angry, and you look angry.

The therapist's emphasis shows the client that she could not hear his anger before. He is encouraged to express his anger that is real for him. But his anger is also frightening to him, which is why he has allowed himself to be 'walked on like a doormat'. Now he *knows* that he is angry, he has experienced it rather than talked about it. What to do with it is the next stage to be worked on.

Person-centred counselling

How would that differ from the person-centred approach? The counsellor may observe the client's manner on entering the room to gauge his feelings, but chooses not to comment on them. The person-centred counsellor's role is to stay with whatever the client feels: to let the client lead. The counsellor reflects back the client's feelings to him, so that he can hear them from another perspective. This clarifies his feelings for him or makes them more apparent. Her empathy encourages him to verbalise the feelings that he has.

The client is looking down at the carpet. He sighs and then speaks.

Client: Well, I'm feeling very fed up right now.

Counsellor: So you are feeling fed up? (By raising her voice at the end of the sentence, this encourages the client to explain if he wants to.)

Client: I don't know what it is about. (He sighs.)

Counsellor: (The counsellor doesn't try to move him away from his feelings, she stays with them and this helps him to do the same.) I can hear how fed up you are. Can you tell me what it is like for you not to know what your fed-up feelings are?

Client: (Sighs, and after a long pause continues) It's horrible. I feel stuck. I feel . . . I just don't know . . . (looks frustrated and irritated).

Counsellor: (The counsellor's empathy enables the client to feel his feelings stronger.) It looks as if you just can't find the words that you need to tell me how stuck you are.

Client: I feel frustrated and . . . (sighs louder, and looks around the room in agitated manner).

Counsellor: (The counsellor notices that she feels frustrated and is tuning into his sense of frustration.) I can really feel frustrated, as if there's something you can't get to. What's happening to you?

Client: I am frustrated, and fed up because I don't want to go on being treated the same way at home.

Counsellor: So you are frustrated and fed up because of the way that you are being treated at home? (She pauses to allow him to hear the words that took such effort for him to bring to the surface.)

And so on . . .

It is important to know that dialogues would be varied in pace and style within sessions, and would probably not sound like the ones demonstrated. There may be silences and at other times lots of content (or story) from clients. Gestalt or person-centred practitioners may not use such obvious techniques in the way that I have demonstrated. Or they may use them more sparingly. Sometimes the dialogue would be like the conversations that you would have with an intimate friend who is sharing something about himself. The focus would be on what is happening moment by moment.

Before getting to this stage, however, there is a great deal of learning to be done. There would be opportunity on a training course to learn and practise skills with trainee colleagues on the course.

Which brings us back to courses and the preparation for starting.

FURTHER READING

Bond, T. (1993) *Standards and Ethics for Counselling in Action*, London: Sage Publications.

British Association for Counselling (1993) *Code of Ethics and Practice for Counsellors*, Rugby: BAC.

Clarkson, P. (1993) *On Psychotherapy*, London: Whurr Publishers.

De Board, R. (1997) *Counselling for Toads*, London: Routledge.

Gurman, A.S., Knoskern, D.P. and Pinsoff, W.M. (1986) Research into the process and outcome of marital and family therapy, in D. Hooper and W. Dryden (eds) (1991) *Couple Therapy. A Handbook*, Buckingham: Open University Press.

Horton, I. and Varma, V. (eds) (1997) *The Neeeds of Counsellors and Psychotherapists*, London: Sage Publications.

Hough, M. (1994) *A Practical Approach to Counselling*, London: Longman.

Hunt, P.A. (1985) *Clients' Responses to Marriage Counselling*, Rugby: NPGC.

Leigh, A. (1998) *Referral and Termination Issues for Counsellors*, London: Sage Publications.

Noonan, E. and Spurling, L. (1992) *The Making of a Counsellor*, London: Routledge.

6

PREPARATION FOR
STARTING A COURSE

This chapter covers the following:

- How do you learn?
- Information.
- Selecting a course.

HOW DO YOU LEARN?

I feel that this is a very relevant question, since you are considering training. It may be quite some time since you were at school, or have participated in any formal learning. Teaching has probably changed since you were at school. I think my generation were taught through a mixture of fear (known as respect for the teachers) of punishment, and disregard for the way that an individual could learn.

One of the most negative feelings of my school days was to be told off for asking questions. When a teacher said 'I have already told you that!' I felt I had done something wrong, and shrivelled.

Considering this question now may be valuable to you when you are on a course. When undertaking any adult training there needs to be a shift from 'school-learning mode' to 'adult-learning mode'. The two are quite different, and it would be a great pity if you went through several years of training still operating from a school-learning perspective.

We can look at making this shift from two stages. The first stage is to get past the learning blocks left over from school learning. This is a personal observation. I have seen people adopt a culturally passive role when they are in a 'classroom'. I say *culturally* because I have not noticed this so much with trainees from some other countries. This may happen when the training is in the form of teacher-transmitter style where you listen, as you do during lectures. You make notes, or there are handouts, but there is no active participation. This is one way to learn, and there may well be some lectures on your course, but it is not the only way – or even the best way to learn.

Asking questions

Most counselling and psychotherapy training today is conducted from a trainee-centred approach. That means that there is participation from everybody, with valuable input from the trainees as well as the tutors. Trainees have valuable life-experiences to offer and questions that raise interesting issues. Trainees *need* to ask questions to understand or find out more. This is part of the self-responsibility for learning. Frequently, what is puzzling to one person applies to others too.

Before enrolling on a foundation or certificate course is the time to ask lots of questions about it. Once you are on the course, you will gain understanding and knowledge that should help you to proceed onto a diploma course. You will need to know more about a diploma course's aims and objectives before starting a certificate course.

There is nothing to be ashamed of if you have scant knowledge of theory. Theoretical ideas are often difficult to grasp, and you are planning to go on a course precisely because you want to learn about them. There is usually a 'language' or jargon that goes with the concepts that may be new to you as well. The use of jargon may not be intended to be inclusive or patronising, but can often feel that way to people who are outside the field.

Asking questions is a natural process of learning. If a tutor has told you something and you didn't understand, or you forgot, then you were not able to take that piece of information in at that time. It may also mean that the tutor has not presented the information in the best way. Asking a question suggests that you have got to the right stage for you. You are ready to receive the information, or at least to begin the learning process.

Asking questions can apply to anything that you are unsure about, or simply don't know, or are even unhappy with. You may not always get the answer that you want, or you may get something different from what you wanted. But if you don't ask, you won't get anything at all.

Being able to ask questions before you commit to a course will help you to make a more informed choice about the course. Throughout the book I indicate questions that you might want to ask administrative staff or tutors. I also give you instances of flaws and problems on courses; these might prompt you to seek clarification about similar matters on the course you are considering. Asking questions is a human need and enables you to process information. It is also a tool for counselling and psychotherapy.

The way you learn

The second part of the learning shift is about the *way* that you learn.

If you think about anything that you have learned recently – whether that was working a particular machine, or making something creative – you might consider what it was that helped you to learn what was necessary. It may be something of the following:

- because you had to;
- because you wanted to;
- because there was some gain or reward to it.

For me, learning something because you have to doesn't work well. The best way is usually because I wanted to learn something for its own sake. The gain or reward is a strong contender. It does depend on what the gain is, of course, and how long the gain lasts.

How you learn

The third part is the *how*. Psychologists have studied this process and come up with a number of ways that people learn:

- Being shown
- Being told
- Doing it yourself
- Feeling safe to ask and make mistakes
- With some humour or lightness
- Changes of presentation that are creative and stimulating
- Through association
- Taking in and digesting over time
- Through repetition or practice
- Through experiences
- Through an empathic relationship
- With support and encouragement from others
- Feeling relaxed and open
- Watching others
- Speaking about it to others.

Take your time to think about this. You may think of other ways for yourself. Which ways would apply to you, and in which circumstances?

We have quite short concentration spans. Were you a child at school who was told off for daydreaming? Daydreaming is the brain's natural way of resting and replenishing creatively. A sort of over-load cut-off point. Daydreaming can be very productive, as it feeds the imagination. The average concentration span is only a matter of minutes unless highly stimulated.

So, learning needs to be interesting, stimulating, and with enough changes to maintain interest. Changing from being active to being reflective in a session. Changing the pace and the medium. From group work to pair work. From flip chart to video.

It is useful to know what the tutorial structure is and whether there is support and guidance given for essay writing. This is important if you have not written since you were at school and have an anxiety about essay writing.

Check on the room that the training is held in. If you are on a course for several years you need to be able to concentrate. The setting needs to be conducive to learning. It needs to be comfortable, without making you drowsy. The temperature of the room is important. Noise and other interruptions need to be dealt with.

If you are bored or concerned about an aspect of the training, and you say nothing, then you have gone into school-learning mode. The belief in that mode is that you cannot say anything: that you do not have the right. If you expect the tutors to give you everything you need, without your active participation, then you are setting yourself up to be very disappointed, and frustrated. Both of those elements are the outcome of being in the school-learning mode.

The adult-learning mode is taking responsibility for your own learning: where you can ask for what you want, or need, to help you to learn. It is the belief that you can give and receive constructive feedback with peers and tutors.

INFORMATION

The duration of training courses in counselling and psychotherapy ranges from half a day, a weekend, correspondence courses, one evening for several weeks or terms, to three, four or more years part time. There are some full-time courses, but these are less common.

Training courses may be titled: introduction, basic, foundation, certificate, diploma, postgraduate, non-award, MA, MSc, on to a PhD, and are held in many different settings: adult evening institutes, universities, hospitals, dedicated training centres and hired rooms.

There may be components of counselling and counselling skills that are included in programmes on other courses. These need to be checked thoroughly, as they may not suit you if you are thinking of furthering your counselling education, and want to proceed to a certificate and diploma. You may find yourself having to start at the beginning again with a recognised or accredited course.

The BAC training directory lists training in counselling and psycho-therapy courses all over the country. Libraries should also hold information on courses. Many training centres advertise their courses in relevant journals and information leaflets.

Requesting training brochures from courses that look interesting is the first step. In the brochures, one should find the aims and objectives of the training courses. The aims and objectives of the course should be spelled out clearly in the brochure. This will tell you what the trainees are expected to learn and what they should be equipped with at the end of the learning. What the theoretical approach is. The different levels of training offered; whether it is a foundation/introduction course, a certificate or diploma course. Whether the course itself is accredited, and what the procedures for application are. The fees should be stated, whether there is a financial contract, and payment schemes.

It is a good idea to send off for a number of brochures from several courses, this helps to compare course content, aims and costs. The geographic location needs to be considered. The exhaustion of travelling from one end of a busy city to another in the rush hours for a number of years may play a part in choice. Trying to fit in your normal lifestyle with travelling and studying is a long-term consideration. The days and times of the course are other points to think about.

You may also find out other information in the brochure that is useful. Whether you can proceed to a higher level with the same organ-isation and what the entry requirement for each level of training is. Whether the course is broken up into modules that you can choose from. What membership of professional bodies the course is associated with. What is the code of ethics and practice that the training adheres to? Whether the training centre offers a clinical and referral service. I discuss this point further on under 'Trainee placements for clients' (pp. 203–24).

Many educational establishments do give a clear statement of their learning content and outcomes. It is worth checking for these details and asking about them if they are not stated. Some brochures describe the learning outcomes in this way: 'At the end of the term trainees will be able to conduct an interview, explore the changes that the client desires and agree on goals with the client.'

This is informative, but lacks the *how*. This sort of detail may be too complex to put into a brochure, but being told how the stages of learning are arrived at will give you an idea of how the course is structured, as well as what actually happens in the classroom.

The more detailed the information the more you will have to help you make a selection. If something is unclear to you, it may help to telephone the school, and to speak to the relevant tutor and request clarification. It is useful to remind yourself that *it is your responsibility to assess the course before applying for it*. Nothing can guarantee that you make the right choice but careful selection can help. It is worth while remembering that because there are many training schools for you to choose from, you can be discriminating.

SELECTING A COURSE

Most courses will indicate the theoretical approach that they train in, but there are still some counselling courses which do not give this information, for which there is no logical reason. Requesting that information is important. Not every counselling or psychotherapy approach is appropriate to every individual, and that follows as much for the individual who seeks counselling help as for the person who trains to become a therapist. Asking what the approach is and requesting that the information be given to you in a form that you can comprehend is highly pertinent.

If you are unfamiliar with the various approaches, you may not know which course is going to suit you. This is highly relevant if the course has a purist approach (i.e. one particular core theoretical model), or whether it is an integrative approach (i.e. an integration of a number of theories from different approaches). Chapters 2, 3 and 4 should help you to have some idea of the different approaches, so that you can consider which may fit better with you.

The way that the training and organisation of the school is conducted should be reflected in their approach. This is not a simple matter, of course, but a well-organised course does reflect that there is care and respect for the trainee. The theory, skills, personal therapy, supervision and all other aspects of the training should be reflected in the core theoretical methods of the course (Wheeler 1998: 134). In other words, the training courses that are the most effective are those where the structure of the course, the trainee development, and the method of training model the approach that is being taught. *Check out this information before committing to the training.*

A humanistic course, for example, that is badly organised, consistently changes dates for giving in essays, changes teaching slots and subjects, and other aspects, is negligent at best. Yet if the course teaches that caring and being supportive and emotionally available to the client is paramount, then a very confused message is being given to the trainee.

Training institutions

Some training institutions hold an open evening (or several) for potential trainees. The topics that can be addressed are:

- What the theoretical approach of the training is. A simplified explanation.
- What the course objectives are.
- What the course entails in terms of study, writing, emotional demands, financial costs, etc.
- Whether fees will be increased during the training.
- How the balance of theory and practice is arrived at.
- What period of time is given for each.
- How many people are accepted on the course – and whether this changes.
- Whether there are any other changes that could occur.
- What the roles and expectations of the tutors, supervisors and any other educative providers are.
- What support is provided.
- What is not provided.
- What is expected of the trainees.
- How assessments are conducted.
- Whether previous trainees are willing to be contacted by prospective trainees.
- Whether trainees evaluate the course, and, if so, whether there are changes effected.
- What questions the potential trainee has.

Most courses would want to see competent and skilled practitioners emerging from their courses: graduates who have gained a solid foundation of theory and method that informs their practice, combined with self-awareness and independent thinking.

The trainers have a responsibility to see that the highest standards of training are offered as well as the most appropriate material to meet the needs of the trainees. This is a formidable task, as trainees on any given course are at different life stages, and have different needs. Their responses to the question of how the course can equip their trainees for the workplace are informative and valuable.

A number of courses offer a short introduction or taster to their longer training. From one to several sessions in some cases, lasting no more than a few hours or a day. If you are at all uncertain about the approach, it is worth taking several shorter courses, or introductions, so that you can see for yourself what they entail. Doing this will also help you to familiarise yourself with the format and procedure of this form of training. Therapy and counselling training are unlike most other training, because there is a high degree of personal insight and development to gain, as well as theory, practice and academic structure.

Courses usually follow the scholastic year, starting in September or October, though there are courses that start at other times as well. Interviews can take place six months or more ahead of starting date.

It is impossible to guarantee that a course will be right for you, even with all the questions asked, the information gathered, comparisons with other courses and careful consideration. The assessors may also believe that you are right for the course, and you may still find that the course is wrong for you once you have started on it. This can be very difficult for anyone. If this does occur it would be important to talk through your feelings with someone you trust and give yourself the opportunity to examine everything you feel. The process of allowing yourself the time to explore: what you feel, what is happening in your life at that moment, your anxieties, expectations and concerns, may be very productive and important to an understanding of yourself.

Leaving a course too quickly because it doesn't feel right, or staying to the bitter end, in spite of the fact that the course may be inappropriate for you, is part of the dilemma or conflict that can arise on the training. There is generally anxiety mixed with excitement at the start of a new venture that may be a turning point in your life. You will find that most people have similar feelings at some point. There are adjustments to be made about going back to studying, and juggling the other parts of your life with study.

Selecting a course for a specific setting

I have spoken of general training so far. A few training institutions recognise that there are people who seek very specialised training to equip them for a specific field. Here are some examples:

The University of Bristol offers a diploma and MSc in Counselling in Primary Care/Health Settings, and a diploma and MSc in Counselling at Work.

Stockton Centre for Psychotherapy and Counselling offers an MSc in Counselling in Primary Care.

Metanoia offers a two-year diploma of modules in Primary Health Care.

The Universities of Strathclyde and Keele both have modules in Primary Health Care at diploma and MSc level.

The Institute of Group Analysis in London offers a year's seminars on Management and Leadership.

The Tavistock offers an MA in Consultation and Organisation.

A two years' Observational Studies and Application of Psychoanalytic Concepts to work with children, young people and families course is designed by The Lincoln Clinic and Centre. This course is a pre-requisite for application to the Tavistock Clinic training in child psychotherapy.

The Portman Clinic, London offers courses in Forensic Psychotherapy and Group Analytic Psychotherapy of Delinquency and Sexual Deviation, amongst other very specialised courses. Eligibility for most of their courses is for professions working in related fields.

To gain up-to-date information on those courses, it is advisable to contact the Centres (see List of Resources, pp. 203–24). Courses change from time to time, but details are beyond the scope of this book.

It is useful to know that some specialised agencies hold their own training. Many youth drop-in centres have free training for their volunteer counsellors who want to work with young people. London Marriage Guidance Council has accredited and validated training in couples' work, and psychosexual counselling. The Richmond Fellowship has an RSA diploma in Post-Traumatic Stress Counselling.

If you are interested in particular fields, then it may be worth your while to investigate these options. Otherwise, it is probably better to undertake an introduction in counselling or a foundation course in psychotherapy or counselling to see how you feel about a general training.

When you have got a better idea of which course you will apply for, consider whether the course has been accredited. The chapter about accreditation will help you to understand this system. If you are considering a long-term course, it would be essential to know that the course had some generally recognisable status, and by whom. If the course is not accredited, you may find that you have to retrain or add many more hours to your original training to come into line with an accrediting body's requirements (see Chapter 8).

If you decide to commit yourself to a long-term course, you need to know the details of the first year as well as the following years' curriculum. Some courses give clear details about the first year but are less clear about the following years. This is bad organisation and many courses are still badly organised, with countless trainees suffering from frustrations. Having an understanding about the kinds of problems that exist on present courses will enable you to raise these points when you are assessing courses for yourself.

Evaluating courses

Training courses could offer the outcome of the previous year's intake of trainees' evaluations as standard practice. Where the trainees made recommendations that are practical and productive, the course organisers could inform the prospective trainees whether the recommendations were implemented. Evaluation is purposeful and goes a long way to improve the standards of training. This benefits both the trainees and the course. There are reports of trainers giving out evaluation forms at the end of their courses, but not acting on the points raised by the trainees. There are reports of tutors behaving defensively when trainees give requested feedback about the course. These reflect badly on the reputation of a course.

Remember that you have the right, and it is vitally important in the assessment interview, to ask as many questions as you can about the course. The questions that I have raised are repeated in Appendix 3. Whilst reading this book you might want to make notes of the questions that arise for you.

FURTHER READING

National Register of Psychotherapists. UKCP 1999, London: Routledge.
BAC (15th edn) *The Training in Counselling & Psychotherapy Directory 1999*, Rugby: BAC.
Dryden, W. and Feltham, C. (1994) *Developing Counsellor Training*, London: Sage Publications.
Johns, H. (ed.) (1998) *Balancing Acts. Studies in Counselling Training*, London: Routledge.

MacMillan, M. and Clark, D. (1998) *Learning and Writing in Counselling*, London: Sage Publications.

Wheeler, S. (1998) Challenging the Core Theoretical Model: a reply to Colin Feltham, *Counselling* 9 (2): 134–8.

7

WHAT TO EXPECT ON A COURSE

Introduction, certificate and diploma

People undertake training for all sorts of reasons, many of them for the positive and enjoyable elements. The practical details also need to be considered. These are examples of the common questions that people who are just starting out ask:

- Which course would suit them in particular?
- What is the academic level of a course?
- Is there enough practical input?
- Will the training equip them to work as a counsellor or psycho-therapist with recognised qualifications?

It is important to choose a course where the appropriate theoretical approach, rigour of academic level, clinical practice, time commitment and financial outlay suits the individual.

This chapter explores the general content of the following:

- Introductory
- Certificate
- Diploma
- Supervision
- Personal development
- Costs of training

Training

Training in counselling is generally 450 hours over 2/3 years. At present, 40 hours of personal therapy is required with a counsellor who is familiar with or practises the same approach.

Training in psychotherapy is longer, and therefore more expensive than counselling. The United Kingdom Council for Psychotherapy recommends that psychotherapy training is a minimum of 540 hours of theory for three years. Some psychotherapy courses are between

600–2,000 hours over a period of 3–5 years part time. Personal therapy should be with a therapist of the same approach for the duration of the course, or longer.

INTRODUCTION COURSE

This may be as little as a few hours, a half day, day, weekend, or 10-week (one term) course. On a weekend introduction to counselling, you might experience some basic exercises and do some listening exercises to practise in pairs. You might get to discuss some of the issues of counselling, and come away with knowing whether you want to continue learning about counselling.

There are distance learning courses, which may offer written and audio material. Some may even have tutorials and occasional weekend residentials. They may have something to offer in so far as an intro-duction to counselling skills is concerned, if you can practise the work satisfactorily, but they are lacking in direct contact, observation and feedback, practise of skills and group participation, which are the core of counselling work.

For many years, I facilitated a 10-week introduction to counselling course. I can describe in some detail the course that I personally was involved in. Other courses of similar time-scale may be different in form, but you may get some idea of what to expect from reading this description.

The centre I worked in was an adult education centre in an old primary school. No amount of light paint, stripped and varnished wooden block floors and modern light furniture could disguise the old Victorian class-room with its ghosts of long-ago childhood lingering in the shadows.

The course was one evening a week for 10 weeks. When the course began in the mid-1980s, there were no other courses in that district, nor any other district nearby that I was aware of. Few people had much interest in the subject of counselling or really knew what it was. It was difficult to get enough people on the course to keep it running. Usually there would be eight or ten, mainly women, participants.

When I stopped working for the centre some seven years later, there were six courses running weekly at that centre and numerous counselling courses running in other centres in the district. There was also a waiting list of people for each course. The numbers had expanded to twenty-five or more participants to each class.

Assessment and entry onto the course was by interest only. The only criterion was that people wanted to come.

I structured the 10 weeks in this way: the first week was mainly helping people to feel more relaxed. At the beginning, some always felt uncomfortable sitting in a circle facing each other, rather than the classroom style they were accustomed to from childhood. People felt more exposed in a circle. The reason that many counselling or psychotherapy training courses use this type of seating is because it encourages intimacy and participation. Everyone can see each other. It is difficult, in a circle, to pair off or carry on sub-conversations when one person is speaking.

There were anxieties to overcome about saying things that could feel disclosing in a group: their names, and the reasons why people had wanted to come on the course; what they expected from it, and what they didn't want; being asked how they were feeling instead of what they were thinking was often difficult. Saying what you feel is to speak about yourself, as opposed to speaking about an idea.

For many, the experience in the main group was not comfortable at first. The difficulty of speaking out could be daunting for some, pleasurable for others. And there were those who felt the group was more comfortable because they did not feel that they had to speak out.

Part of the skill of facilitating is to see that everyone participates, when they are ready to and at their own pace. Helping reluctant speakers to express themselves, and to feel better about doing that. Containing or curbing the over-zealous from taking too much time in the group.

Once they started to work in pairs on a given and timed exercise, the participants generally felt better. They could get to know each other, and assuage their fears of being the only ones who felt nervous, or who weren't doing it right. I always emphasised that there was no right or wrong, and that these were learning exercises. If I made a mistake – got someone's name wrong – or forgot something, I would say that I had made a mistake, very firmly. I felt it was very important that people could see that I was human too, and that it is really normal and expected that we make mistakes.

I think that very many people have had some bad experiences of school (including myself) and having to get things right, so that the feeling of going back to school reawakens those old fears.

The exercises at first were listening exercises; listening to each other without making any comment, and then saying back to the speaker what they had heard, in their own words.

Fortunately, it was never difficult for most people to find a subject for them to speak about when their turn came to take the client role. If they did find it difficult, I offered suggestions.

The trainees would practise the exercises in pairs. Then they would practise in threes, where one was an observer and could give constructive feedback to the person doing the listening. Time was spent in agreeing what constructive feedback was before doing the exercise in threes. The trainees would then discuss their experiences and observations in the main group. As the weeks went on, they would become more relaxed in the group and more adept at talking about the exercises, as well as how they were using them in their lives outside the course: in their relationships or their place of work.

Through the feedback that they gave and received from each other, and from me, and with practice, they gained in confidence in the skills. I always enjoyed the trainees' enjoyment in their own sense of progress and learning. It was also a rich, growing stage for me to learn how to impart these skills: to make them interesting and understandable, which was sometimes challenging.

Further on in the course we looked at the whole span of feelings, which I would list. The group would discuss them: which ones they would find difficult to express or never expressed, which ones they found difficult in others and so on. This always led to a lively interchange.

We looked at an overview of counselling, but the time limit did not permit us to go further. We looked at some of the theory and the goals for counselling. We explored how to begin and end a counselling session. We would discuss why 'rescuing' someone who was distressed in a session was not appropriate. What being non-judgemental meant. How allowing the client to lead the session felt through trying it out in pairs. These concepts are basic person-centred core skills.

Half the session would be for the practice of a skill and half would be for discussion. Towards the end of the 10 weeks most felt that they wanted to go on to the year's certificate course. That centre did not have the facilities to do that. A year's course entails two facilitators and written work that must be assessed for certification with a recognised board. The board may be the training institute's own certifying board, or there may be a college or university board that certifies the course.

A selection criterion for a certificate in counselling skills in a training centre may require:

- Age requirement (over 25 might be a starting age).
- Candidates should be working in or planning to work in jobs that require counselling skills (paid or voluntary work).
- No formal qualifications are required, but reading and written assignments will have to be completed during the course of training.

- Candidates should be personally suitable to engage in and benefit from training.

COUNSELLING SKILLS

Counselling skills are valuable in themselves and as a foundation for a career in counselling or psychotherapy. All good counselling courses teach counselling skills, whereas not all psychotherapy courses do. Whether someone trains as a counsellor or psychotherapist, counselling skills are invaluable for understanding the way that we interact and communicate with others.

The basic skills that are taught on a counselling course are:

Listening skills. It takes time and patience to learn to listen authentically to another. That means not hearing what you think someone is saying, but hearing what they *are* saying. Checking out with them that you have understood exactly what it is that they are saying. It also implies learning to listen to others with respect – without judgement or interpretation.

Most of us do not listen to others in the way indicated above. Sometimes we wait for others to finish what they are saying so that we can talk about our own opinions and thoughts. This means that we will not have listened carefully because we were focusing on our own thoughts.

We may interpret the other's words to fit our own world-view; hearing what we want to hear, or what we think we hear. It can be hard to try to see the world as the other person views it, but if we do not truly listen we distort the other's meaning. Too often this can lead to misunderstandings, hurt and a breakdown in communications.

Understanding our own feelings about a situation enables us to communicate this more openly to others, and we can help others to do the same. Learning to make requests instead of accusations and demands also improves communications and consequently relationships. Accusations are blaming and counter-productive, since they generally provoke defences or counter-accusations. Questions that are asked for the sake of clarity are constructive.

Reflecting – communication skills. Using listening skills lets the other person know that we have heard what they are saying; that we have understood them. Reflecting back what we have heard is another listening skill. When someone hears what he has just said reflected back to him with openness and genuine interest, he feels understood by the listener. It is as if the listener has acknowledged and validated what the speaker has been saying. If we haven't understood, asking for clarification also helps the other person feel they are being listened to.

Clarifying the client's feelings by checking them out demonstrates that the counsellor is (a) interested in the client and wants to understand him, and (b) is being genuine, not pretending to understand. People use words in many different ways, and there are nuances of meanings. Asking the client what their own meaning is can enable the client to reflect more deeply, and to understand that they have a right to their feelings.

Owning feelings is taking responsibility for the self, and is central to the skills in counselling. Saying 'I' when speaking about events, situations or feelings, instead of 'you', or 'one', is a start. For example: 'I don't feel comfortable when someone shouts at me', instead of 'you (meaning "I") don't feel comfortable when someone shouts at you'.

Another example of owning feelings is where two people are having an argument. Instead of blaming, it is better if one person speaks about his own feelings, and what is happening for him. There is more possibility that the other will not feel attacked and may begin to hear the person's viewpoint. Owning feelings in this case could sound like this: 'I feel really upset when you shout at me, and then I don't feel that I understand what's happening, so when I'm confused, I want to blame you.'

Owning feelings enables the person to see the choices: they can express the feelings and they do not have to act on them. What is repressed, i.e. buried, and therefore not able to be expressed, is more likely to be acted out. Acting out means doing something (to someone else) rather than speaking about the feelings.

This form of communication may not be familiar, as many people have not learnt how to express their anger.

Open-ended questions are another form of counselling skill. Used with genuine concern and not with pre-conceptions, these are questions that enable a client to open up their thoughts and expand on them. An example of seeing somebody looking upset would be to ask: 'what are you feeling right now?' This encourages the person to explore or explain, which helps them to understand more about themselves. This form of questioning is intended to help dialogue to take place and move forward.

Closed questions usually only elicit a yes/no response, which does not always help conversation or relationships; for example: 'are you feeling upset?' Someone could answer just 'yes' and the conversation could dry up. Frequently, someone says: 'Are you all right?' There is a sort of cultural expectation in the person responding, 'Yes, I'm OK.' There is a place for closed questions when factual information is required; for example: 'are you living at home?'

Focusing on one particular aspect of concern for the client is helpful. When a client feels that everything is difficult and doesn't know where to begin, there is a sense of being overwhelmed. There is confusion and a loss of one's own resources. Paying attention to one part and working through that can bring relief as well as lessening the feeling of being overloaded.

Summarising what has been said, either used intermittently or at the end of a session, can help the client to grasp the essence of that particular session. Counsellors can do this, or they may ask the client to do so. This is valuable for all clients and particularly those who find it hard to stay with what has been talked about, for one reason or another.

With practice, these skills become absorbed into a natural way of communicating generally. For more thorough training towards becoming a counsellor there are courses of up to 250 hours part time, where both skills and theory are taught.

CERTIFICATE/FOUNDATION COURSE

There is an assessment of candidates for a course that is more than an introduction, usually referred to as a certificate or foundation course. The rigour of the assessment may be in keeping with the quality of the training centre.

The information about entry requirements should be stated in the course brochure.

Assessment for entry onto a certificate course

The suitability of your personal qualities will be assessed, and you will be required to show your interest in working with people. There is almost certainly a formal interview or assessment procedure for prospective trainees. This may be a group process, an individual interview, or a mixture of both. Not all courses conduct their interviews with advanced expectations, but they will need to see whether a prospective student will be able to withstand the rigours of group dynamics.

How the interview is conducted tells a lot about the training. A number of trainees have reported feeling uncomfortable at the interview stage. It may be that in those particular settings assessors are interested to see how the candidates cope with the stress of the interview procedure. This gives some insight into how the candidates would cope with the stresses of the course and the therapeutic work.

There is a high demand for courses. And there are many training courses, which means that there is also a commercialised aspect to enrolling trainees. Filling up numbers for a course may well be a criterion for many training courses in the struggle to compete. You will get a clue to this by the kind of interview you have. If it is not rigorous, that may be a relief if you are feeling nervous about it, but it could suggest that the course is more concerned with the quantity than the quality of trainees. If this is the case, you may have cause to regret it later on.

There is unlikely to be an expectation that an applicant has a sound knowledge and understanding of therapeutic process and theories. There may be an expectation that you have an interest and healthy curiosity about the subject and can demonstrate that. Having curiosity is a positive ingredient in counselling and psychotherapy.

Read something before applying for a course

It is a good idea to have read something, however simple (in fact the simpler the better if you have no knowledge of the subject), before you attend an interview so that the concepts used may register with you even if you are unclear of the meaning.

It is frequently easier to read an explanation of the theory, rather than the theory itself. Having some awareness of the approach taught on the course will give you an opportunity to ask some questions about it.

Some established training centres have a library for their trainees to use. Others, particularly the less established centres, do not. It is worth enquiring about a library, as well as the number of copies available for each year's intake of trainees. Most courses tend to give out very long required reading lists, and it is costly in terms of money as well as the time and effort to go to bookshops to locate the books you need.

If there are too many expectations of your abilities before you have even started, it may mean that you will have to adapt quickly. On the other hand, if you do have some theoretical knowledge and/or experience it would be informative for you to ask what *they* can teach you in addition to what you already know.

You may feel anxious about getting on a course; the interview may bring up reminders of school and exam nerves. Yet this is an important place and time to find out as much as you can about the course and to raise your questions and concerns.

Some of the more orthodox training centres, such as the psycho-analytic and psychodynamic schools, may assess applicants partly on the basis of having some experience of working with individuals in a therapeutic way, or other related field experiences: social work, counselling, caring for others. They will assess the applicant's capacity and potential to work long term with a patient. Having experience of personal therapy is also a means of demonstrating serious intent and ability to stay with the rigours of prolonged therapy.

For more general courses in counselling and psychotherapy, a certificate or foundation course is usually one year and is part time (one evening a week). For entry onto such a course, the course organisers may be interested in your personal life-experiences and your interest in the field.

Most courses will want you to demonstrate that you can cope with the academic part of the training. For this reason, you may be required to have a degree, or to have undergone some other academic course of similar level, or be working in an allied field. For psychotherapy courses, being in a related profession is usually a necessary requirement. You may have to have some relevant experience of working with people in a responsible role.

As a mature student, you may not be required to have a first degree – life-experience is considered an important element in selection criteria. You may have to submit a page or an essay on why you want to do the training and why you wish to enter the profession, before being considered. They will need to be assured of your genuine interest and commitment in the subject.

Communication is another criteria for a profession that relies on two people talking together. This does not mean that you have to be eloquent, but rather that you have the ability to communicate your thoughts and feelings, and you can facilitate others to do the same. Perhaps the most important element regarding communication is that you are receptive to others and can listen to them.

Experience to be eligible for a course

There is a common complaint that applicants may not be eligible for a course if they have not had any experience. Showing that you are very interested in the subject by having done some voluntary work, telephone counselling, or allied relevant voluntary work, is more likely to demonstrate your serious intention and work in your favour. Working in a related caring profession such as social work or nursing is an advantage, whether this is paid or voluntary. If you are already involved in some related work, or do relevant volunteer work, this does demonstrate your interest and commitment and will assist your entry. If you have some experience of working with people in a caring or supportive role, this will be invaluable.

If you have done an introductory course with another training centre, you may wish to apply for a diploma course and not take a certificate course. If you have had experience of working in the profession you may be permitted to forgo the certificate course. Most courses do prefer their trainees to follow the route of their certificate course and then onto their higher, diploma course. The course organisers may consider that continuity and covering the syllabus are essential.

You may want to know what the entry requirements are for proceeding onto their higher course from the certificate. Some postgraduate diploma courses require you to have a degree and others do not. If you are already on the certificate course, how do you proceed? Is it through selection? Do you automatically go on to the diploma course providing you have successfully completed the certificate? Knowing the answers to these questions is useful before you decide which certificate course to start on.

What would you expect on a certificate course?

Unless the course states that it is psychodynamic, or Gestalt or some other purist approach, it is likely that a general counselling certificate course may be person-centred based with a combination of humanistic approaches, such as TA and Gestalt. A framework of Egan's model may be employed, and some cognitive-behavioural approaches could be introduced. This eclectic approach does give a wider look at the range of approaches, but does not satisfy the person who seeks in-depth knowledge and an identifiable orientation.

Courses that deal with the teaching of humanistic counselling generally emphasise that counselling is a non-directive practice. Non-directive means, literally, not to give direction, influence or advice. Whilst this may be humanly impossible at some unconscious level, counsellors are trained to be alert to their own feelings, wishes and thoughts regarding how these can affect their client's welfare. The practitioner's own optimism, goodwill and beliefs in the client's desires to heal, change or come to terms with his own difficulties are also important elements of counselling and psychotherapy.

There would be some similarities of content to the description of the 10-week introduction course that I facilitated, but with the realisation that a year's course is three terms, or approximately 30 weeks. This enables the content to be more expansive, and there is time for set reading and writing of essays, discussions and presentations or projects.

Some of the following, generalised, examples are likely to be in evidence, and I will say something briefly about each one. This is not an exhaustive list, and depending on whether the course is in counselling or psychotherapy may make a difference to what is included or excluded. This applies to the particular theoretical approach as well.

The general objectives for counsellors and psychotherapists on a first year's training are:

- learn theory and the philosophy of the theoretical approach taught
- to learn some skills
- to apply theory to practice
- to learn the stages of human development, and how development is impaired
- how changes can be facilitated
- an understanding of boundaries and confidentiality and their relation to process
- knowledge of the process of counselling/psychotherapy: the beginning, middle and ending phases.

The aims of counselling and psychotherapy vary according to the objectives of the theoretical approach.

One element of training that is considered necessary across theoretical approaches, though varying in degrees of rigidity and flexibility, is the subject of boundaries that I discussed in Chapter 1. It may take a trainee both time and experience to understand the necessity and implications of boundaries within the therapeutic relationship and the process.

Teaching assessment and referring

Whilst it must be noted that there are as many people who seek self-knowledge and more effective ways of living their lives who enter psychotherapy as those who enter counselling, a psychotherapy training does include the understanding of personality disorders. This gives the psychotherapist the ability to diagnose and treat someone who is disturbed, as well as the whole range of emotionally neurotic disorders that counsellors will see. Diagnosing may mean that someone gets referred on for psychiatric treatment, or medication, or some other form of therapy that may be more appropriate.

Because people who are in psychotherapy may be more ill or have more severe neuroses than those who seek counselling, the risk of personal disintegration (or breakdown) is greater in the psychotherapeutic process. Treating psychic illness requires training in appropriate assessment. Diagnostic skills are taught in psychotherapy training and may not be included in a counselling training. There is an emphasis on the elements that produce change or curative factors (Yalom 1975) that are studied in psychotherapy training.

Counsellors would greatly benefit if they learned during their training to assess their clients for referring on to other forms of treatment where necessary. Referral may mean to psychiatrists via a doctor if the counsellor considers that a client is in some danger or need. There are still counselling courses that do not equip trainees to do so, which is regrettable and irresponsible.

Learning one's own limitations is about learning to be competent. I consider that training courses have a responsibility to their counselling trainees to teach assessment and referral skills, for the safety and welfare of clients and counsellors.

SUPERVISION

During clinical practice, whenever there is any doubt or clinical concern, the trainee consults with a supervisor.

In psychotherapy and counselling training, there has to be supervised client work. Many counselling courses do not provide clients for the trainee counsellor to work with, whereas many psychotherapy courses do. In psychotherapy training, clients are assessed as suitable to work with trainees and the trainees are encouraged to work with a variety of different people with different presenting problems to gain the experiences they need.

The following is an outline of a course content.

Theoretical framework

The theory of the model that is being taught is presented as input in lecture form, required reading and through essay writing and discussion. The understanding of therapeutic process, knowledge of human development, interventions, strategies and process are the academic and practical skills aspects of a course.

The theory is a structure that a therapist uses in this work. The theoretical structure helps the therapist to understand the problems that the client presents.

Before trying to make sense of the client's presenting issues, the therapist needs to consider a context for the client. The context contains the client's life stages. What is happening in a particular client's life stages is explored at the very beginning of the work. The exploration covers:

- Why the client has come at this particular time.
- What issues they wish to focus on.

The group

A lot of the learning on a counselling or psychotherapy course takes place in groups. There is the large group, which may be thirty or so trainees, and smaller sub-groups. Groups change and evolve as they pass through the various stages of development. They can feel threatening to some individuals and safe to hide in for others, whilst some people revel in the attention. Either way, there is much to be learned from the experience of several years with the same group. There will be challenges from the tutors in raising points for you to reflect on, and individuals within the group can be challenging in their interactions with peers.

A good course will not push people beyond their limits, but neither should they permit people to 'hide' in the group. A balance of trainees learning and growing at their own pace and being stretched is a paradox and an example of a good course. This blend cannot be expected to happen all of the time, but needs to happen some of the time for trainees to gain from it.

Experiential group learning

Some of the group work may focus on experiential learning. This is where the trainees direct their own learning within the allotted time of the group session. The tutors observe or say very little even though they are usually present. This type of work can be alive, stimulating, challenging and demanding – a place to take risks or not – and certainly can help trainees to notice how they behave in group situations.

During the experiential learning time, trainees raise any subject that they feel is relevant to the group. Subjects may include: how they are feeling at that moment, how they feel about someone else, what is concerning them on the course, and what is not being spoken about in the group. Feelings can surface and are either expressed or hidden but felt none the less in the group. A group member may ask for feedback from the group, which can be an opportunity for personal insight for the person receiving the feedback. It is also an opportunity for others to practise giving constructive feedback. This practice enables group members to view things from another perspective.

The experience of sharing personal feelings and thoughts in this way, and how the individual and the group deal with them, is the learning experience. A tremendous amount of learning about the self and the self in relation to others can be gained in experiential groups. This experience also gives an understanding of how clients will feel when faced with speaking about their thoughts and feelings that they would not normally share with others.

This type of learning is challenging and is often a struggle. People have to tackle the difficulty of not having a structure or a tutor to tell them what to do. The stages of this learning are well noted in the literature, as are the dynamics of the group; that is, the interchanges that take place and the undercurrents that are felt.

There are stages that the group passes through before the group can become a cohesive working group. This is a very powerful learning place for most people, and can be very uncomfortable. Some groups do not become a cohesive working group.

The criticism of this form of learning is that it is not always clear as to when the session has become a therapy group, and when it is a training group. I discuss this in more detail below. You may want to ask about this kind of learning in your interview.

Training group or therapy group?

There are some courses, particularly among the less established ones, that seem to blur the boundaries between whether the group work is a training group and when it is a therapy group (or personal development group). Some facilitators themselves are not always clear about the difference. The questions that could be raised in an interview include:

- Is the training group a therapy style group, and if so is it made clear to trainees from the outset? If this is the case, is there enough support from the facilitators to make it safe for trainees to risk working on their own process within the group?
- Do the tutors facilitate trainees to end the therapy part of a group session, and to make the adjustment to the training part?
- How would this type of group affect the assessment of the trainees?
- Should a therapy group be an integral part of the training?
- Should it be separate from a training group?

The advantages and disadvantages could be made clear to prospective trainees.

Very often this information is not forthcoming. There are courses where trainees have felt very unhappy with the way that some group facilitators encourage feelings to be roused in a group, but are then unable or unwilling to support the trainees. The facilitators may have the expectation that the trainee can take those feelings to their therapist, but it seems to be an unclear and uncaring structure. Whilst I have heard facilitators stress that the feelings of the trainees are their own responsibility, this cavalier approach is not a reflection of the supportive and caring philosophy of therapy.

Stating intentions honourably

Courses that practise this maintain that the trainees are responsible for their own learning. There is, in my view, a shared responsibility for the learning from the course organisers, tutors and the trainees. Part of the organisers' and tutors' responsibilities is to inform trainees what to expect. They should state their intentions honestly and openly.

As part of taking responsibility for themselves, this may be an essential part of a course; trainees need to learn to gain support from their peers.

The trainee will have the time, during the course, to self-reflect and self-examine so as to gain insights about themselves. Being part of a group, trainees can become aware of their own process, their blocks and blind spots, their unresolved conflicts and how they react and relate with others.

Role play

This is a mode of learning that is popular with tutors, and whilst it can be very powerful it can be contentious with some trainees. The objective is to enable the practice of interventions and strategies in a creative way. The usual way of using the role play is for one person to take the role of a client, and the other the therapist. The client presents with a specific issue so that the therapist can practise something that was taught earlier. Some trainees complain that they find it hard to act a role, or feel that the situation is contrived. In effect, whether a situation has been contrived or someone is acting, the person who plays the part is still being themselves in the role. Whilst the character they are portraying may not be real for them, their feelings are theirs and are real.

Role play has its use but is also limited by the brevity of time that there is to practise. It works better if people bring their own real issues, but they have to be selective because of the difficulty of time and the fact that their partner is not, at this stage, a trained therapist.

Observing therapy

On most courses, this will be live work with two people and a tutor or third trainee observing. Two trainees can be asked to work in front of the group. There may also be videos of therapists working with clients, for the group to observe, followed by discussions.

Assessments: peer, tutor and self-assessments

The assessment is on the trainee's progress, their personal and professional development, and their strengths and weaknesses. Tutors assess through group work and from tutorials. Trainees in small groups assess each other throughout the year.

The ways in which you will be evaluated on the course are varied. The obvious one is through essay writing, which can evaluate your grasp of concepts and later on, the application of relating theory to practice.

Writing and submitting a personal journal of your experiences on the course is another form of evaluating how you are using the learning to gain insights into your own process. The more open, searching and reflective you are, the more you will gain from it.

You may be expected to self-evaluate, which is a way of learning to reflect on your own progress and to monitor your effectiveness.

Your supervisor will give feedback to you and to the course.

Skills and interventions

Techniques are taught that fit to the theoretical approach of the course, amongst which are:

- listening skills
- open-ended questions
- what, why and how questions
- observing the process whilst listening to the content
- not leading the client
- focusing the client
- looking for what is being avoided
- observing the client's body language

- reflecting on the meanings of the client's words
- enabling the client to ventilate feelings
- disclosing appropriately.

On humanistic courses trainees are taught how and when to disclose feelings or be transparent. On psychodynamic courses, trainees would learn how to work with transference, resistance and other defence mechanisms.

Confidentiality

Tutors ask trainees to keep issues that arise from the group to the group itself, not to discuss them elsewhere. There may be small groups within the course training, and confidentiality is required in the same way as in the larger group. This practice allows trainees to accustom themselves to maintaining confidentiality when they are working as practitioners.

Principles of ethical practice

Ethical practice is learnt through direct teaching input, group discussions, essay writing and case histories. If the course is accredited through an organisation, it is useful for the trainees to be given a photo-copied handout of the appropriate code of ethics in practice. A course may have its own code of ethics related to practice in its handbook.

Boundary setting

The implications and reasons for setting boundaries are usually thoroughly explored and discussed in training. Throughout the course, trainees become used to time, confidentiality, ethical and other professional boundaries. The aim is to maintain a balance of professional boundaries for the safety and trust of the therapeutic alliance whilst allowing the warmth and care of the human relationship.

DIPLOMA COURSES

On the diploma course, the standards and depth of learning will be more thorough and demanding. More is expected of the trainee; and the trainee can expect to be challenged more. The trainee is expected to be more critical, reflective and willing to take more risks.

Entry requirements

Entry requirements are that a trainee has successfully completed a prior certificate course, usually with the same training organisation. A required number of hours of theory, group work and supervised practice needs to be in place. Some psychotherapy courses would expect applicants to have been in individual therapy with a training therapist for a year before applying. Permission from the personal therapist may be sought for suitability to enter the course.

On other courses, individual therapy would be required during training. Applicants usually need to be working in a related field or voluntary capacity.

Applicants for psychoanalytic psychotherapy courses are expected to have a degree in medicine, psychology, social science, or a relevant professional qualification equivalent to a degree. Some experience working with psychiatric patients is required. Those who do not have the necessary psychiatric experience would be expected to undertake a placement within a mental health setting.

On some courses, applicants will be expected to be working with clients; on others they are not permitted to do so until they are assessed as ready to.

References will be taken up. A detailed questionnaire may be required. Personal suitability, an aptitude to work according to the standards of the course, a commitment to the course, and an ability to support oneself financially throughout the training are general to all courses.

Once you have decided on a diploma course, you are going to spend a great deal of money and time investing in a long and sometimes arduous training. It is a training that has many stages of development, with the likelihood of a fair amount of anxieties and difficulties. As well as the stress of managing the training requirements, there are the rewards, satisfaction and positive values. Training in therapy or counselling can change your life.

The content of a typical diploma course, over 2, 3 or 4 years, includes:

- Introduction to concepts
- Reading
- Comparative theoretical concepts
- Essay writing
- Theoretical seminars and lectures
- Group work
- Intervention, strategies and techniques

- Application of concepts to different types of pathology (psycho-analytic studies)
- Assessment of patients
- Ethical issues
- Clinical management
- The relevance of research

Some of the above are very dependent on the particular theoretical approach of the training. Not all apply to every course. Essays are expected on training courses. They demonstrate a trainee's understanding and abilities.

Essays

You need to know how many essays are required in each year, and what duration of time is set for writing them. On some courses, you may be expected to write one essay a term. The word length will vary from 3,000–5,000 words. There are courses that require 10,000 words in their fourth year. There are usually topics to choose from that will involve research and substantial reading. Most courses suggest that trainees allow for 5–8 hours a week for reading. Writing essays is time-consuming and a demanding aspect of a course.

There is certainly a technique to be learned about writing essays in the ways that are acceptable to the course. Using tutor-allocated time for this, if you are unsure about writing essays, is pertinent.

Courses will have a time limit when essays should be handed in. It is worth asking if the time limit is fixed or if it is flexible. There are courses that categorically state a time limit for essays and then extend the dates because either the time period was not realistic for trainees (or tutors), or not enough trainees handed their essays in on time. This can be very frustrating for those trainees who work hard to get their essays written in the time that has been allocated.

What sort of feedback can you expect from the essays? Do tutors mark/score or evaluate/give feedback? – another worthwhile question to raise at an interview.

There is a great deal of trainee criticism around the marking of essays – on masters' dissertations too. There are far too many tutors on courses who do not read essays thoroughly, or who make superficial or unhelpful comments. Encouragement and constructive criticism or feedback are both necessary attributes to the learning curve. Receiving constructive feedback encourages the trainee to reflect on their work, which is a necessary practice.

Other aspects of learning on a diploma course curriculum in either counselling or psychotherapy can contain the following:

- Values, principles and philosophies of theories
- Stages of human development
- The dynamics of the therapeutic relationship
- Understanding the therapeutic process
- Group and individual supervision
- External personal therapy
- Personal development within the course
- Assessments
- Keeping a personal and professional journal
- Group meetings
- Issues of specialised topics and client groups
- Loss and bereavement
- Beginnings, middles and endings of sessions and the overall process
- How to relate theory to practice
- Understanding of referral and agencies in the community
- Professional liability (insurance)
- Accountability
- Contracts
- Placements
- Case management
- Case discussions
- Recording notes
- Presentations to the group
- Tutorials
- Tape recordings and/or video of trainees counselling each other

The recordings make a lively and interesting part of the training and are usually carried out for the benefit of the group as well as the individuals who can see and hear themselves working. Assessments and feedback have a richer quality when someone can observe or hear themselves, in spite of the anxieties and inhibitions. Written transcripts usually accompany a video.

According to the type of course, there would be skills practice. It is interesting to ask whether the tutors themselves model some of the skills. Some do and others flatly refuse. Some tutors would not model out of fear of their trainees' criticisms. I personally feel that seeing tutors can help the trainees to see how it is done, providing that the tutor is confident about making mistakes. Making mistakes or struggling a bit would be a positive learning experience for the trainees. The message would be that even tutors are human, and making mistakes in the training room is an important part of the learning.

There is also the disadvantage of tutors modelling their own style, especially if they do not make many mistakes! This may have the opposite effect; that is, of making the trainees feel inadequate at not being able to have the skill and confidence that the tutor displays. The trainees may believe that the tutors are demonstrating the correct way, rather than *a way* of practice (Dryden and Thorne 1991: 26).

Apart from the individual learning, there is likely to be pair work. People may be paired up for supporting each other for a certain time, as well as to become used to working in pairs because this is the nature of the profession. There can be large and small group work.

The theory of the course will probably come under one of the three main theoretical orientations, i.e. psychodynamic, humanistic or cognitive-behavioural. The applicant can enquire what the training methods are and whether they are consistent with the core theoretical model. A course should strive to create a balance between theory, skill components and personal development, consistent with the core theoretical model.

There could be a good deal of overlap between a particular counselling course and a psychotherapy course. Psychotherapy training could contain some of or all of the list above and (depending on the approach) could also include the following:

- Diagnostic skills, particularly early detection of mental illness
- Treatment strategies/planned structure
- Theoretical concepts and philosophies
- Critical analyses of theories
- Principles and techniques of the approach
- Lectures or seminars on particular topics
- Personality development and personality disorders
- Sexual development and the sense of self
- Psychological development
- Transcultural issues in psychotherapy: race, gender, disability and sexual preferences
- Seminars on psychopathology: psychotic and neurotic functioning, sexual problems, depression and manic defences, dreams, anxiety and defences, obsessions, addiction
- Case histories
- Supervised clinical placement work
- Clinical observation of infant and mother
- The unconscious processes between the patient and the therapist

- Attachment theory
- Knowledge of psychosomatic illness
- The psychological effects of chronic or terminal illness
- Different stages in the life cycle of loss and the negotiation of life crises
- Structuring and managing the psychotherapeutic sessions
- Taking and giving referrals, and working with other agencies

A number of psychoanalytic and psychoanalytic-psychotherapy training courses require trainees to observe a mother and baby in their family setting, once a week for an hour. The observations are written and discussed at weekly discussion seminars. Trainees are required to write a paper based on their observations at the end of the first year.

On psychoanalytic courses, trainees would be required to treat one male and one female patient each for a minimum of three sessions per week, usually during the second year. One training patient would be treated for at least two years and one for at least eighteen months. Trainees are required to submit written six-monthly reports describing the progress of treatment and to attend seminars once a term to discuss these reports. All clinical practice would be in conjunction with an individual weekly supervisor who would be approved by the training institution.

The acquiring of skills and knowledge, and having mastery in developmental psychology and psychopathology, is an aim of psychotherapy training.

Having a balance of the list of the above objectives on any course is what makes the course interesting and thorough. The tutors' creative input, skills and attitudes are fundamental to making a course enjoyable or otherwise.

Topics that may not be included on a course

Topics that are generally not seen to be relevant to general training courses may have a small slot in a course, under topics of interest. Very often, these topics that are not considered relevant are highly relevant once the trainee has left the course and begun to work as a practitioner. I would like to see courses include such topics as:

- Intercultural counselling (see Chapter 9)
- Prejudice awareness
- Awareness and prevention of secondary traumatic stress disorders in therapists

- Working with the client who becomes threatening or dangerous
- Becoming familiar with the appropriate code of ethics and practice to which the course adheres
- How to evaluate practice

Prejudice awareness

Human beings make assumptions about others and have prejudices. The term 'prejudice' means holding a negative, preconceived opinion about someone even after further information is received to the contrary. It is very uncomfortable for a counsellor or psychotherapist to have prejudices about a particular person they are working with. Trainees, inexperienced practitioners and experienced practitioners alike may feel ashamed of such feelings. They may choose to deny the feelings. Raising the subject on a training course enables a trainee to understand that such feelings can arise and that they can be taken to therapy and worked through.

Awareness of secondary traumatic stress disorders

People who choose to work in the caring and mental health professions are usually people who are sensitive and empathic to others. Having empathy is one of the important qualities of effective counsellors and psychotherapists, but the more empathic a practitioner is, the more likely they are to be open to the transmission of trauma from working with traumatised clients.

Research has shown that strong emotions can be transmitted, and it is possible and expected for practitioners working with traumatised clients to suffer from similar affects. These secondary traumatic stress feelings can become *disorders* if the practitioner is unaware of them, and if they are not picked up in supervision. They include physical, emotional, behavioural and interpersonal disorders. There are short- and long-term symptoms; sleep disturbances, anxiety attacks, depression, phobias, hypervigilance, exhaustion and burnout.

Working with threatening and dangerous clients

Having an understanding of your limitations in your work is a sign of competency. This stage of awareness may not be recognised in trainees or inexperienced practitioners, who may find it difficult to turn someone away who has asked for help. Through inexperience, it may be difficult to recognise when someone needs more help than you can offer, or a different type of help from that which you can offer. Supervision of course is essential, but learning where and how to refer is necessary.

Working on diagnoses of mental illness in training is relevant. Being aware of the possibilities in a work setting and discussing what you can do in the event of a crisis, are issues that need to be raised and explored in training. This preparation is a safeguard for clients and therapists.

Become familiar with the code of ethics and practice to which the course adheres

Tutors can supply a copy to each trainee of the code of ethics and practice that the course adheres to. It would not take very long to read through with the trainees and to answer any questions that are raised. Many of the points that are covered by codes of ethics and practice are helpful for trainees to reflect on and discuss during their training.

How to evaluate practice

Courses do not specifically help counsellors or therapists to develop their own methods of monitoring their therapeutic practice effectiveness. Designing evaluation forms to give to clients at the end of therapy and following up with further forms after a period may be very useful. As all experience is subjective, it would be interesting for the practitioner to see if the client's experience of the therapy process was different from her own.

The trainers may not consider that self-regulating practice is a practical part of training; that this is beyond the training course and therefore beyond their responsibility. This is unfortunate, as counselling and psychotherapy practice monitoring is a part of increasing effectiveness and competence, as well as supporting research into the validity of therapy. Using one's records in a specific way to chart or define blocking of progress could also be taught. Other ways of evaluating practice effectiveness could be raised on training course.

Trainee placements for clients

Trainees will need people to work with in order to practise their skills, and to gain the amount of practice hours that are required on the course. There is the practice of counselling or psychotherapy that takes place on the course between trainees. At some point in the course trainees are expected to find clients or patients outside the course. These are clients from members of the public.

There are training schools that insist that

- trainees do not start a course unless they have already acquired clients.

There are schools that have a policy of

- assessing trainees working with colleagues on the course first, before they are permitted to work with members of the public. If trainees are not considered ready to begin working with clients, their training could be extended.

There are training schools that

- have clients assessed by an experienced assessor for suitability to work with trainees.

And there are training schools that ensure that

- trainees receive regular supervision whilst they are on placement.

And there are training schools that do not provide supervision within the costing of the course.

> *What is expected and what is provided are extremely important to be checked out before committing to the course.*

My own opinion on this matter is that the training institute should have the responsibility to assess the trainee's stage of development and suitability to take up placements, as well as selecting clients who are appropriate to work with trainees. Close supervision should be an integral provision of the cost of the course.

Some of the analytic and psychoanalytic psychotherapy schools supply patients for their trainees who are considered ready to work with the public. The patients are usually carefully assessed beforehand and are fully aware that they will be working with a trainee. On those courses, there may be a requirement of working with several patients, several times a week for a number of years. Each one presenting with different problems. The trainee is strongly supported with individual supervision.

The majority of training courses do not supply clients however, and it is for the trainee to find their own. Asking in the assessment interview about placements is a vital question. This is an aspect of the course that puts pressure onto many trainees, both in terms of finding clients and in the hours that are needed to work with them. Between two and four clients a week is a number that each trainee must work with. This may not sound a great many, but it is if a trainee is working as well as managing the course and her personal life. Finding your own clients who are happy to work with an inexperienced trainee may not always be easy.

There is also the question of where to see the clients once you have managed to find them. If the training institute does not provide the accommodation, and you do not have the privacy or suitability at your home, where can you go? This will possibly take time and energy to research. There are volunteer agencies that might be glad of the help and will provide the accommodation, and there are hospitals and many doctors' surgeries that are happy to have trainee counsellors and therapists.

Tutors

An assumption about the suitability of tutors on the course is that they are all qualified and experienced. Another assumption is that they are adequately briefed about the stage of development and the learning of the group of trainees they are to facilitate. Regretfully, this is not always the case. As in all teaching settings, there are good and bad facilitators or tutors. Some tutors are also better prepared than others. Visiting tutors need good direction if they are to work with a group of trainees for only one or two sessions.

Frequently brochures may give details about their teaching staff, who may be qualified and experienced, but their ability to impart information satisfactorily may not match their qualifications.

It is useful to find out the ratio of tutors to trainees on the course. The general recommendation is twelve trainees to one tutor. In many training courses there are one or two tutors working with large groups, one tutor with small groups, and occasions when two tutors are working with sub-groups. There are seminars, lectures, practice groups and study groups, and there may be different tutors for this variety of teaching. Asking about the format of teaching gives an idea of the structure of training support that exists on the course.

SUPERVISION

An important aspect of that support is the supervision arrangements of a course.

The supervisor on a training course is accountable to the course and has some responsibility for how the trainee works and learns within the supervision session. Supervision is a powerful form of learning and gaining insights for the trainee.

A supervisor closely monitors a trainee's stage of development, interventions and skills, feelings that arise as a result of working with a particular client, and the trainee's part in the therapeutic relationship. A supervisor also monitors the progress of therapy.

A supervisor is a person who should have a lot of experience of therapy work and has preferably undertaken training in supervision herself. The supervisor on a training course should be well versed in the particular approach of the course. The supervisor should know the aims and objectives of the course and for the trainees so that the supervisory input is in accordance with the course requirements. Each trainee may have two supervisors, one for the group on the course and another external supervisor. In the group, the trainee learns from seeing how their colleagues work in supervision.

The external supervisor may see an individual trainee or may see two or three trainees together.

All the supervisors on a course should be working in accordance with the course requirements. There are courses where this does not happen and one of the supervisors may tell a trainee something that is in contradiction to another or something contrary to the tutors on the course. This is highly confusing to the trainee, and undermines the training ethos of the course.

Asking for an explanation of the supervisory arrangement, as part of gaining information about a course, may give you clues about the organisation of the course.

Supervision may be a whole new experience for you. Your openness to learn from the supervisor and to use the sessions productively will be valuable to you in your work. In order to ensure that you have as positive an experience as possible, it is realistic to be aware of your expectations, anxieties and needs regarding supervision. If they are not expressed you could become frustrated. If you are aware of difficulties, it is better if they are addressed and explored within the early supervision sessions.

A supervisor may help the trainee regarding the keeping of client records. This is a discipline that becomes automatic, but takes time to develop. What to write, how much and how to make use of it are the usual points. Some trainees begin by not being able to write very much at all, and others write far too much detail.

Presenting case material may be difficult for the trainee, and the supervisor can suggest ways to do this. Some supervisors suggest that the trainee brings an audiotape of a session. The trainee may choose a particular point in the session to play back to the supervisor. This method of supervising can be very instructive and helpful for both supervisor and trainee. What is important to explore in the supervisory sessions, and how to make best use of the time, is all part of the learning.

At the training interview, it is worth while asking what happens if you find that you cannot work with your supervisor: whether you can change to another one or find your own. There may be all sorts of reasons why this is not permitted, but it is helpful to know at the outset as supervision is an important element of the training course. You will be with your supervisor on a regular basis, so the relationship is important. Depending on the course, you may see your supervisor every few weeks for the duration of the course.

The course may stipulate the number of required clients. Where this is not done, the supervisor discusses with the trainee the number of clients that the trainee can work with. This number will accord with the level of experience, and the capacity to work with different issues at the trainee's stage of development.

Courses usually have their own list of external supervisors from which a trainee can choose – or trainees may be allocated a supervisor. A trainee may expect to pay extra for individual supervision, or the supervisor's fees may be included with the course fees. This is important to consider when reckoning your outlay for the whole course.

PERSONAL THERAPY AND PERSONAL DEVELOPMENT

Few courses would expect a prospective student on a long-term course to have worked through most of their own personal issues, but some courses are interested to know if you have some self-awareness. An important criterion is that you show openness and a willingness to be self-reflective.

There are a number of routes to help trainees become self-aware and self-reflective. One is through writing a personal journal throughout the course. Trainees will demonstrate their understanding of the objectives and goals of therapy through writing essays and keeping personal journals. The course may include some introduction to writing a formal journal, or may not have such expectations, and leave the style and format to the trainee. Some courses will want to see the journal and consider it as part of the assessment of progress. Receiving the written feedback from tutors can be constructive and informative. This is both a personal and professional form of self-awareness, as the journal relates to what is happening for the individual on the course.

Being on the course itself is a major source of personal awareness. Reading the required material, the lectures, experiential group work, discussions and films and learning the skills will undoubtedly open up many personal issues.

Trainees learn a great deal from their own personal development. Most courses require trainees to be in their own personal therapy, at least for the duration of the course. All the theory and learning come together through the experience of personal therapy.

More and more counselling courses are making therapy a requirement of training, but may not stipulate a lengthy period.

To some, the idea of paying out more for personal therapy may seem like a heavy burden of extra financial cost, especially if someone is struggling to fund their own training. But there are extra costs to be considered anyway, and the idea that someone can practise on another person that which they have not undergone themselves is questionable and untenable in this particular helping profession.

The experience of personal therapy is often said to be the greatest learning for a practitioner. You become aware of experiencing the process for yourself, as opposed to learning it theoretically. It is easier to see what is helpful and what is unhelpful – at least for you. It is beneficial to apply what you have learned in your own therapy to everyday life, which facilitates the understanding of how clients change.

You will gain insight into your own vulnerabilities and unresolved issues; the familial, social and cultural influences that have affected you. You will also gain an understanding of how you are in relationships and what difficulties you may have in them. Lastly, how would you know that something works unless you have experienced it for yourself?

As with the supervisory provision, you need to check out exactly what is required of you with regard to your own therapy. Does the course have its own list of practitioners to choose from? How frequently will you be required to be in therapy? Courses and theoretical approaches vary, of course. Therapy for yourself can range from once a week counselling for 2/3 years (or whilst the course lasts) to five times a week for 4/5 years minimum for psychoanalysts. The extra cost of your therapy is a large part of your expenses. Again, it is important that the practitioner's orientation should be compliant with the orientation of the course

Some courses offer personal development (sometimes also called self-development or self-awareness) on a course in addition to requiring the trainee to undergo personal therapy. Personal development (PD) is often a form of group therapy through exercises.

PD groups are not the magical, quick and definitive answer to all the changes the individual desires for himself. Neither are they training for life. What they do offer is an intense and concentrated period of time to try out, through risk-taking, different ways of responding to situations in a permissive and safe setting. There is an opportunity to be challenged if one allows it. As an adjunct to personal therapy and to the learning on a course, PD groups are invaluable if they are facilitated well by a skilled and experienced facilitator.

The early existence of the PD group began in the 1960s and 1970s with encounter groups in the States, notably at Esalen in California. The idea was to weaken people's defences through prolonged hours and emotionally draining cathartic exercises, public confessions and confrontations from the trainers. Participants were locked in and unable to leave until the end of the weekend.

An example of a personal development weekend course

PD courses have come a long way since their US origins. Training institutes that include a PD element may either build it into the ongoing regular, group meetings as an integral part of the course time schedule, or have a specific weekend (or more). The PD is either included in the cost, or is extra. There are courses that make one or more residential weekends a requirement of the course, where PD is conducted.

On a weekend PD course an outside facilitator may be brought in. The level of the PD will depend on the stage of the group, whether they are in their first, second, or final year of training. The facilitator will work with whatever the individual members bring up. This may be from an exercise that she has set, through questions that she asks the group to think about, or some stated input that she makes. An example of an exercise follows.

At the beginning of the course, the facilitator could ask each individual to tell the group their name, what they know about it and what their name means to them. During this exercise, someone may say that they have never liked their name. The facilitator may ask this person if she can work with him and she may spend a short time exploring with the participant what this dislike of his name means to him.

A number of things can happen. The participant may gain some deeper personal understanding. Other members of the group may also begin to think about something significant for themselves. Feelings, such as anxiety, may grow. Another participant may raise an issue directly or indirectly related to the exercise and the facilitator may work with that individual.

Participants also work in pairs and in smaller groups as well as the larger group. The facilitator may use a range of creative exercises such as guided imagery, asking people to draw particular things on paper. There maybe movement and music, and exercises to test trust, as well as discussions and working with individuals.

The facilitator has to be highly skilled and attuned to the pace and level that the individual members of the group can work at. Too much confrontation, or challenging inappropriately or at the wrong time, creates distrust. Too little and people become bored.

For an outside facilitator this can be more difficult if she has had no contact with the group before leading the course. But this is still preferable to a known tutor from the course leading the PD weekend. A known tutor will already have a relationship with the group which could interfere with the process of the group. Some participants would feel more inhibited to work on themselves with tutors they knew. They could be reluctant to take risks with tutors, as very often the tutors are a source of ongoing assessment for the trainees. Keeping the roles of tutor and PD facilitator separate is to keep a clear boundary.

This form of learning needs to be clearly defined beforehand and conducted by an experienced facilitator. The trainees need to be aware that they may need support during the personal development training and following it, as strong feelings can arise from a focused and concentrated weekend of personal work. Having their own therapist and therapy session to turn to is important.

Why personal therapy is necessary

There is a saying in this profession that the client can only reach the place that the practitioner has got to. If therapy seems at an impasse it could mean (amongst other things) that practitioners have not worked through for themselves something that they and their clients are troubled with.

It is from one's own therapy, struggling with ambivalence, conflicts and defences, that a trainee/practitioner resolves her own issues that frequently resonate with those of her clients. Accepting what cannot be changed helps her to empathise with those clients who are in a similar position.

In personal therapy, the learning is more than how the process works, more than learning from one's own therapist who models the approach, and more than the application of theory to practice. It is the felt-experience of working through the personal issues within the therapeutic relationship. No classroom theory can replace this experience. For the trainee, there is the evident experience of knowing how it feels to be a client with all the range of emotions that being in therapy contains.

Self-reflection is central to the therapeutic experience. It is a creative capacity that either someone is capable of before entering therapy, or learns to develop during therapy. Self-reflection leads to awareness and insights and ultimately to what can and cannot be changed.

A client or patient has the right to expect that the therapist will have resolved many aspects of their own difficulties and have reached a level of maturity. Age and life-experience in themselves are not the only criteria. Wisdom and understanding about the work, and respect and empathy for the person, come from the experience of the personal therapeutic work.

COST OF TRAINING

Finally, we look at the cost of training. Courses may quote specific fees in their brochures, but it is not unusual for the fees to rise during the training. This may be due to inflation. The fees quoted may not include the extra costs of:

- Registration.
- Supervision. Group supervision may be included, individual supervision may not be.
- Professional indemnity (for seeing clients).
- Personal therapy.
- Extra-curriculum workshops that are 'part of' the core training.
- Books. There is always a substantial reading list and textbooks are costly. Libraries may not hold specialised books.
- Photocopying. (Photocopying of long sections of material is against copyrights.)
- Personal tuition on help with writing essays, reports and disser-tations.
- Membership of an association.
- Fares to and from training centre.

I phoned approximately thirty training institutes to enquire about the cost of the first, second and subsequent years' courses. I asked how much each year would cost, and how much fees would increase annually.

I had a great deal of difficulty in getting clear and precise information. Administrators often did not have the appropriate information. Many thought that there would be some increase, but could not tell me by how much. At best I was offered 'a bit of an increase'. I eventually gathered that the cost of many courses increases yearly by between 3–5 per cent.

There is a wide range of fees for different training courses. The fees are not necessarily related to the quality of tuition or the duration of the courses. As a consequence of this the following figures are for guidance only.

Adult education institutes that run courses in basic counselling skills: these cost in the region of £60–70 for about 20 hours. Concessions are often available. Someone in receipt of benefits would pay about £15.

There are very few subsidies or grants beyond those mentioned above. If you are already employed in a job where you could use counselling skills, your employer may help you with part of the costs. The BAC has a few educational bursaries for people accepted on BAC-recognised courses. Check with BAC for the details of availability and the application procedure.

The voluntary counselling agencies may provide their own training. Some of these agencies will provide free training in exchange for an agreed amount of your time for voluntary work. Relate is an example of an agency that does this.

There are many commercial training institutes. The fees are likely to be high. You could expect to pay in the region of £250 for an introductory course of 20–40 hours.

A certificate year in counselling skills course could cost £800.

Advanced courses are nearly all part time. They will last a minimum of two years for a diploma, three for a master's and more for a doctorate. Most colleges tell you the fee per year and the number of years a course will last.

Annual tuition fees for diplomas could be in the region of £1,000 to £2,000 per year. This is substantial if the course lasts for three or four years. Although many educational establishments are competing directly for your custom, one cannot assume that a more expensive course is better.

Some psychotherapy training that takes in personal therapy can cost £20,000 in total.

Some additional costs will apply to more advanced courses. The additional costs may well be hidden in the details of a college's brochure, and if you are not aware of them it can come as a shock later on. Many colleges charge separate fees for registration, administration and tuition.

The cost of personal therapy once a week could be £1,500 per year. Supervision cost is dependent on how many clients you are seeing. An average sum would be around £750 per year. Professional indemnity is about £50 per year.

If you are planning to do a master's course, there may be separately itemised costs to tutor you through the dissertation. Your research project will incur expenses. These will depend on what you do, but common costs include travel to libraries, books, photocopying, postage, word processing, telephone, stationery, and finally the costs of binding your dissertation.

How fees are payable

Many courses operate a non-refundable deposit, which can vary from £100 to £500. Most courses permit payments to be made by several amounts over a year. More courses are introducing a contract of payment for trainees to sign before commencing a course. The contract binds you to a completion of the full payment, whether or not this is through payments made by arrangement. Failure to complete can mean that the institute will take legal action.

Training centres can also retain the right to increase fees for the second and subsequent years.

QUESTIONS FOR SELF-REFLECTION BEFORE APPLYING FOR A COURSE

1 Do you enjoy studying?
2 What are your anxieties and expectations about going on a course?
3 How do you feel about writing essays?
4 How do you feel about sharing personal feelings in a group?
5 Are you anxious in large groups, small groups, or both?
6 Do you dominate, shrink or behave in particular ways in groups?
7 Can you manage your time constructively for studying and other parts of your life?
8 Are you able to accept and make use of others' constructive criticisms?
9 Can you give constructive criticism to others?
10 Can you give and accept support from others?

FURTHER READING

Abram, J. (1992) *Individual Psychotherapy Training – A Guide*, London: Free Associated Books.

Dryden, W. and Feltham, C. (1994) *Developing the Practice of Counselling*, London: Sage Publications.

Dryden, W. and Thorne, B. (eds) (1991) *Training and Supervision for Counselling in Action*, London: Sage Publications.

Stevens, R. (ed.) (1995) *Understanding the Self*, London: Sage Publications, in association with The Open University.

Wallace, S. and Lewis, M. (1998) *Becoming a Professional Counsellor*, London: Sage Publications.

Wicks, R. (1994) *Helping Others*, London: Souvenir Press Ltd.

Yalom, I.D. (1975) *The Theory and Practice of Group Psychotherapy*, New York: Basic Books.

8

QUALIFICATIONS, REGISTRATION, ACCREDITATION AND RESEARCH

QUALIFICATION OF COURSES

Gaining a certificate or diploma in counselling or psychotherapy is a mark of training standard, but it may be the standard of the particular school or training institute that has awarded it. A certificate may be nothing more than a simple certificate of attendance from the institution itself, or the award can be external to the institution:

1   A valid counselling training would mean, at this stage, that a counselling course had applied for and achieved accreditation through a recognised body. The course must meet with the accrediting body's requirements, thus ensuring that training institutions raise and maintain the standard of training acceptable to that body. An example of an accrediting body is BAC.

2   A psychotherapy training course that carries recognition would mean that the graduate trainees could be eligible to apply for membership of the United Kingdom Council for Psychotherapy (UKCP).

3   A training institute that has membership of The British Confederation of Psychotherapists (BCP) would be a training centre with high standards. They would publicise their membership in their prospectus.

4   The British Psychological Society (BPS) has a division of counselling psychology that publishes its course and examination requirements for the BPS diploma in counselling psychology.

There are other awarding bodies that validate courses, such as the Associated Examining Board, British Accreditation Council, Counselling and Psychotherapy Central Awarding Body, City and Guilds of London Institute, Royal Society of Arts, Northern Examinations and

Assessment Board, The Scottish Qualifications Authority, and Welsh Joint Education Committee. (For further details see the List of Resources, pp. 203–24.)

There are courses that do not carry the status of these organisations and award bodies. They may be courses that have sought recognition from those associations and not been accepted, or they may have chosen to seek validation from a university.

Courses have the right to state in their brochures that they are applying for (a particular) accreditation. But the course may not gain the accreditation they seek, or they may not gain it whilst you are there as it takes time for application and formal procedure. There are courses that have failed to obtain accreditation through the more established associations and, recognising the public awareness of standards control, have set up their own.

You need to consider who validates a training course, as it is very likely that you will want to apply for accreditation or registration after your training. As the general trend is towards licensing or statutory regulation, then the recognition of the training that you undertake is important.

If the course does not have the desired accreditation or eligibility for registration then this needs to be made clear. During an interview/ assessment, assessors should tell candidates whether the course is applying for accreditation or registration, and with which organisation. It is equally important that they declare that they have not yet gained it and may not do so. Candidates are then aware of the situation and can decide for themselves about the course in the light of that information.

You need to know not only what the quality of the training is but what recognition the course has, and by whom.

QUALIFICATION OF INDIVIDUALS

In order to be awarded a qualification at present, trainees have to have successfully completed the course requirements. This usually means regular attendance, successful presentations, the required number of essays, and other written work satisfactorily completed; a set number of supervised clinical work, and personal therapy hours. The trainee's suitability and progress should have been charted and accepted according to the institution's evaluation. This is usually agreed between tutors and supervisors, with peer and personal assessments taken into consideration on some courses. A viva (oral interview) or written examination may be held at the end of some courses.

If an external body validates a course, then the scaling for the examination has to be in accordance with those requirements.

As yet, there is no nationally recognised training standard or qualifications in either counselling or psychotherapy.

NATIONAL VOCATIONAL QUALIFICATIONS

As Europe proceeds to becoming more unified, qualifications will need to be standardised so that they can be recognised in all countries of the European Union. National Vocational Qualifications are intended to serve that purpose of recognition in counselling and psychotherapy.

National Vocational Qualifications (NVQs) are new to the field of counselling. They are standardised qualifications that are divided into numbered levels. They are intended to assess knowledge and practical skills directly relevant to the workplace. The levels are based on competencies and abilities. The emphasis is on evaluating the things which can be evaluated, such as skills, the results of using the skills, and competency.

There has been a conflict within the counselling and psychotherapy world as to whether NVQs have a place. Those critical of the intro-duction of this form of qualification stress that the philosophy and personal experiences of the practitioner are not taken into consideration, and neither is the therapeutic relationship or the process of counselling or therapy. In short, the components that form the basis of the therapy that are deemed invaluable and contribute to the development of the practitioner and the profession cannot be measured.

It is not yet clear how these qualifications will work in practice or how they will fit in with the systems of accreditation and registration being developed by BAC and UKCP. In other fields of work NVQs are regarded as safeguarding standards at levels well below those expected for full professional status. For example, there are NVQs concerned with tending animals, but these are not comparable with veterinary qualifications.

The BAC and the UKCP have nevertheless worked tirelessly on presenting National Vocational Qualifications in advice, guidance, counselling and psychotherapy. There are five levels of competence. Level 3 for counselling is due to be in operation in 1999.

The move towards NVQ for counsellors is part of the general move towards auditing competency and efficiency in the field. It is not possible at this stage to know how this qualification will work in practice. No doubt there will be change and improvement as it is tested and worked with, before reliable measurements of what constitutes competency are accepted.

This qualification may help to bring about the implementing of statutory registration or licensing of practitioners. Quite how this will affect the great number of voluntary counsellors is not clear. There is also the problem that if standards are to become more rigorous in order to regulate them nationally, then counselling and psychotherapy training courses may need to subscribe to full-time courses, as for training social workers. Existing part-time courses are already expensive, but they do permit trainees to continue working in their current jobs if necessary.

One of the doubts about the trend of evaluating and auditing is to wonder whether there will be a future for counselling, when there may be fewer candidates for training courses because of prohibition of costs and time?

One of the great shifts, brought about by the counselling world in the last decade, has been to open up the training possibilities for people who would not have had access before. The dominant psychoanalytic training requirements prevented many people from applying for training. The financial burden, length of time training, and one's own analysis, were all beyond reach for so many. It would be a regressive step were such obstacles to be placed in the way again.

LICENSING

In parts of Europe only psychiatrists and clinical psychologists are allowed to practise psychotherapy. In order to practise they have to follow a licensing procedure. A licence to practise is intended to ensure accountability. This is a protection for the public against bad practitioners, but a licence cannot actually stop the practice of bad practitioners. An offending therapist can have their licence withdrawn following a complaints procedure, and would not be given a licence to work again.

Licensing is not implemented at present in the United Kingdom for counsellors or psychotherapists, but may well be in the future. As more countries in the EEC practise a standardised regulation of therapists, the UK will undoubtedly join them. At present, the system is accreditation or registration.

REGISTRATION

United Kingdom Council for Psychotherapy

A decade ago, a conference was held in Rugby to discuss the route to regulating psychotherapists. The conference gave birth to the United Kingdom Standing Conference for Psychotherapy. As it was a standing conference, it was an ongoing body that discussed issues of regulating psychotherapists, and monitored relevant professional events in Europe. In 1990 the conference delegates voted to form a voluntary register of psychotherapists and the first move was made towards forming a European Psychotherapy Association.

In 1992 the conference developed into a council. In January 1993, the UKCP was established and the National Register was published that year. The register is published annually, and only psychotherapists who meet the training and ethical requirements of the UKCP are included.

Within a very short time, the UKCP has evolved into being the national umbrella organisation for 78 psychotherapy organisations of all theoretical orientations. The list of member organisations is extensive, covering humanistic and integrative psychotherapy, behavioural and cognitive psychotherapy, family, couple, sexual, systemic therapy, hypno-psychotherapy, analytical psychology, psychoanalytic and psycho-dynamic psychotherapy, and psychoanalytically based therapy with children.

The criteria for an individual psychotherapist's inclusion on the UKCP National Register of Psychotherapists is through training with a UKCP-recognised organisation, or becoming a member of a UKCP-recognised organisation. An individual training course will state such information in its brochure.

The member organisations must comply with common areas of curriculum and rigorous standards agreed jointly by all organisations within the UKCP. If you choose to become a psychotherapist, it is impor-tant to consider whether the organisation you train with is an approved member of the UKCP.

If you were a humanistic psychotherapist, for example, you could become a member of The Association of Humanistic Psychology Practitioners (AHPP), which is a member of the UKCP. The following details about the AHPP will give you an idea of what is required in order to be registered.

The AHPP is a professional organisation of members of different occupations who use humanistic psychology in their work. The AHPP is an independent accrediting body. Once a member has been accredited with them, they can then apply for inclusion on the UKCP National Register.

The requirements for successful membership/accreditation through the AHPP are the completion of at least three or four years' training, comprising 900 tutor contact hours (which does not include any pre-requisites to entry requirements, individual therapy, personal study time or peer group work) and a substantial piece of written work.

The psychotherapist's training should include knowledge of:

- the main humanistic theorists
- the main analytical theorists
- existential and phenomenological theory
- human growth and development, including sexuality
- the therapeutic relationship, including transference and counter-transference
- psychopathology: traditional, medical, humanistic and social models; the ability to recognise clients who are too disturbed to take advantage of once- or twice-weekly therapy; to cover referral services as appropriate
- the nature of science and the importance of research

The AHPP requires a psychotherapist to have personal therapy throughout training to be over a minimum of four years. A therapist must have regular supervision of client casework, and must be supervised with the same supervisor for not less than two years. The therapist must have completed 450 hours of client contact at a ratio of at least one hour's supervision to six hours' client contact.

After completion of training a therapist should have worked with at least six clients for both short and long periods, over a minimum of two years. A practising therapist must have professional liability and malpractice insurance.

Full membership and accreditation is applied for via application forms that are supplied by AHPP. A non-returnable application fee of £500 must accompany the completed application forms. After consideration of the completed application forms, the membership committee may interview candidates for full membership. Annual membership fees in 1999 are £155 for psychotherapists. Accreditation lasts for five years, after which full members must show that they continue to meet AHPP criteria in order to be re-accredited.

Some psychoanalytic psychotherapy training centres accredit therapists. Successful graduates are invited to become members of their association and are then entitled to registration with UKCP in the Psychoanalytic and Psychodynamic Psychotherapy section.

If you train with a psychoanalytic or psychoanalytic psychotherapy organisation like the British Association of Psychotherapists (BAP), they are a member of the BCP and the UKCP. They do not use an accreditation system for their psychotherapists. A trainee is considered qualified as a psychotherapist on the recommendation of her training therapist, supervisors and adviser. The council elects the trainee as an associate member of the BAP.

British Association for Behavioural and Cognitive Psychotherapies

Membership of the British Association for Behavioural and Cognitive Psychotherapies (BABCP) is open to anyone with an interest in the practice and theory of behavioural and/or cognitive psychotherapy. Accreditation as a psychotherapist for registration with the behavioural and cognitive psychotherapy section of the UKCP is available to members who fulfil the criteria.

British Association for Counselling

Counsellors apply for accreditation through the British Association for Counselling (BAC). This is an independent counselling association, and is the largest counselling organisation in this country, representing many different counselling and psychotherapy approaches. There are over 15,000 individual counsellor members of the BAC and 908 organisational members.

ACCREDITATION OF INDIVIDUAL COUNSELLORS

The BAC is recognised nationally, and whilst accreditation is not a statutory requirement to practising as a counsellor, nor a measure of superiority over non-accredited and experienced counsellors, the accreditation is often a requirement by employers and therefore carries status.

Since 1983, the BAC has accredited individual counsellors. Accreditation is part of the process of post-training. Application can be made after (450) post-training hours of supervised client work have been accumulated. The required number of hours gives the newly qualified counsellor the time to gain experience and insights into the work, as well as to absorb their training and apply their theories to practice. I list in some detail the BAC criteria for accreditation further on to show accreditation requirement.

The pre-accreditation period is an apprenticeship period and a productive time for practitioners to reflect on their own personal and professional progress. Reflection is the very essence of counselling and therapy. This is a space to pause in between the end of training and growing in experience. It is the transition from being a graduated trainee to being an experienced practitioner.

After training, a practitioner will be keen to go out and work in their chosen field. Most organisations that employ a counsellor will expect the individual to be accredited. For employers and the public, accreditation is a way of telling them that the counsellor has reached a particular level of knowledge and experience.

Rigorous efforts are being made by specific bodies to maintain the standards and reputation of the counselling and psychotherapy profession. Thus, the accreditation or registration of practitioners operates for the protection of the public and to ensure that their members are aware of a particular code of ethics and complaints procedures.

Since 1997, the BAC has offered accredited independent counsellors the option of voluntarily registering as a United Kingdom Registered Independent Counsellor (UKRC). There is a cost for this inclusion, which at present is reasonable. Registration is recognition of experienced and accredited counsellors. Being a member of the Confederation of Scottish Counselling Organisations (COSCA) is also a route to being registered with the UKRC. From the summer of 1999 the UKRC published the first edition of its register. It contains the names of Registered Independent Counsellors and Registered Sponsoring Organisations.

What is accreditation?

A candidate first becomes a member of the accrediting organisation. Then they apply for the accreditation papers. A charge is made for application, which is generally not refundable.

The accrediting committee assesses and ratifies applications four times a year, so papers will have to be returned by a stated time.

The application forms for the BAC accreditation currently cost £155. (There is a reduced fee for those on a reduced membership subscription.) The original and three additional copies of the completed application form, and the same number for the supervisor's report, have to be submitted.

BAC has three routes to accreditation, which in summary is that:

1   The applicant should have completed a BAC accredited counsellor training course, comprising 200 hours of skills development and 250 hours of theory. The applicant should have had at least 450 hours of counselling practice that has been supervised in accordance with BAC requirements.
2   The applicant is claiming little formal counselling training, but can provide evidence of ten years' experience in counselling that is acceptable to BAC, with a minimum of 150 practice hours per year under formal supervision. After the end of December 2002 this route will no longer be available.
3   The applicant can provide evidence of a combination of some formal counselling training and several years of practice, which includes 150 hours minimum per year under formal supervision.

By the year 2000, BAC intends to implement several notable amendments and additional criteria for accreditation.

Accreditation is a system of ensuring, as far as possible, that counsellors and psychotherapists have arrived at a post-training, post-apprenticeship stage. A place where the practitioner is judged to be competent by their supervisors, and evaluated through the accrediting procedure by a board or accrediting body.

The accrediting body may specify that the training course that the candidate undertook should have a recognised accreditation, or be validated by an institute or university that has a recognised accreditation.

Submission of documentation as evidence of gaining a qualification is required. A declaration must be made that the candidate has not been subject to any formal complaints procedure with any professional body, or if they have, to give an explanation of the details.

A section of the accreditation application will ask for the specific hours of theory and practice that were taught on the course. Precise details of what was taught, including the method, content, philosophy and approach, are requested. Other areas that are relevant to the training details are asked for, i.e. hours spent in group work and whether videos and tapes were used.

Written case studies are submitted to show how the candidate works, as well as how the candidate uses supervision. The candidate's supervisor has to submit a report and a testimony that case studies presented reflect the usual clinical practice of the candidate and show the use of supervision.

The candidate's commitment to personal and professional development is required. The personal development is usually evidenced through submitting the name of the candidate's personal counsellor or therapist, with the dates and regularity of sessions attended. There may be other forms of personal development that the candidate submits, such as attending personal development groups.

A description is required of personal and professional development, including involvement in relevant groups, membership of relevant organisations and ongoing training and study. Continued training in the form of attending advanced training, workshops, lectures and conferences.

One of the aspects that an accrediting body looks for is that the individual has understood the theory that they have trained in and the ethos of theoretical approach adhered to; also, that they have obtained the required skills and can write a satisfactory description of how to use them appropriately. For this purpose, a client's case study forms part of the accreditation requirement. A diary of sessions over a period of time may also be required, showing the themes that arose in each session. This gives the assessors some idea of the work that the candidate covers.

Candidates should be able to have formulated their own philosophy of counselling or psychotherapy, which demonstrates their depth of understanding and self-reflection. This is usually given as a further piece of written evidence.

It is necessary that the candidate has been in their own therapy for at least the duration of their training course. Details about the candidate's counsellor or psychotherapist are required: the qualifications and theoretical model used, the date therapy started and number of sessions, etc. A description is expected of how personal therapy has contributed to the candidate's professional development and work with clients.

Supervision details are also required. It is necessary to have been in supervision with the same supervisor for a specific length of time, usually for a minimum of two years. The accrediting body specifies that supervised practice should be one and half or two hours a month, but frequency of supervision must be according to the number of clients seen weekly. Six client hours to one supervision hour are a general recommendation for counsellors. The supervisor will have to submit a report. The more clients a candidate sees, the more supervision they need. The type of workload also has to be taken into consideration for supervision requirements.

One or more referees will also be required to make a statement about the counsellor's work and the counsellor's qualities as a person in a helping profession.

If the counsellor is successful in their accreditation application, they are asked to subscribe to the code of practice and ethics of the professional association. The accreditation usually lasts for a period of five years and is upheld whilst the counsellor is a member of the organisation or association who has accredited them. In this way good practice can be monitored and maintained over time. Accreditation represents the practitioner's standard of practice and efficacy.

Current methods of training, accreditation and regulation of counsellors and psychotherapists are constantly being questioned, both inside and outside the profession. This is as it should be. The existing system in the counselling and psychotherapy profession does not suit everyone and does contain many flaws. In a profession that deals with the caring of people, reflecting on and challenging the methods is the pathway to evolution and improvement (which are not necessarily the same thing!).

By being involved within the profession an individual can exercise their rights, and make positive contributions towards improvement. This can be done through voicing personal disquiet and offering constructive feedback, or through publishing articles or research that enables open and informed discussion. An aspect of working for accreditation is that it gives a practitioner several opportunities:

- to self-reflect;
- to consider the stage of professional development that has been reached;
- to consider the procedure of evaluating and assessing practice;
- to be more involved in the organisation that awards the accreditation.

Registration or accreditation of practitioners is about meeting with subscribed training and standards of good practice. The labels may be different, but they suggest the same thing: to monitor ethics, good practice and standards.

You may choose not to go along this route, preferring to be independent. There are other practitioners who feel this way and have come together to form their own regulations and self-evaluating. The details of the Independent Practitioner Network (IPN) are in the List of Resources (see pp. 203–24).

CODE OF ETHICS

An individual organisation should supply a copy of their code of ethics and practice on request.

Each organisation may vary the wording of their codes according to their own values and interpretation of ethics and good practice and standards. In general, however, the bodies who set out their codes of ethics and practice expect their members to sign to and adhere to a framework of integrity:

- Responsibility of the individual to the organisation
- Responsibility to the profession and to one's colleagues
- Accountability
- Confidentiality
- Respect for the client/patient
- Maintaining high levels of professional standards
- Continuation of supervised practice
- Ongoing commitment to the practitioner's own professional competence and growth

The member practitioner is subject to the individual organisation's complaints' procedure.

MASTER'S DEGREES AND RESEARCH

There is an increasing number and variety of master's degree courses that take study beyond the level of diplomas. Universities who are responsible for the syllabus and standards, award master's degrees.

Some institutes view the master's degree as an expansion of study in theory and practice. A master's degree is an academic award, not a professional qualification. It is a route along an academic path. A master's degree is frequently another step towards a doctoral research, and can also be a prerequisite for entry into advanced courses in particular institutes.

If you are an experienced practitioner who wants to undertake a master's degree you need to examine your motives carefully. The study generally takes three years part time. It requires a tremendous commitment of your time, energy and money. If you want a master's degree primarily because you think it will help you get a job or it has a desirable perceived status, you should reconsider. A master's degree will not necessarily help you to get a job; it is evidence of academic achievement rather than your effectiveness as a practitioner. If you want to develop an academic career, however, a master's degree will be a necessary prerequisite to further study, teaching or research jobs.

The entry requirement for a master's degree in counselling or psychotherapy is that a student should have a thorough, practical and theoretical knowledge of psychotherapy or counselling, and hold a postgraduate diploma (or equivalent relevant qualification). These degrees are primarily academic qualifications for those with a desire to acquire more knowledge for its own sake. Studying for a master's degree should be considered as studying for the pleasure of it: for wanting to know more about a specific issue.

Teaching structures vary from institute to institute, and some training courses offer modules for flexibility. There may be a structure of achieving a pass in each element or module before proceeding onto the next. A number of courses now offer a master's programme after the completion of a diploma. It is important to know as much as you can about the master's component that is offered on a course that interests you.

Most courses with a master's programme are not flexible enough or compatible with others to take on students from other courses. This is a pity. I feel that a credit system that allows students to transfer onto a master's programme at a different institute would be welcomed by many students, enabling an exchange of ideas that keeps stimulation and creativity flowing.

Gaining a master's degree is a rewarding personal process. You will learn more about topics that interest you and it will help you to be more confident and informed about your work. Your thirst for knowledge and enjoyment of the course should be paramount, otherwise it will be an expensive, arduous and disappointing experience.

Types of master's degrees

The two most common types of master's courses in counselling or psychotherapy are Master of Arts (MA) and Master of Science (MSc) There is no fixed definition that distinguishes between these degrees. An MSc places a greater emphasis on the use of research methodology. It is usual for a student to undertake a research project that is then written up as a dissertation. In an MA the dissertation is primarily a literature review and personal analysis of the subject. There is considerable overlap and both aim to help develop critical faculties.

The details of the syllabus and the teaching methods are up to the individual institution running the course. Both types of course usually contain a mix of lectures, prescribed reading, discussion groups, clinical practice, analysing data and methodology of research, designing questionnaires and surveys, supervision and tutorials. These learning methods usually occupy two-thirds of the course. The remaining third is devoted to a personal dissertation, commonly around 20,000 words.

An assessment process may be continuous throughout the entire training, designed to ensure that students are able to demonstrate development, depth of knowledge, and understanding in their chosen subject.

RESEARCH

The desire for the therapy world, like any other trained and qualified body of people who believe in their work, is to be accepted as a legitimate profession with substantiated knowledge, audited accountability, and having proven testing of outcome.

We live in a climate that encourages the acquisition of knowledge, in order to make informed choices. We want to know more than why things happen, we want to know how they happen, when they happen, and what their outcome is. We want to know if things work, and if they do, what it is that makes them do so. To link this process and outcome it is necessary to prove, or disprove, certain factors. This evaluating of effectiveness is done through research.

In order for the profession to develop it is essential that there are people who are involved in research. Making papers available and publishing articles based on research contributes to this development. The word research may put some people off; it may be helpful to think in terms of exploration or enquiry, which is what research is about.

What is involved in research

A master's is a degree whereby the student undertakes a project or experiment that has an outcome that can be measured or evaluated. The methodology for the experiment is taught on the course. Statistics may be used and the methods may be qualitative or quantitative, or pluralistic (using both methods). Because of the difficulties of scientifically evaluating counselling and psychotherapy, narrative and heuristic methods are frequently used.

The components of a master's degree course include a taught programme and a completion of a research project or dissertation. The structure of the course may contain:

- An academic aspect: theory
- Clinical practice
- Lectures
- Prescribed reading

- Discussion groups
- Methodology/research skills (on an MSc)
- Completion of a brief research project (as above)
- Supervision/tutorials
- Written dissertation
- There may also be a viva

A master's degree in counselling or psychotherapy provides an opportunity to research in depth a very particular aspect that is of interest to the individual, learn about a disciplined procedure and methodology of investigation, and make an informed and positive contribution.

Research projects can be costly in terms of time to study and design the form of research you desire. A research project may involve designing a questionnaire, contacting and interviewing people, travelling to places, buying books, reading papers and talking to people. It is learning about different methods to see which method would be appropriate for the particular piece of research you are going to do. Lastly, writing a lengthy dissertation, editing it and presenting it for assessment within a given time-scale.

It is not usual for counsellors and psychotherapists to have a science background, so it is important to know what research a scientific approach entails. There are two major approaches to research: quantitative and qualitative. Quantitative (quantity) research is more concerned with counting and precise statistical analysis. Qualitative (quality) research is more concerned with evaluating concepts such as emotions that are difficult to count or measure.

Traditional quantitative scientific research and number crunching are of limited importance in counselling and psychotherapy. The profession is developing more appropriate qualitative research methods. An MSc course should develop an ability to undertake research and also the ability to critically appraise the research of others.

Some of the difficulties of researching counselling and psychotherapy is the confidentiality issue. A student on a master's degree who wants to research into an aspect of therapeutic effectiveness has to rely on outcomes from clients and their therapists. Every individual has their subjective experience. Each may vary by degrees as to what elements created the effectiveness. Every person may, unconsciously or otherwise, wish to please the researcher and give him the desired information. The individuals may also wish to appear in a particular way and emphasise information accordingly.

Long-term research, with large numbers of people involved, as well as a control group for contrasting and comparing, may help with these particular difficulties. This form of research is, however, costly and complex.

Research should be important to all of us, and a fear of statistics or belief that science cannot measure emotions should not put you off. Research in counselling and therapy is about trying to evaluate what practitioners do in order to make the work more effective. Research is not restricted to proving or disproving a hypothesis. Research should make us open to new ideas, be critical, and adaptable to change.

Further reasons to consider why research is important to counselling (and therapy) include: gaining a wider perspective, accountability, developing new ideas and approaches, applications of counselling in new areas, and personal and professional development (McLeod 1994: 2–3).

Therapeutic interventions, treatment effectiveness, diagnosis, treatment strategies, therapeutic process, therapists' countertransference reactions, are all examples of clinical factors that have been the focus of much research. Yet more research is needed to keep pace with the changes in society that affect the individual's expectations.

There are many practitioners who do not avail themselves of research material, nor consider research to be important and relevant enough to their work (McLeod 1994). This is regrettable, and is something that could be explored and addressed on training courses.

Other relevant, caring professions, such as medicine, social work, nursing, teaching, psychology and mental health, make use of research to legitimise and further the understanding of those professions, for the benefit of the practitioners and the welfare of the public who use their services. Counselling and psychotherapy are still comparatively young professions and need continuous access to research to inform counsellors and psychotherapists about all aspects of their practice. Research supports the advancement of the profession, and the professional.

The discipline of study and research enables students to become more discerning about information, and more critical and informed about their chosen subject. Reading and researching large amounts of material on a specified topic and writing a dissertation takes self-motivation. Evaluating, understanding process and the results of a research have to be well organised.

The structure of a master's degree course should include good support from supervisors and tutors to facilitate students, especially in the early stages when the procedure and aims of the degree may not be fully understood.

Methods

The profession employs techniques used by social scientists and psychologists, with methods that are sensitive to the unique aspects of counselling and psychotherapy. You might have heard of the commonest research methods such as focus groups and questionnaire surveys. Focus group methodology is a formalised way of recording and analysing the feelings expressed in a discussion on a particular topic by a group of people.

You have probably been a participant in a questionnaire survey at some time. You may be surprised by how much knowledge and effort is required to design and analyse a questionnaire to achieve reliable, unbiased and valid results.

The anti-scientific debate: Master of Science

Preparing for a Master of Science in counselling or psychotherapy assumes a readiness to test the scientific enquiry. There is an ongoing debate as to whether counselling or psychotherapy can be tested scientifically, because the model is very particular. There are people in the profession, happily, who are willing to research and quantify the worth of both counselling and psychotherapy.

There is an ongoing debate about counselling and psychotherapy: are they a profession; if not, then what are they? Are they valid? Are they scientific? Can their components be measured? Can they be proved to work? If they can, would they be more acceptable to those who need to have scientific proof that something works? How do they work? Are they reliable, and consistent?

There are arguments that counselling and psychotherapy are non-scientific, that they just simply do not work, and there is no empirical evidence to prove that they do. Although counselling and psychotherapy have been the subject of much research, particularly in the last few decades, it is still difficult to prove scientifically, over time, that people change, get better or improve purely because of the counselling or psychotherapy that they undergo.

Critics of the scientific approach to therapy claim that scientific research is misguided and unworkable in counselling and psychotherapy. To try to test individuals on the same level as physical or concrete objects, they reason, is inappropriate.

Physics, medicine and chemistry are scientific models, for example, that can be proved or disproved by rigorous testing, comparisons, analysis and results.

Just because many people feel that the therapeutic work they engaged in was of immense value to them, or that their lives have changed dramatically, is not acceptable as scientific proof that it was necessarily the counselling or psychotherapy that did it.

There are counsellors and psychotherapists who believe that the profession is not good enough because others do not accept it, and that it would be made respectable and acceptable through empirical validation. With this opinion, the profession must therefore follow the path that has already been trodden by others, regardless of the difficulties that this entails.

The counter argument is that counselling and psychotherapy are different paradigms and need different approaches in auditing and evaluating their outcomes.

Counselling and psychotherapy researchers are working in a relatively new field and may well have to shape their research accordingly. There are newer research methods being developed by counsellors and psychotherapists trying to evaluate the process and outcome between individual therapists and their clients.

Whilst there is a rejection of scientific paradigms by some in the field, effectiveness, reliability and validity are elements that can be measured in other fields. Reliable instruments may still have to be devised to cope with the very special human, emotional components that exist within the counselling and psychotherapy relationship.

It is difficult to give precise details about the newer research methods because they are not well established. What will be important to assessors on an MSc course is that a student can show an understanding of the principles of scientific appraisal and evaluate the benefits and shortcomings of their work and the work of others.

More longitudinal research is needed with control groups to evaluate and audit the outcome of therapy, both in terms of reducing human misery and in terms of time and cost.

Whether or not you regard yourself as a scientist, you may find it exciting to think that you could have an influence on the development of research methods in counselling and psychotherapy.

FURTHER READING

BAC publish Information Sheets, price £1, on Evaluation of Counselling: *How effective is counselling in*:

1   Medicine?
2   Situations of Bereavement?

3 Higher Education?
4 Primary Care?
5 The Workplace?
6 Helping People with Eating Disorders?
7 Those who were Sexually Abused as Children?

BAC, Information Guide 4, *Ethical Guidelines for Monitoring, Evaluation and Research in Counselling* (£1.25 for members, £1.50 for non-members.
Dryden, W. (ed.) (1996) *Research in Counselling and Psychotherapy*, London: Sage Publications.
McLeod, J. (1994) *Doing Counselling Research*, London: Sage Publications.

A national Register of Psychotherapists is published annually by the BCP, available at booksellers (ISBN 0-9524565-3-2). All the member organisations of the BCP are psychoanalytic in nature. The Register can be also found at some public libraries; it gives information about the training and qualifications of practitioners, and their geographic location.

9

OTHER FORMS OF THERAPY AND SPECIALISED TRAINING

There may be topics that interest you, but will not be introduced on a general training courses. Subjects, such as eating disorders, HIV and AIDS, substance abuse and self-mutilation.

Working with children and young people requires long-term specialised training.

An understanding of the unique needs of the elderly, and of disabled clients is necessary to work effectively with them.

These subjects are very specific. To have an in-depth understanding trainees should consider specialised training courses after completing a general course.

Brief and short-term therapy is in high demand by many organisations in the NHS, private and voluntary sectors. At present, there are very few training centres that are offering this approach. Counsellors and psychotherapists need specific training in this work. Many in the therapy world view brief therapy with great suspicion, believing that it must be superficial and unsatisfactory. However much resistance there is to the practice of brief therapy, it is a reality. Time and funding difficulties are creating the demand. Training centres have to be aware of this fact.

This chapter looks at integrative, group, family, couple, psychosexual, bereavement, and post-traumatic stress disorder therapies. They are introduced here as examples of specialised training.

Included in this chapter is intercultural therapy, a subject I believe should be incorporated into all counselling and psychotherapy training. The importance of this subject has wide-reaching implications for practitioners and their clients. It should also be taught as a subject on longer, specialised training courses in its own right.

INTEGRATIVE THERAPY

Whilst there are certainly training courses in integrative therapy, and it is not, strictly speaking, a specialised subject, I have nevertheless chosen to include it in this chapter of specialised training to differentiate it from the purist forms of training.

Integrative therapy is generally a broader-based approach. The purist approaches cover more depth.

Some practitioners, who have trained in a number of theoretical approaches, would describe themselves as eclectic.

A simple and straightforward definition of the difference, in counselling, between eclecticism and integrationism is suggested as:

> An eclectic approach to counselling is one in which the counsellor chooses the best or most appropriate ideas and techniques from a range of theories or models, in order to meet the needs of the client. Integration, on the other hand, refers to a somewhat more ambitious enterprise in which the counsellor brings together elements from different theories and models into a new theory or model.

(McLeod 1993: 99)

Integrative therapy is the combining, synthesising and blending of specific theoretical models. This form of therapy appeals to people who are unconvinced by the total belief in any one purist approach as the cure for all. Since research has shown consistently that no one approach is the cure for all, this may be one of the reasons for the beginnings of growth in the integrative approach.

Clarkson (1993: 129) describes integrative therapy as 'a process, a development and an evolution'.

Through an integrative knowledge, there is an appreciation of the therapeutic process that goes beyond the limitations or dogma of any one particular approach. There is flexibility, and in today's pluralistic society the integrative approach reflects the needs of the society.

It is likely that the massive flourishing of different therapies is another of the reasons why there is a trend towards integrative therapy. It could be a valid attempt to positively contain the differences and intolerance between schools of therapy and approaches.

There are those who believe that it is impossible to integrate such variant theoretical approaches that may be incompatible with each other. In spite of the warnings, the integration of psychotherapy approaches is a developing practice in the western world, particularly in the USA, and increasing in Britain.

Critics of the approach counter these points and state that integrating different therapies is not a desirable development. Some even maintain that the substance of an approach is watered down by integrating others. They suggest that integrating approaches is no different from eclecticism, or a mishmash of approaches that endangers the integrity of therapy – that it is not a satisfactory solution to the problems of healing psychic pain.

The approach is seen as a threat to the competency of the therapist and therefore the therapy to such critics. In spite of the opponents, there is a rise in integrative courses that have their own emphasis on a particular blend of approaches.

Training courses need to be thoroughly investigated to satisfy the individual's requirements, and this applies equally to the training of integrative therapies. If there is no substantial and thorough-based theory and understanding over a period of time, the trainee may leave a course feeling confused and inadequately trained in any theory.

The humanistic integrative therapist maintains that there is an integration of the best of both the humanistic, psychodynamic, behavioural and other therapies.

There is frequently a framework that considers phenomenological, dynamic and existential schema and that incorporates cognitive strategies and behavioural patterns. There are also integrative therapies that do not contain a humanistic element, and are psychodynamic, systemic and cognitive-behavioural combined. This combination is frequently used in couple therapy.

Cognitive-analytic therapy (CAT) is used in brief therapy work, using cognitive-behavioural approaches and employing Freudian concepts of defences. There are other combinations that individual practitioners will have devised that work well for them.

The strengths of an integrative approach are illustrated in trauma work combining elements of *self-psychology* and *cognitive-behavioural* therapy: self-psychology employed for its emphasis on self-soothing; cognitive-behavioural therapy to deal with the reframing of thoughts and beliefs; and guided imagery to transform the intrusive traumatic fantasies.

Influences

Practitioners engage in reflecting on and exploring their own work in supervision and continuing training. It is highly unlikely that some integration of other schools does not seep in to challenge a freethinking and flexible therapist, regardless of their disciplines.

It is virtually impossible for practitioners not to be influenced by the amount of information that comes to them via journals, books, lectures, the media and discussions with colleagues. Through this means alone, therapists will be absorbing, unconsciously or consciously, the latest thinking in the great debate of therapy approaches.

Reflective practitioners develop their own style over time. They modify their approach at different life stages, to accommodate their own personality and character determinants, as well as their clients' needs. These are the human qualities that reflect the human service that is being worked in.

Integrative therapy does not have to threaten the integrity of the therapist, but needs rather to confront the rigidity of dogmatism.

McLeod (1993) emphasises the need to regard integration, not as abstract theoretical exercises but as choices intimately connected with the process of counsellor (and psychotherapist) development.

Integrative therapy is very young, younger than the history of purist therapies. It still has a long way to go – as do the other therapies – to demonstrate its value. Integrative therapy represents a determined step towards realism; if no one theory is any more effective than any other, then combining the best of a selected few increases the possibility of improving quality and effectiveness.

Integrative therapy of whatever combination is only as good as the therapist who utilises it. 'Utopian wishes for one finalised, true integrative psychotherapy with consistency, coherence, scientific rigour, conceptual clarity, practical value and aesthetic appeal, will probably have to wait a while to be satisfied' (Clarkson 1993: 129).

GROUP THERAPY

Group therapy has two meanings, according to Bion and Rickman (Bion 1961). One meaning refers to a number of individuals who have come together for the purpose of receiving therapeutic treatment, and the other refers to a planned endeavour for the purpose of carrying out a co-operative activity; this could be a committee or a staff team. Training for leading groups could therefore be specific to the type of group that is desired.

All groups are a dynamic social entity that each member influences and is influenced by and that develops over time (Bertcher 1994).

Groups can be exploratory or supportive, educative, scientific, informative, task-oriented, problem-solving, voluntary and therapeutic.

Groups can meet in private premises, in voluntary agencies and in therapeutic communities. They may be open, meaning people can join at any time, or closed, meaning that once the members are assembled no one else can join in; they may be ongoing for years, or time restricted for a set number of sessions. They may be informal, formal, professionally led, hierarchical or democratic and peer-led as in self-help groups.

One leader or two can facilitate a group. The person directing the group may be called leader, therapist, conductor or facilitator. The leader can take an active, facilitative or directive role, or passive observer and non-participatory role.

Group participants can be seen individually by a therapist/facilitator in addition to participating in a group.

Group therapy is used in organisational consultancy, management effectiveness, teaching and training. In the NHS, group work is used for its cost effectiveness in relation to numbers of people seen.

Some of the areas of group application in the NHS are in parent craft, effective relationship skills, learning disabilities, psychosexual and psychosomatic problems, alcohol and drug dependence, eating disorders, mood and personality disorders, psychosis and long-term mental illness.

An advantage of being in a group is the realisation that others have similar feelings and reactions, and that one is not alone. The disadvantages are the complexities of sharing space and time with a number of people; needing attention and possibly having to jostle for it, or trying to avoid the attention or feelings of exposure.

The group can represent a painful reminder of deepest vulnerability and shame, as well as a healing place where universal fears are recognised and contained.

In the therapeutic group, there is an emphasis on the individual developing self-awareness and understanding of their relationships with others through their relationship to the group, and their participation in the group.

One of the most rigorous group training is the Institute for Group Analysis in London that has developed an integrative approach. Group Analysis is primarily a method of group psychotherapy that was originated by Bion and Rickman during the Second World War with a military psychiatric unit. In the early 1960s Bion was particularly interested in group dynamics when he was working at the Tavistock.

Bion termed the characteristics of the groups that he saw. These terms refer to the emotions and assumptions that happen within groups and can affect the behaviour of an individual that in turn affects the behaviour of a group. He called these characteristics *basic assumptions*, which are characterised by:

- *Dependence*: where the group expects the leaders to be responsible for the outcome and resolution for the group.
- *Fight–flight*: where individuals flee from or fight with others.
- *Pairing*: which is set up by individuals for support, dependency or protection of the self or their ideas.

Bion noted that someone in contact with the complexities of a group could regress to primitive processes similar to an early mental stage that Melanie Klein had described. Freud also had noted a 'loss of individual distinctiveness' (Bion 1961). Bion observed that groups pass through a series of complex emotional episodes.

The intense anxieties and other feelings that so many individuals experience in groups are due to the heightened feelings of individuals who transmit their feelings to the rest of the group.

Groups have the possibility for the individual to feel empowered. Equally, the individual can feel humiliated and shamed, which adds to the anxieties of regression and survival.

Group dynamics are concerned with understanding the anxieties and defences within the group.

A number of group psychotherapy approaches combine psycho-analytic insights, with an understanding of social and interpersonal factors, and cognitive-behavioural tasks. Analysis of individuals is through transferences that are worked with.

There are also other approaches used in group training, notably Gestalt and psychodrama. S.H. Foulkes was the founder of the Group-Analytic Society. Foulkes was influenced by Gestalt psychology and used small groups for clients with personality disorders in the 1960s.

Moreno developed group work in the 1920s with psychodrama, having the client enact aspects of his life with other members in the group. The individual member directs all the actions so as to re-experience or recon-struct situations that give more productive meaning to the individual.

Group therapy is a newer addition to the field of therapies. Individual therapy has its share of criticism, and, as may be expected, group psychotherapy comes in for its share. A criticism is for the apparent

> confusion of theoretical concepts used in group interventions; the limitations in the empirical understanding of group process and outcome, and inadequate interface between research and practice.

> (Dies 1992: 265).

There is still a long way to go and a lot to learn about the very complex phenomenon known as the group.

According to the style of the leader and the approach used, the leader will negotiate a contract with the group, which may or may not be reviewed or changed but from which there is a basis for starting. Mediating skills are important, and learning how to deal with confrontation amongst group participants, as well as having to confront and be confronted by participants. Dealing with confrontation in a group takes experience, skill and maturity on the part of the leader. The leader needs to be able to contain the group and his own feelings. A defensive leader demonstrates his inability to do this. A group leader is automatically and consistently modelling his behaviour to the group.

For anyone interested in training as a group leader after completing and qualifying in a general counselling or psychotherapy training, I would recommend that you participate in a variety of groups first. You will, of course, have experienced your own training within a group and that is both relevant and valuable to your understanding of groups.

Participating in further groups, with the express purpose of observing what happens within the group, is the suggestion here. It can be very difficult to monitor the dynamics of the group, the individuals, and yourself, whilst participating. It may only be possible to carry out such activities intermittently; monitoring, then participating.

FAMILY THERAPY

There are a few family therapy clinics that are private, but they are costly. Their advantage is that there is unlikely to be a waiting list. Family therapy is also practised in the NHS. Family therapy is considered appropriate when there is a persistent problem over time that interferes with the functioning of family life. An illness such as schizophrenia in one member of a family that causes problems for the whole family would be considered appropriate. The illness could be viewed as a family problem rather than the individual member's problem.

Family therapy might also be considered when one of the members, usually a child, acts out in an aggressive and destructive way over a period of time, and no intervention from school or outside agencies rectifies the situation. Child psychology may be used, and if this fails then family therapy may be recommended. Family therapy is viewed as a development of child psychiatry.

Illness, redundancy, death and divorce can have traumatic consequences on families. Families that are experiencing problems through second or third marriages and have difficulties in trying to integrate the children of the multi-layered families may also need therapy to help them adjust.

There may only be one therapist working with the family, but very often there is a one-way screen that is used where a supervisor or colleague is observing. The family knows of the colleague's existence but cannot see him or her through the mirror. The therapist may leave the room at intervals during the session to confer with the colleague in live-supervision. This system is used because of the difficulty, for one person, in trying to contain and make interventions with a group of people. Having someone outside the room, who is not seen or does not participate directly, is invaluable to the therapist and the family.

Systemic theory

We are all parts of systems or series of systems, and thus a systems theory was developed to work with families. A systemic approach looks at the problems inherent in how each member has an impact on the others and how that affects the whole family unit or system. Change or disturbance in any part of the system affects the whole system. There is the wider system also to be taken into account, which includes interactions with the outside influences of extended family, work, school, neighbourhood and community.

From the systems theory approach, the therapist does not see the 'problem' person as seen by the family, but looks at the whole family in a circular rather than linear method. The therapist focuses on the relationship of the family, not the individual; how each member relates to the others, consciously and unconsciously.

It can be one child who is presented with the problem for school refusal, or bed-wetting, for example. The therapist explores the whole system to find the meaning behind the behaviour, and may discover that the parents are arguing and that the mother is depressed. The child's behaviour can then be seen as a means to elicit help.

The advantages of working with a family group as opposed to the individual are that the therapist can gain a much wider perspective of the presenting problems.

Provided that the whole family has agreed to work with the therapist willingly, and that there is some degree of mutual responsibility and co-operation, then family therapy can benefit the whole family through increased understanding and improvement of more open communication. The family also has the opportunity to continue the open communication at home. As a further maintenance of therapeutic interventions, there is usually at least one member of the family who can point out when another is closing off or slipping back.

Criticisms of family therapy hold that family therapists are manipulative and coercive. Many family therapists would agree, and would probably point out that any form of therapy and counselling is covertly or overtly manipulative of the client at some level. The argument goes that trying to avoid manipulation is probably pointless. Rather, therapists should learn how to influence the client or family in ways that are most productive and appropriate for them.

Therapists learn a framework of systemic concepts and terms that help them to analyse, understand and assess presenting problems. Exploring the existing family triangles and enmeshment, enables members of the family to differentiate from each other. Challenging the family rules and behaviour whilst supporting the fragility of the system is important to open the gridlock that the family may be in.

Analytic interpretations may be offered to give insight, and behavioural techniques may be implemented through direct challenge and instructions. Family therapists tend to adopt a more directive and active role: asking members to role-play how other members of the family may think or behave can be instructive and powerful for all the members. 'Family sculpting' – where the family physically creates a representation of their closeness or distance to each other – can be enlightening to the family.

The goal of family therapy is to identify and change dysfunctional behavioural patterns. Examples are: parents can learn to put boundaries in place where they have been too rigid or too loose; secrets and other avoided subjects can be named and their power diminished; the therapist can support a passive father to acquire and develop the authority he needs.

Therapists are taught techniques and strategies, such as:

- how to convene family meetings;
- how to conduct interviews;
- how to devise interventions according to systemic principles.

In effect, there are many ways of practising family therapy, and therapists may use many creative techniques to achieve systemic changes. The therapist offers new perspectives and different solutions to old problems, whilst maintaining minimal involvement.

The principal training establishment in this country is the Institute of Family Therapy in London, where psychodynamic and behavioural therapy has combined to create the systemic approach that is taught.

There is no prescription in English family training for a trainee to work within their own family as a part of the training, although the experience has been shown to be valuable to the trainee at developing unusual skills and flexibility. Bowen, in the USA, worked with his own family in the late 1960s and later presented the account at a family therapy research conference. There are, of course, problems about working in a therapeutic way with members of one's own family, which is possibly why the procedure has not been formally adopted on training courses.

There is an Association for Family Therapy that has regions and branches throughout the country that will have the name and address of a training institution nearest to your area. (See List of Resources, pp. 203–24.)

COUPLE THERAPY

Couple therapy has been in practice in this country since the late 1940s, predominately in Relate (formerly the National Marriage Guidance Council) and the Tavistock Institute of Marital Studies.

There are individual practitioners who work with couples, in a triadic therapy, or two therapists working with a couple, in a foursome. Two therapists working with two people as a couple is known as conjoint therapy. Probably the most frequent method of working with couples is with one practitioner.

Couple work is difficult and demanding for one practitioner, who has to contain so much alone. But there are advantages and disadvantages to working with a co-therapist. One of the advantages is that there is someone else to help observe the dynamics. Through discussion together outside the session, meaning and insight can be gained. Each of the practitioners can play an important role for the individuals in the couple. A disadvantage is if the therapists' relationship is affected in some way, creating disequilibrium within the foursome. The therapists can become enmeshed with the couple. There may be unresolved conflicts or other difficulties between the therapists that can interfere with the couple work.

It is not always feasible, practically or cost-effectively, for a practitioner to work with a colleague in couple work.

Why couples come to therapy

A crisis is likely to bring the couple to therapy. It may be something destructive that has developed over a long period before the couple is prepared to consider outside help. An example is when disappointment of one or both partners is felt, at not being the all-containing, all-providing partner. This is when the relationship begins to flounder and therapy is sought, sometimes as a last resort. Many couples come into therapy only when their relationship is really at an impasse and has been so for some time.

Couples may also come into therapy because they have decided to separate and want help to do so.

Working with couples is very different from working with individuals, as the focus needs to be primarily on the interaction or the dynamics between the couple. It is the *relationship* that is focused on by the therapist. The dynamics of the relationship between the individuals and the practitioner, and the couple and the practitioner, can happen very fast. The practitioner needs to watch that she does not get pulled in to siding with one partner against the other. There are two people's material to be aware of, as well as the relationship that is being presented. The difficulties of trying to work solo with two people should not be underestimated.

Theoretical differences permit different perspectives for the therapist to work with. Some orientations focus on the shared unconscious fantasies (see Glossary) of the couple. This is an unconscious image or belief that they have of their relationship.

A couple's historic difficulties create a 'fit' with each other. Such fits can be seen in the aggressive–passive couple, or the dominant–submissive couple. A couple who fight but seem not to resolve anything share a fit, as do a couple who fear confrontation. This unconscious process may be considered as a mutual attempt at personal resolution through the presence of the other person.

There are many possibilities for attention in the work. The transference and countertransference that operates within the couple, and between the therapist and couple, plays an important part. How to negotiate and resolve differences can be practised within the safety of the session. The faulty beliefs and behaviour that are obstructive and destructive to the relationship can be challenged. There may be life-cycle problems that are affecting the couple, which are creating conflicts and stress. Learning how to make appropriate adjustments and to cope with conflicts and stress may be valuable resources for the couple.

Further aspects of couple work are:

- Effective communications
- Boundary setting
- Hidden agendas
- The power balance
- Fears of intimacy and abandonment
- Psychosexual issues
- Negative thought patterns that are acted out
- Defensive and destructive interactions

It is vital that both partners should be equally committed to the work. If one feels resistant to coming it is doubtful that there will be a successful outcome.

Couple therapy can be brief, with a set number of sessions agreed between couple and practitioner at the beginning. The sessions may be weekly or at longer intervals. Therapy may be longer, more closely resembling the type of individual therapy that is open-ended. Couple therapy is practised with homosexual and heterosexual couples, and with practitioners who are homosexual or heterosexual.

Couple therapists from any approach may give homework tasks to the couple and ask them to try out different interventions in the session.

Schroder (1989: 60) has outlined five basic options of counselling that couples could choose from:

1 The couple has individual work with separate therapists.
2 Collaborative counselling, where the partners are seen by different therapists who communicate together about the couple.
3 Concurrent mode, where the couple are seen separately by the same therapist.
4 Conjoint counselling with either one or two counsellors.
5 Conjoint group work with other couples.

A thorough theoretical understanding of dyadic relationships and the stages that they go through is required to undertake couple therapy. There are a number of different approaches that may be used in couple therapy: systemic therapy, which is grounded in family therapy; psychodynamic and Gestalt therapy; and a blend or integration. Cognitive-dynamic and cognitive-behavioural approaches work with the couple and therapist jointly identifying the problem, setting the goals and agreeing the method of treatment.

Whilst there are a number of diploma courses in counselling and psychotherapy that offer a taster or brief introduction to couple therapy, there are relatively few specific couple training courses. Relate train their volunteers, London Marriage Guidance Council offers a 4-year part-time psychodynamic course. The Tavistock Institute of Marital Studies in London offers both long and shorter courses. They run a one-term introduction to couple therapy entitled 'Looking at the unconscious processes in couple work', which focuses primarily on object relations theory; participants have to be practising therapists, but do not have to be working with couples.

One further interesting aspect about couple training is that *practitioners are not required to be in couple therapy themselves with their partner*, although they may be required to be in individual therapy. The training institutes have not addressed this issue.

PSYCHOSEXUAL THERAPY

Confusion about sexual identity in one partner that has not been acknowledged may bring a couple to therapy. Doctors can refer couples to a psychosexual clinic in a hospital, and couples can self-refer. There are also private clinics and individual practitioners.

'Sex is a psychosomatic activity' (Skrine 1998: 169). Both the body and the mind have to be working reasonably well and in some form of harmony for sex to be good enough. The body/mind link relates to symptoms of sexual dysfunction that frequently have their link with hidden or unexpressed feelings.

The causes may be from physical or psychological (emotional) sources. Traumatic events, medical negligence, life stages, personal injury and illness cause or compound sexual difficulties. The couple may have first visited their doctor, who will have eliminated any physical problem or suspicion of illness.

Psychosexual therapy may be with an individual client, but is generally with couples. Bisexual, hetereosexual and homosexual couples are treated in psychosexual therapy. For a homosexual couple, this may be about lack of support from families and fears of coming out, which adds or complicates sexual dysfunction.

Couples usually present for psychosexual therapy when there is a dysfunction in their sexual activity that is causing distress, sexual avoidance and relationship stress causing the most common problems. Sexual problems lead to a lack of confidence, loss of affection and touch, feeling rejected or isolated by one or both partners, and low self-esteem. This can result in a breakdown of marital or couple relationship.

Masters and Johnson in the 1960s and 1970s and Kaplan in the 1970s contributed enormously to the understanding and treatment of psycho-sexual dysfunctioning. They changed the approach to this form of treatment by enlisting the co-operation of the clients in the planning of their treatment programmes.

The conducting of treatment in psychosexual therapy focuses on the sexual issues of the couple (or individual) who present for therapy. This form of therapy may be technique- and education-driven and cognitive-behaviour based. The therapist is explicit in naming and exploring the sexual behaviour of the client, whilst being sensitive to the emotional consequences of the problems that are presented. Understanding what different aspects of the sexual act mean to each partner is important. Penetrating may have particular significance to a woman who was sexually abused as a child.

The nuts and bolts of what people actually do during sexual intercourse have to be spoken about in detail. This may be highly embarrassing for one or both partners, and communication may be one of the difficulties that inhibit satisfactory sexual activity.

Couples (and individuals) who come to psychosexual therapy may find great difficulty in having to speak so explicitly about a subject that is culturally not spoken about. The therapist may sometimes have to work at enabling the couple to feel less inhibited. The therapist needs to be sensitive to the fact that she may also be seen as intrusive in this most private of human intimacies.

The therapist works at making the setting as safe as she can, whilst normalising the sexual words and descriptions that are used. Sexual terminology has to be clear and explicit whilst fitting to the clients' own use of words.

The practicalities of sex are explained and taught if required. Corrective techniques over time may be employed, teaching someone how to prevent a variety of difficulties, such as premature ejaculation, retarded ejaculation, erectile difficulties in men; orgasmic difficulties, vaginismus (painful spasms of the vagina during intercourse) or desen-sitising phobias about semen in women; and losses of desire in sex by either gender. Advice on preferred sexual positions or non-penetrative options can be given.

After a history has been taken, the minutiae of the problem are explored. When the couple and the therapist understand this, the thera-pist devises a programme of treatment that is discussed with the couple before they engage with it. The progress of the programme is monitored by the couple and reported to the therapist during the sessions, and altered if necessary. Most psychosexual practitioners, if appropriate, generally take a collaborative approach with the couple and other advisers.

Training

The phases of human sexual functioning and sexual dysfunction that are general or specific are taught in training. Training can be challenging and demanding. Exploring personal attitudes towards sex, and learning to speak about sex comfortably, are relevant to the practitioner. The practitioner must become open and accepting of their own and others' sexual attitudes. Some medical and anatomical knowledge is taught. Effective interview techniques and diagnostic skills must be learned. Watching explicit film and video material for sex education and therapy, and discussing case histories, are all aspects of this training.

Other comprehensive elements of training are taught on courses such as Relate. This is a British Association for Sexual and Marital Therapy (BASMT) approved syllabus. It is a diploma course to practitioners (in relevant professions) in psychosexual therapy and offers:

- Effective strategies to help clients with sexual difficulties
- Assessment and diagnostic skills
- Negotiation of an appropriate contract for treatment as well as the specific treatments for dysfunction in males and females
- Medical and psychological causes of dysfunction
- Ethical issues
- Sessions on work with adult survivors of sexual abuse
- Therapy with individuals and people with disability
- Gender and orientation issues
- Ethnic minorities and ageing.

The course is spread over 16 months and has seven interdependent elements. A nation-wide supervisor support system operates. (See the List of Resources, pp. 203–24, for address.)

Practitioners need to have couple skills or to be trained in couple work as part of psychosexual therapy training.

Psychosexual therapy training may be included in couple therapy training, or may be a distinct and separate training. Practitioners need training awareness of the particular needs and stresses at different life stages, and in couples from different sexual orientations.

Synthesising counselling skills with psychosexual practice is relevant and needs to be taught. Training should also take into consideration the assessment and treatment of a couple who may need psychotherapy or counselling about other issues. Someone suffering from any kind of physical or emotional loss, or post-traumatic stress disorders, needs to work through their bereavement before dealing with sexual difficulties.

INTERCULTURAL THERAPY

Considered the 'fourth force' of therapy (psychodynamic, humanistic and cognitive-behavioural therapies being the first three), it is important to mention that this form of therapy is becoming recognised in its own right. Intercultural therapy stresses equality and empowerment of the individual whilst recognising and acknowledging differences.

Therapeutic approaches need to integrate an intercultural awareness in their training. The traditional theories of therapies have been formulated according to a dominant, western way of viewing the world. This approach applies to white, heterosexual westerners. Intercultural therapy has made a significant contribution to the evolution of therapies in respecting the persons' differences, whilst also appreciating the similarities of humanity that we all share.

Any approach, behaviour, attitude, role or view that systematically denies access to opportunities or privileges to members of one group, while perpetuating access to opportunities and privileges to members of another group, is the very opposite of intercultural understanding and practice. Equality of opportunity must be applied in all training institutions and as a normal ethos of therapy and counselling. Intentional (overt) and unintentional (covert) prejudices and racism should be explored in training.

All training courses should subscribe to an anti-discrimination policy, in terms of gender, race, colour, religion, sexual orientation, age or disability.

Seeking changes through the human relationship, intercultural therapy brings the client's cultural diversities into the therapy. This includes:

- social
- customs
- linguistic
- political
- historic
- ethnic
- national
- religious
- age
- class
- disability
- gender
- sexual preference
- family
- individual roles and identities

These dimensions have only recently been explored in the literature.

The definition of 'culture' is expanded to mean all aspects of a person's identity. There are collective, personal and familial elements of culture. Identity is concerned with the many different ways in which people see themselves. Individuals are a dynamic blend of multiple roles and identities.

Clients are not only representatives of one group; they are members of a variety of synthesised groups at any one time. All individuals are heterogeneous, and no one person from one culture is necessarily the same as another from that culture or even within the same family. The assumption that people have only one cultural identity is to dismiss the uniqueness of people.

Intercultural therapy is a holistic model that facilitates human development through awareness, acceptance and respect for identity and culture. Identity and culture are the ways in which we belong to groups. Belonging is a profoundly human need.

Counselling and psychotherapy has been developed from a white, western cultural view. Many trainers of counselling and psychotherapy are themselves white and middle class. Practitioners in the public sector will not necessarily work with clients from the same class, or other defined cultural background similar to themselves. Yet the ways of thinking and reasoning, the values, customs, class and religious-based beliefs are reflected in the practice.

Emphasis in the counselling and psychotherapy culture is placed on being articulate: describing and expressing feelings. Self-responsibility and personal growth is valued in many counselling practices. Autonomy or individuation is prized. Ending is considered very important; it is the stage of working through unfinished issues, with a chance to resolve and to let go.

Trainee counsellors and psychotherapists learn to practise from this viewpoint. If the trainee is not from this culture, she may have some difficulties with these values, assumptions and expectations of the training. In many Asian cultures, which are communal-based, self-responsibility is a very different concept.

Death is not finality in many eastern cultures. The western therapy practice that ending with a client needs to be addressed as finality does not have the same meaning and significance for someone from an eastern culture.

Amongst the qualities most admired in women in an Indian culture, for example, are modesty of manner and self-effacement, not independence or assertiveness. The Indian culture is a communal-based culture, not an individualised culture as this society is. The female, white practitioner who models both assertiveness and independence, may covertly expect her client to behave in the same way if she is unaware of the difference in cultural values.

In the intercultural training that I have led, I asked groups to think about their own culture and what it means to them. What is always interesting for the group is that people from the dominant culture (British) have not generally considered this before. This is understandable, as we are only aware of such things when we are outside our own culture; when we feel ourselves to be noticeably different from the majority.

Awareness grows as individuals begin to identify regional differences and other variations. Very soon, the question of what we carry in our 'collective culture' is raised. For white, Anglo-Saxon people there is the troublesome question of the 'oppressive' culture from a relatively recent past. An individual from an empire that once dominated other cultures may still, unconsciously, hold feelings of superiority and power over other peoples.

It is essential to explore these uncomfortable ideas in a non-threatening setting for white counsellors who will work with black clients, and for black counsellors who will work with white clients.

Low self-esteem has been linked to poorly formed and seldom explored ethnic identities, in studies that included black and Asian subjects (Phinney and Chavira 1992). In other studies, both social class and colour are found to be associated with the way that mental health is viewed. Lower social classes and blacks are more likely to be hospitalised for psychiatric problems, whilst middle classes and whites are treated for the more socially accepted 'depression' with anti-depressants by their GPs.

There is a myth that we are all the same. Telling a black person that there is no difference between them and a white person is to be colour-blind. Respecting a person's differences is to be open to and interested in the differences, and to be interested is to discover and appreciate differences.

The same can occur for religious differences. Practitioners need to explore their feelings and beliefs in relation to other religious practices, and not to assume that every white person has come from a Christian background, even if they don't practise, or that every Indian is Hindu.

Practitioners who work with people from another culture may lack empathy and impair therapy if they are not aware of differences in the client's cultural attitudes, needs, expectations, values and beliefs; this also applies if they have no understanding or awareness of the person's historical links that have helped to form their identity.

Prejudice

Homophobia is an example of a more subtle and pervasive prejudice in our society. Heterosexual practitioners need to have challenged their own prejudices and explored their own sexual identity. Working with gay and lesbian clients means to be aware of the stage that the client is at

– whether the client has 'come out' or not – and to understand the meanings and fears of the client, as well as the feelings regarding their sexuality. Practitioners need to be supportively challenging the internalised homophobia of the gay or lesbian client who has accepted the prejudice in order to be socially accepted.

> *When a person's identity is attacked they feel shame and injury that can range from the insignificant to a 'small death'.*

Humans have prejudices about differences, stemming from two main sources. One is the fear of being overwhelmed by another; this stems from a primitive survival need. The other is the fear and hatred of our own unacceptable feelings that we project onto others. Training in intercultural therapy incorporates learning to understand and tolerate primitive feelings and those that do not fit into our self-image.

This training enables a practitioner to listen to clients in a non-judgemental way. Being non-judgemental is to be relatively free of assumptions, prejudices and mistrust of differences. It means not perpetuating stereotypes.

Intercultural therapy training explores the practitioner's role in how to challenge racist, sexist and other negative and discriminating attitudes when they arise. Challenging others may be intimidating if individuals have not considered this and learned how to do it.

Being aware of differences is the task that the counselling and psychotherapy practitioner has to apply herself to. To be able to do this for a client is to confirm the person's humanity. The opposite, therefore, is to deny their humanity.

Culture shock

Culture shock is a dramatic feeling of being in confrontation with a physically, sensationally, linguistically and psychologically different culture. Refugees and immigrants can be so desperate to be accepted and conform that they may dismiss their own culture. They may suffer from depression, grief, resentment, apathy, anxiety and shame, which are all aspects of the difficulty in adjusting, precisely because they are anxious to conform. Yet their continuity and connections are through the very culture that they may choose not to identify with.

Respecting the stage that the client is at in trying to acculturate means that their culture can be honoured by acknowledging and valuing it.

Helping the client to make the connections is to help him to connect to himself. Understanding the client's stage of assimilation and adaptation to the host culture is essential.

Accommodating clients' needs

Reframing language is communicating verbally and non-verbally the therapist's understanding of the client in a language that the client can understand. In this way, the therapist accommodates the client's needs.

In some cultures the professional carries a status of great authority. This image is applied to counsellors and therapists. Waiting for the client to speak and direct the session has to be weighed up with telling the client how counselling is conducted. The client may have unspoken expectations that the counsellor will take an active and directive role, advising him on practical details and writing letters or making phone calls. Discussing and negotiating these issues at the beginning is necessary.

Practitioners may need to modify their approaches to accommodate other cultural needs of a client. Modifying my approach with a client is illustrated in the following example:

> A client who came from a culture where small children were normally with their mothers most of the time, expected to bring her two small children into the room for her session with me. I explained that this was her time, but I could see that she had very little concept of such a notion. We agreed to try different ways of working over several weeks. First, she brought the children to the session with toys to amuse them. Second, she arranged for someone else to be in another room with them. Third, she arranged for them to be looked after whilst she came to her session. After we had experienced all three ways, we discussed it, and she felt that she wanted to have more of her time. She proceeded with her sessions and rarely brought the children along if she could help it.

Had I been more rigid about my boundaries and my cultural approach, the client may well have left and never had the experience of time for herself that she came to prize.

Feminism

Feminism has played a major role in redefining the way that women think about themselves and the way that men view them. It has also had an effect on the way that therapy has evolved. Through the outspoken voice of feminism, we have been encouraged to see that the personal is also political. The oppression of women has been, until recently, completely normalised in all spheres and at all levels of societies – in education, organisations, business, politics, religion, law, etc. – and has been knowingly or unknowingly perpetuated by each one of us, women included. Low self-esteem in women has been linked to the oppression of women.

Female clients may react submissively to a male counsellor or therapist just because of the gender and power difference between them. Male practitioners therefore have to be particularly aware of this.

We live in a pluralistic/multicultural society which means that, as therapists, we now meet people from a wider range of cultural, religious and ethnic groups than in the past. We also meet a greater number of people with a range of personal sexual preferences. We need to develop an awareness and sensitivity to their specific issues.

In the same way we need to develop specific understanding and sensitivity towards those clients who come from a very different social class background than the one in which we may have grown up in.

It is not possible to have empathy without first developing sensitivity to the client's variables.

BEREAVEMENT TRAINING

On many general courses there are certain subjects that may be included for their wider relevance to the whole subject. Bereavement and loss is one such subject. As there is ending and loss in every phase and part of life it is a natural subject for inclusion.

To gain mastery over any subject, however, it is necessary to study it in more depth and over more time than may be possible on a training in general counselling or psychotherapy.

The voluntary agency CRUSE is nation-wide and gives a number of weeks training.

Bereavement courses do not usually consider application from someone who has been bereaved within two years of applying for a place on a course. Being on such a training may bring up unresolved personal losses which need to be addressed and worked through if the trainee is to be of help to someone who is grieving.

The content of a course in bereavement may contain:

- The study and process of grief – the human response to loss
- Abnormal grief or extended grieving

- Multicultural aspects of grief
- Inability to mourn
- Losses at different stages of life
- Personal losses and grieving awareness
- Death of an infant
- Traumatic death (i.e. suicide) and multiple deaths
- Death from war (hero or sacrifice?)

Bereavement is a time when the mourner tries to hold onto or resurrect the loved, dead person. Trying to overcome the reality of the death in their fantasy does this. It is not uncommon to hear someone say 'If only I had done this . . . or that . . . then he would still be alive.'

Understanding the whole process of grieving is essential to bereavement work. Understanding one's own attitudes and feelings of grieving are essential to this work. Being able to stay with the ways in which people express powerful feelings of grief, without feeling overwhelmed, angry, anxious or wanting to change the subject, is essential.

The learning incorporates being able gently to facilitate people to talk about and express their feelings. For people who control their feelings, it is helpful for them to understand more about their need to control them. This understanding can help them to work through the grieving process.

Humans need meaning from losses, and the struggle in grieving is the struggle to make meaning. The trainee learns what aspects of death can be processed by the mourner, and at what stage. Staying with another's pain without trying to rescue them, take it away, make it better or any of the other ways that our society generally deals with death, is difficult. This is the very essence of training in bereavement.

It is to be hoped that training courses fully allow for the processing of the traumatic effects on the trainees through focusing on the subject of loss, endings, trauma, death and grieving. Everybody has known loss of one kind or another, and this training inevitably reawakens painful or sad losses for the trainee. Support on the training course and outside must be considered.

POST-TRAUMATIC STRESS DISORDERS

This is another subject that may be included in a general training, but needs very specific training in order to gain mastery and for someone who wishes to specialise in this subject.

Trauma is the outcome of the deepest shock that reverberates through, and affects, the whole system. It is the individual or collective response to helplessness in the face of felt or realised catastrophe.

Like bereavement it is a stressful subject to study and work with, and affects trainees and experienced practitioners alike. Training in this subject varies enormously. Courses should be carefully checked to see what aspects are covered. Trainees need to learn what causes trauma and how it affects people; how stress and trauma can develop into post-traumatic stress disorders (PTSD); how to work with traumatised clients and to manage the clients' strong feelings and their own. Trainees also need to learn how it affects people who are in direct contact with those suffering from trauma.

Trauma can be transmitted to counsellors, psychotherapists, mental health workers and carers who are working with someone suffering from PTSD. The disorders that affect practitioners can also happen through being exposed to knowledge of trauma.

One of the factors that makes a practitioner more susceptible to traumatic stress disorders is empathy. Practitioners need to be empathic to do this work, but the more empathic a person is, the more likely they are to suffer from the effects of the trauma they are exposed to in their clients.

Stress is the inevitable result of working with clients who are suffering from PTSD, and is unavoidable. It is the natural response to working with trauma. It is the *disorders* that result from the stress that need to be recognised and understood.

Disorders may be physical, emotional, behavioural and interpersonal. The affects can result in depression, sleep disturbances, anxiety, strains on relationships, substance abuse and burnout.

How disorders can be recognised and diminished or prevented should be taught on training courses.

Trainees need to learn assessing skills, to be able to recognise the signs and symptoms of stress and disorders. Knowing how to take care of the self and to maintain a balanced lifestyle is an important aspect of training. Practitioners who don't take care of themselves and don't lead a healthy lifestyle are also at more risk of being vulnerable to stress disorders. The practitioner's reaction (or countertransference) to the traumatised client and his situation is inevitable. Practitioners therefore need safe, supportive settings to off-load their own difficult feelings.

Acknowledging that personal and professional support is essential should form part of the learning on a course.

Some courses deal with crisis intervention. This is a training that holds the notion of restoring the person to his previous levels of functioning, and uses strategies and techniques to this end. This is usually taught in brief therapy, from 1–12 sessions.

Other courses that are considered long term, and address trauma that may be historic, will concentrate on:

- containment
- stabilising
- coping skills and strategies
- desensitising
- phobia avoidance
- normalising feelings
- debriefing
- narrative therapy (retelling the client's story)
- addressing self-blame or guilt
- facilitating meaning
- anxiety and stress management
- encouraging sensory associations
- eye movement desensitisation and reprocessing (EMDR)
- employing metaphors
- integration of trauma

If practitioners are dealing with someone from a family that has been traumatised, they need to know the relevant details of the critical events that have affected their client. Identity to a group that has been traumatised affects both the personal identity of the person and their continuity. Trainees can learn how to gather such information sensitively. Working with shame and self-esteem are also relevant factors for this training.

FURTHER READING

Archer, J. (1998) *The Nature of Grief*, London: Routledge.

Bertcher, H.J. (1994) *Group Participation. Techniques for Leaders and Members*, London: Sage Publications.

Bion, W.R. (1961) *Experience in Groups*, London: Tavistock Publications.

Burnham, J.B. (1986) *Family Therapy*, London and New York: Tavistock Publications Ltd.

Clarkson, P. (1993) *On Psychotherapy*, London: Whurr Publishers.

Culley, S. (1990) *Integrative Counselling Skills in Action*, London: Sage Publications.

Dies, R.R. (1992) 'Models of group psychotherapy: sifting through confusion', *International Journal of Group Psychotherapy*, 42: 1–17.

Dryden, W. (ed.) (1992) *Integrative and Eclectic Therapy. A Handbook*, Milton Keynes and Philadelphia: Open University Press.

Dryden, W. and Feltham, C. (1992) *Brief Counselling*, Milton Keynes: Open University Press.

Freeman, D.R. (1990) *Couples in Conflict*, Milton Keynes: Open University Press.

Hawton, K. (1985) *Sex Therapy: A Practical Guide*, Oxford: Oxford University Press.

Kubler-Ross, E. (1973) *On Death and Dying*, London: Routledge.

McLeod, J. (1993) *An Introduction to Counselling*, Buckingham: Open University Press.

Mahrer, A. (1989) *The Integration of Psychotherapies: A Guide for Practicing Therapists*, New York: Human Sciences Press.

Pedersen, P.B., Draguns, J.G., Lonner, W.J. and Trimble, J.E. (1996) *Counseling Across Cultures*, London: Sage Publications.

Phinney, J. and Chavira, V. (1992) 'Ethnic identity and self-esteem: an exploratory longitudinal study'. *Journal of Adolescence* 15: 271–281.

Rack, P. (1982) *Race, Culture, and Mental Disorder*, London: Routledge.

Ridley, C.R. (1995) *Overcoming Unintentional Racism in Counseling and Therapy*, London: Sage Publications.

Schroder, T. (1989) 'Couples counselling', in S. Palmer and G. McMahon (eds) *Handbook of Counselling*, London: Tavistock/Routledge.

Skrine, R. (1998) Emotional contact & containment in psychosexual medicine, *Sexual & Marital Therapy*, 13 (2): 169–178.

Skynner, R. and Cleese, J. (1983) *Families and How to Survive Them*, London: Methuen.

Wilson, J.P. and Lindy, J.D. (1994) *Countertransference in the Treatment of PTSD*, Guildford: Guildford Press.

10

CAREERS IN THERAPY

This chapter will help you to consider the possibilities for work. This is relevant, whether you are at the stage of considering which type of training to undertake, or whether you are at the end of your training. Two points are considered:

- What job prospects there are as a counsellor or psychotherapist.
- Whether to go into private practice.

A CAREER AS A COUNSELLOR OR PSYCHOTHERAPIST

There are many more counsellors and psychotherapists finishing a training course than there are jobs for them to apply for. A career in counselling is generally low paid with difficulty in finding employment and unsatisfactory conditions of employment. Counsellors with experience and who are BAC accredited are likely to be given priority in the job market.

There are organisations that do employ full-time therapists, but there is high competition for places. Within the NHS psychotherapists fare somewhat better, as there is more opportunity for psychotherapists with training in adult or child psychotherapy. Psychotherapists who are UKCP or BCP registered have more recognition.

After your initial general training, it may be valuable to undergo specialised training in a particular field that interests you. It is a mistake to assume that all training courses equip therapists to deal with every subject. Research shows this not to be the case. Many occupations for counsellors and psychotherapists are in particular settings, as mentioned above, and therapists are employed who have the necessary therapeutic approach, knowledge (and preferably experience) of a specialised subject.

Individuals wishing to work as a counsellor or consultant in an organisational setting need to consider specific counselling training for the workplace. There are relatively few courses available in the country at present, but it is growing. The Tavistock NHS Trust offers a course for professionals at managerial level, and Bristol University offers a course that helps to equip people with the necessary skills and understanding of the organisational context and workplace counselling practice. The Institute of Group Analysis in London also offers psychodynamic training in organisational group work.

There are a number of different theoretical approaches that seem to suit counselling and consultancy in the workplace, including Gestalt, cognitive-behavioural, systemic, TA (transactional analysis), NLP (see Glossary), psychodynamic and solutions-focused brief therapy. These are sometimes noted in the advertising section of courses that offer training for the workplace.

Specific psychotherapeutic approaches are more called for in some settings; for example, brief therapy or solution-focused therapy is preferred with many commercial and industrial settings.

Cognitive-behavioural therapies tend to be employed in the NHS for treating patients with problems, such as phobias, anxieties and obsessive-compulsive disorders. Psychodynamic and systemic therapies are also the more traditional approaches used in medical settings, but the humanistic approaches (and many of the alternative therapies) are gaining some entry into this setting.

There are organisations that want staff to have counselling and communication skills as part of their ongoing jobs, and there is a lot more scope for jobs requiring those skills. Some organisations are prepared to send particular staff onto courses to enhance their skills within their existing jobs.

Becoming a member of the BAC gives an opportunity to join one of the seven divisions dedicated to particular counselling settings. Each of these divisions keeps their members advised of information that is relevant and of interest to them. The divisions are: Association for Counselling at Work (ACW), Association for Pastoral Care & Counselling (APCC), Association for Student Counselling (ASC), Counselling in Education (CIE), Counselling in Medical Settings (CMS), Personal, Sexual, Relationship, Family (PSRF), Race & Cultural Education in Counselling (RACE).

Looking through relevant magazines and journals, as well as newspapers, for vacancies for counsellors or psychotherapists will give you an idea of the requirements of a post.

The places to look for counselling and psychotherapy jobs are in the national newspapers – the *Guardian* is a good example – and health-care related journals. There are counselling agencies that are part of social work and social care agencies, where you can register. There is also the *Jobfile*, which is a fortnightly information news sheet, advertising jobs, and is available on subscription from the BAC.

Counsellors and psychotherapists as educators and promoters of the profession

Training in counselling or psychotherapy should ideally include difficulties that therapists will encounter in the workplace. Some of those difficulties relate to insufficient knowledge of counselling and psychotherapy by employers.

The profession itself has to address the lack of understanding of counselling and psychotherapy in the public arena. This means that members of the profession ensure that those who employ them as counsellors or psychotherapists are very clear as to what the contributions and limitations of therapy are, and why supervision is required. The objectives, for both practitioner and the employer, need to be clarified: how the practitioner is to practise, and the ethics involved that may be viewed from a different perspective between practitioner and employer.

A counsellor or psychotherapist can take a role as an educator where necessary and offer the required information about therapy.

Counsellors and psychotherapists may be called upon to run training courses within an organisation. The wide and varied issues that have to be dealt with in the workplace include conflict mediation, interpersonal relationship difficulties, alcohol and substance abuse, stress, PTSD, depression, debt, redundancy, career change and retirement.

In large organisations, there may be teams of counsellors. The national emergency services and London Underground are examples of this. As part of their occupational health service for their staff, London Underground provides short-term general counselling, as well as long- and short-term trauma relief counselling. The counsellors are trained to work with crisis interventions and PTSD. Stress- and trauma-related problems are common difficulties that counsellors would be expected to deal with in such settings. The counsellors use tests, inventories and questionnaires as well as the usual counselling skills.

Counsellors are employed in a very wide variety of settings, dealing with expansive general and specialist areas. Examples of other areas where you might find counselling are stress management for organisations, Age Concern, Mind, Rape Crisis and other voluntary agencies; in careers advisory services, drug addiction centres and youth drop-in centres, bereavement services, crisis work, family planning clinics, hospitals, special needs schools, colleges, HIV and AIDS centres, couple counselling and psycho-sexual clinics. There is specific counselling for men who batter women, women in refuges, lesbians and gays and ethnic minorities.

Many alternative therapies like voice, dance, movement, music and art, are recognised as valuable and employed in varied work, medical and educational settings.

If corporate organisations pay for their staff to see a counsellor, it is common for counsellors to see clients for as little as one or two sessions, with 6–10 sessions very often being the maximum. The brevity is dictated by the demand, the time factor and the cost. Brief therapy, goal-oriented and task-oriented therapies are frequently sought in commercial and organisational settings.

There is the issue of how many hours a counsellor should actually counsel to take into consideration. In a BAC leaflet (see further reading list, p. 202), they advise that 'Counselling is a very stressful occupation and it is recommended that in any one week . . . full-time counsellors spend no more than 16–20 hours in face-to-face counselling.'

Psychotherapists are employed in similar settings to counsellors. They will also have access to work in hospital psychiatric units, mental health day clinics, couple therapy, family therapy units, hospital clinics for mentally ill children and adolescents, group therapy units, prisons, psychotherapeutic communities (residential, hostels or day-care settings), work closely with Social Services, as well as working as consultants in organisational settings and private practice.

Support within organisations for therapists

Some organisations may be keen to employ a counsellor but without having a clear idea of what counselling entails. It is important to check with them about supervision; whether this is provided and under what conditions. Would the role of supervisor cross boundaries (i.e. someone who would be your line manager who would also supervise you)? Would you have the choice to find an external supervisor and would the company pay the cost? Would they cover training costs? How does the company expect the counsellor to structure her counselling time?

I was employed full time in a resource centre for the unemployed for a number of years, and was expected to see clients back-to-back, with no spaces in between for note taking or reflection. This is not good practice.

Medical settings

There may be a number of therapists in a NHS hospital, within a hospice, day centre, rehabilitation centre and within commercial organisations. Counsellors and psychotherapists usually work as part of a team within those settings. Counsellors, psychotherapists, psychologists, creative art therapists and others in those settings work with bereavement, people with terminal illness and work-related issues. They may work in a one-to-one setting, or with groups.

GP surgeries

Trainees on most courses have to find their own client placements. In general there is high demand for placements in a GP practice, as trainee counsellors find doctors' surgeries useful places to work the client hours that are required by the course.

This may leave some doctors less inclined to employ trained and experienced counsellors who want to be paid for their services. Fund-holding GPs have had a choice about paying for counsellors in their practices until recently, when the government abolished fund-holding GP practices.

Primary care counsellors with some basic medical knowledge are still new to the profession. They are not being given the recognition they deserve in either status, pay conditions or the greater acceptance and use of counsellors, in spite of the enormously valuable resource to a doctor that counsellors can be in a busy surgery.

If you are able to secure a post in a GP practice, you can expect to earn about £15 per hour for a set number of hours per week, in London. In some practices the doctor may suggest that you negotiate your own fee with the patients.

It is important to consider whether there are clients that you would not want to work with, or feel limited to work with. Depending on the severity of the presenting problem, you need to advise the GP accordingly, so that you are both clear about the patient group you will see. The appropriate matching of the patient's needs with the counsellor's competence is paramount. If you are in doubt, you should discuss with your supervisor first.

There are doctors who do not have a clear understanding of what counselling is and may have different expectations from the therapist regarding outcome expectations. The medical system in this country is organised so that general practice doctors are required to diagnose effectively within the space of about seven minutes per patient. They must investigate possible life-threatening illnesses and refer where necessary, all within that time-scale.

Counsellors on the other hand are trained to go at the client's pace and to work with underlying emotional causes. The changes may be slow and not always apparent.

A counsellor may not want to work in one of the medical consulting rooms. Setting aside a room for counselling is a way of validating the work. Research has shown that designating rooms for counselling within a medical practice has made a marked difference to the client's perception of counselling, and their relationship with the counsellor.

The CMS Guidelines have a section under Job Description which states that each general practice should provide a job description that outlines:

- the role of the counsellor
- the time allocated for seeing clients
- supervision
- administration and record keeping
- confidentiality and professional accountability
- terms and conditions of service

Education and young people

Counsellors, art therapists, psychologists and psychotherapists are employed in education: in special needs schools, colleges, institutes and universities. There are young people's drop-in centres, birth-control clinics, drugs and substance abuse clinics that all offer counselling and mediation services to young people. Short-term or brief therapy is frequently offered in these settings, again because it is the most cost-effective, where funding has to be given priority consideration. There is also a view held by some that brief therapy is more appropriate for young people at their life stage.

As a consequence of low budgeting, however, there is still wide use of voluntary counsellors in education.

An added difficulty for counsellors wishing to practise in education settings is frequently the lack of understanding of counselling. There is also a lack of appreciation for trained and qualified counsellors and the regular provision of supervision. Social workers, teachers and other personnel may attend very short courses or introductions to counselling skills and believe that they are qualified to counsel pupils and students.

Whilst good teaching incorporates child-centredness, caring and supportive qualities that are enhanced by the use of counselling skills, teacher training does not include the depth of a 2–3 year counselling training. That understanding cannot be gained in a few short training sessions. There is also the issue of combining the role of teacher and counsellor. Busy teachers cannot fulfil the role or give the time to a child that a school counsellor can. Keeping the two quite separate makes for uncomplicated boundaries and less confusion for all concerned.

In educational and medical settings there is now a shift away from the isolated counsellor to the counsellor being a part of a multidisciplinary team. A team may consist of teachers, social workers, health workers and a counsellor. This involves counsellors being more accountable for their work, but which also places limits on confidentiality.

Accountability of counsellors and therapists applies to many workplace settings. Counselling in Education (CIE), one of the divisions of the BAC, acts as a link between local education authorities, teaching staff and counsellors in education. One of its objectives is to promote counselling in schools.

Traditionally the theoretical training in psychotherapy for working with young people has been in psychodynamic psychotherapy. Training centres such as the WPF, the Institute for Group Analysis, the Tavistock and the Lincoln Centre, are all in London. The Tavistock NHS Trust in London holds seminars and conferences for professionals working in education, health, social services, psychology and counselling related areas.

The interest in working with young people is, of course, paramount. Particular issues for training would be bullying, anger and violence, drugs abuse, sexuality, family problems; age-appropriate legal issues, and information about statutory organisations. Counsellors who work in the field of young people also need to have such specialised training.

In the tertiary sector, universities and colleges, there is the link with employment, and the concerns that young people have regarding careers. Training in career advice would be essential.

Freelance

We come now to working freelance, which gives the therapist a choice of organisations to work with, rather than being employed by one organisation full time. An example would be working for Employee Assisted Programmes, or EAP for short. An EAP acts as an agency, supplying counsellors to organisations for the benefit of their staff.

The EAP contacts counsellors all over the country, usually from the BAC list, asking them if they are interested in working for them. EAP agencies prefer to select BAC accredited counsellors to contact.

There is usually a contract to be signed between the counsellor and the EAP. The contract will tell you how many sessions you will work with a member of an organisation's staff. The sessions usually number between 6–10. This is brief therapy, which needs specific skills. This form of therapy does not mean that a practitioner is simply working fewer sessions.

For EAP freelance work, you will be paid a set sessional rate, and will have to sign a contract to declare that you will not arrange meetings with clients outside those contracted for. This prevents the counsellor taking away prospective clients for themselves.

You will probably have to write a report on the clients you see and send it to the EAP. As you are accountable to the EAP agency, you will not necessarily know what happens to that report.

It is important to clarify what the terms and conditions of note taking and reporting are, and therefore the confidentiality. You will need to know where the notes will be kept; whether they are for the private use of the counsellor; whether the company expects a report on each member of staff who is counselled; and what details are to be reported, etc. This consideration needs to be explored and clarified whenever someone is employed as a counsellor or psychotherapist.

The advantage of working freelance is that you can look for work amongst other organisations and not solely in one. Agencies that employ therapists freelance are alcohol units, HIV and AIDS projects, women's refuges, drug abuse units, mental health projects, pregnancy advisory services and others. The work may not be regular, but there is generally a positive recognition of the value of counselling and psychotherapy in these projects.

Working freelance brings you into the area of private practice, which is the next point.

SETTING UP IN PRIVATE PRACTICE

I facilitated a day's workshop on the above subject for some years. It was a popular workshop because:

1   Most training courses do not provide the information necessary to consider how to set up and maintain a private practice.
2   There are so many people graduating from the great number of training courses, and there are not enough jobs on the market to accommodate them. Private practice is an obvious option.
3   Private practice is a very attractive option to people who are comfortable with the setting.
4   Therapists need to know about the business side of running a practice.

There are many therapists in private practice, and if the numbers of practitioners continues to rise, the competition will become ever greater.

I have been in private practice for the last nine years, and would not want to work for anyone else. Working for yourself can be immensely satisfying and rewarding, providing you are aware of the difficulties and prepare yourself accordingly. The following section is intended to help you to do this, when you are ready to consider private practice.

The pitfalls of private practice

I shall look at some of the things to be aware of before you commit yourself to working on your own:

Time

You may have to keep unsociable and inconvenient hours when you are in the early stages of setting up a practice. Clients want to come at times convenient to themselves, which may be after their working hours. You may be twiddling your thumbs during the day, and working late in the evening.

A business

It will take time, effort and money just as in any other business to get started. Setting up a business means acquiring premises and clients, gaining a reputation, keeping accounts, filing tax returns, opening a separate bank account, having printed leaflets and cards, sending invoices and receipts, taking up professional membership, paying for professional indemnity and liability, etc. You are solely accountable.

Having spent three or more years on a course, learning how to be empathic and being there for the client's needs, there is a paradox in reconciling a caring profession with a business. But this is what it is.

Money

If you have worked before, unless it was for yourself, the chances are that someone else will have paid you. You may have worked in the voluntary sector and not been paid at all. If you start your own private practice, this may be the first time that you have had to ask for money in this way. Money put into your hand by the person you are working with in a session is often a strange experience at first, for a therapist.

Working as a therapist for an hourly session rate does not make a lot of money. Remember that even when clients are not there, you will have to provide and pay for your own supervision, ongoing training, personal therapy, liability insurance, and save for your own pension fund. You also lose money when you take time off for holidays or sickness.

There can be a problem, especially at the beginning of your practice, in that you need to have a certain minimum number of clients in order to pay your bills. If you are financially dependent on each client, waiting for another one to start can create anxiety. A client may use therapy or counselling as a form of habitual self-absorption, which may suit the practitioner who has financial worries. This idea of needing clients or needing clients to stay, is contrary to the ethics and principles of counselling and psychotherapy.

Integrating the self, internalising therapy as a means of self-reflecting and self-regulating are the objectives of counselling and psychotherapy. Obviously there is a reality about financial practicalities, but the underlying needs and insecurity of the practitioner must be addressed in both supervision and personal therapy, not through clients.

Your home

If you work from home, keeping a conscious dividing line between the practice and your living space is important. If you are able to set aside a room just for the practice, then it is easy to close the door on it at the end of your working week, and not open it until the following week. This is a separation ritual that makes a boundary between your business and your home.

If the therapy room is not a designated room and is used at other times, then it is worth while considering how you can make some adjustment at the end of each working period. Even shifting around the chairs that you use for yourself and your clients can be a valuable ritual for separation.

If you decide to work from home you will have to bear in mind the following:

- That it is quiet – that family, neighbours and traffic will not disturb you.
- You will need to invest in a telephone answering machine.
- That the accommodation is suitable: the chairs need to be comfortable, especially for yourself, as you could be sitting for six hours a day.
- The room should, ideally, be light and airy and a comfortable temperature.
- Consider the decor and ornaments. Too many things create a distraction from the work, but too bare a room can be sterile and off-putting.

- Do your clients have easy access to a toilet?
- Is there a separate room that could be used as a waiting room if necessary?
- Are there parking facilities within easy access?
- Will they meet your family in the hallway?
- Are there pets in the house? There may be clients who have allergies to animals or just dislike them. Animals can cause disruptions by coming and going.
- There is the wear and tear on your carpets and furniture, and the extra heating and lighting costs.
- Your own safety if you are in the house on your own with clients. What safety precautions would you use?
- Working alone can be very isolating.
- Sitting all day can create lethargy. Getting out of the house regularly, exercising and keeping a balance in your life is important.

After contemplating all the practical considerations of using your home, it is important to think about the information your home gives to clients about you.

The importance of taking care of yourself cannot be overstated. A total involvement in therapy, supervision and talking about therapy to colleagues is not a balance, but the relentless fascination with therapy is an easy trap to fall into. Remember that therapists suffer from burnout too.

Referral system

Some of the well-established psychodynamic psychotherapy training centres operate a register of therapists who trained with them. Trainee therapists and the general public who are referred to the centre can then obtain the details of a therapist. This system assures the newly qualified therapist of some clients to work with.

There are some humanistic training centres that hold a list of their qualified therapists and give out the list to the new intake of students who are looking for a therapist. If this is not the system of the training centre, then setting up a referral system is probably the most difficult hurdle for the therapist to overcome when starting in private practice. Once you are known and reputable, word of mouth will be your best form of referral; but how do you get yourself known?

Going to lectures, workshops and conferences enables you to network. It is also a form of socialising and getting out of your isolation. If you do decide to work on your own, it is a good idea to form a study, supervision or support group. The sharing of case studies, information and frustrations can be immensely supportive. You will also have a ready-made referral system.

It is as important to know how other people work as it is to let them know how you work, so that you can exchange referrals with them. If the colleagues you choose as a group have different approaches from yours, and if they specialise in something that you do not work with, these are advantageous to you.

There is also the matter of filling appointment times. Evening appointments are the more favourable. A potential client may phone you and you may not be able to see them in the time that they want; being able to refer them to a colleague is helpful to them. Your colleague will appreciate this and will do the same for you.

If you do not form a group, you could consider finding one other trusted colleague. This is helpful in both exchanging a list of your clients so that clients could be contacted and provision made for them in the event of an emergency, such as an accident or the death of one of you. Both of you could also arrange for very vulnerable clients to telephone the other if they needed to, when one is absent.

Medical back-up support

The BAC advice regarding medical back up is worth noting. I have quoted it from their Information Sheet 6 in private practice:

> A firm arrangement with a psychiatrist or other medical consultant is advisable. This means that if you are in any doubt about the medical implications of a client's difficulties or need some specific information about disabilities, drugs, etc., advice is readily available. A fee for such an arrangement may be required. Co-operation between yourself and your client's GP can sometimes be important, especially if your client is currently receiving medical treatment. Some counsellors [and psychotherapists] do not accept a client unless permission is given for the GP to be informed, while others leave it to the client to decide whether the GP should be informed or not. Others again will vary their policy in this matter according to the needs of the particular situation.
>
> (BAC 1993)

How to let people know you are there

How else can you get clients to know about you apart from your support group or your training institute? Becoming a member and getting your name and professional details in the BAC directory if you are a counsellor or psychotherapist, and being eligible for the UKCP or BCP register if you are a psychotherapist, is important. UKCP or BCP have a register of psychotherapists who are members of an association that those bodies recognise. Although this takes time, obtaining BAC accreditation for counsellors and UKCP accreditation for psychotherapists is an advantage. (See Chapter 8 on accreditation.)

The Central Library in your area may hold community information on computer, and you can ask to have your professional details added to their list. Churches, colleges and other learning institutions also hold lists. Do not forget to give your details to the centre where you did your own training and to check each year that your name still appears on the list.

Ask your own supervisor to refer appropriate clients to you. If you are practising from home it is useful to keep a list of the source of client referrals. You will soon be aware of the sources that are most productive.

I am doubtful of advertising in shops or newspapers where people can walk in off the street, unless you can satisfy yourself of their serious intent as a client. Equally, it is still a problem amongst the public of how to find a professional and reputable therapist, and some people may not want to go to their GP.

Advertising in a directory like Yellow Pages is expensive and may work better if you are with a group practice rather than in business as an individual.

A word on leaflets and cards. Make the wording clear and simple and avoid using jargon. If you cannot find a suitable design it is better to leave it quite plain. Most people want straight information. State something about yourself, your experience and your qualifications. If you specialise, it is important to put that in.

You cannot use membership of an organisation as a qualification, as it is misleading, and could be construed as a professional qualification. You may not describe yourself as a member of the organisation, either as an organisational member or as an individual member. This may give a faulty impression to the public, who may assume that membership letters stand for qualifications.

Many organisations have a policy on what can and cannot be stated on letterheads, writing paper, business cards, fliers, promotional papers, advertisements, prospectuses, etc., wherever the public have sight of your details. The wording that is allowed is quite specific.

If you do leave your cards or leaflets with GP surgeries, health food shops, educational centres, CAB, libraries, etc., remember to replenish them every few months.

Consider offering free talks about the benefits of counselling or psychotherapy to groups, schools and colleges. If you are confident, write articles for newspapers and magazines. One further step is to approach local radio and even TV. You will certainly get known in this way and will be helping to demystify therapy, as well as informing the public on how they can find reputable therapists.

As anyone can set up in private practice this has, unfortunately, led to some malpractice that has been highlighted by the media. We are all responsible for the standards of our profession. One of the ways that we can redress the balance of bad practice is by letting the public know who we are, what we do, and that we do it with integrity and commitment.

Tell your friends and colleagues and when your clients are ending therapy (if it feels appropriate) that you have vacancies and that you are happy for them to refer people on to you. Telling others is an equal opportunity for you and them.

Boundary setting and contract

Therapists know that maintaining boundaries is a vital part of the therapeutic relationship. The meaning of the term 'boundaries' refers to limit setting, either in behaviour or time. It is important to set limits in therapy, so that clients and therapists know where they are. Not discussing the work or the client with anyone except your own supervisor is a confidential factor or boundary. Not working with friends and relatives therapeutically is another. Although it may seem like a good idea to work with people you know, resentments and expectations can get in the way of the work. Boundaries are designed to make the work clearer, uncomplicated and more effective for the welfare of the client and in the interest of the therapeutic relationship.

In some ways, it may be easier to set boundaries when working from home than in a work setting. Setting limits on clients phoning or writing to you between sessions in your home has to be considered carefully, as does non-payment for missed sessions.

I cover the latter in a written contract. The contract is set out in Appendix 1. As you will see, observance of the boundaries is considered regarding the session time and day, cancellations, confidentiality and working to an ending.

We both sign and exchange a copy to keep. Signing each other's copy is a commitment of our intention to work together. I usually give this to the client after the initial assessment session, when both therapist and client have agreed to work together.

An initial assessment interview is important for a number of reasons. It is an opportunity for both client and practitioner to meet, without obligation, where both can assess each other. The practitioner can assess the client's needs and decide whether she can help, and whether she wants to set up a commitment to work with the client. A client may be unsure of what he wants, or what therapy is about. He has an opportunity to find out how he feels with the therapist, and to ask questions if he chooses.

Recording sessions

Clients have the right to know about their notes and to see them if they wish. The BAC Code of Ethics and Practice for Counsellors B3. 5. Management of Confidentiality refers to the recording of session notes. Working on your own means that you are entirely responsible for your records. Due care and attention must be applied to the keeping of clients' records. This means that you must provide a secure and confidential container for your notes. If you keep notes on computer, contact the Data Protection Act Registrars for information about storing your notes in this way (telephone: 01625 545745).

You may be requested to write reports for injury or other compensation or criminal proceedings. Some practitioners tape every session with every client, and will not work with clients who are not happy with this arrangement. These practitioners prefer this method to notes, believing that taping portrays a more accurate rendition of the subtleties of a session, which writing cannot do. Practitioners who write notes will be selective in what they write, because of difficulty in remembering each detail, and the time it takes to make notes.

It is better to be prepared and face the fact that as litigation is becoming more common there is always the possibility sometime in your career of having your notes read in court. For this reason and others, professional indemnity liability is vital. These points need to be considered before you begin your practice.

Not working from your own home

Upon reflection, you may prefer to work from hired rooms, or share with a group practice. There are many advantages to the latter. The company of others is one of them. Another advantage is that you would have a ready-made referral system with other therapists in the practice, especially if they practise different or alternative therapies. You may be able to arrange a receptionist between you, and a waiting room, and share other costs, such as advertising. Having your leaflets or cards on show in the reception area is a permanent and inexpensive form of advertising. It is worth investigating working with others in a group practice. It is equally worth the time and trouble to investigate the charges of hiring rooms as they vary enormously.

Part time

Having considered all the possibilities of setting up your own practice, you may think that working part time, whilst you try to build up your clients and your experience, suits you better. At least you will be assured of some regular income. This will save you worrying about the gaps. These occur when clients leave and you don't know when the next one will come to take their place.

It is relevant to consider how many clients you feel you could work with each week. Generally, 20 client contact hours a week is a maximum number suggested by most therapeutic organisations. BAC has produced a guideline which refers to the workload of counsellors. They advise 16–20 client contact hours in any one week, which has to take into account the nature of the workload, the support available, and the competence and experience of the counsellor.

Particular attention is drawn for practitioners in private practice, to the absence of a supportive administrative, managerial and peer framework, and the dangers of burnout if a practitioner's load is excessive.

Any more than the suggested maximum numbers of clients makes it difficult to hold each person's story in your head. The work is very focused, and therefore tiring. Knowing your limitations is part of being a competent therapist or counsellor. This also includes knowing which client groups you want to work with and those you do not. It is not humanly possible to work effectively with every person.

Fees

The last point to mention about private practice is the fee. Many newly trained therapists are uncertain how much to charge. There seems to be a conflict about fees in general that may be helpful to discuss here at length.

I suspect that it is the paradox of the profession that causes the conflict. Training emphasises a therapist's empathy and compassion: not bringing their own needs into the session. These qualities are paramount to the relationship and to the effectiveness of therapy. The therapist may have difficulties therefore in charging people, as the fee is the therapist's need. Charging fees adds a dimension to therapy that is missing in voluntary work and where employers, not clients, pay therapists.

The work of therapy is frequently around healing problems in the present that originated in a person's early life. The client has already paid heavily for this psychic wounding, resulting in difficulties in areas of his life before coming to therapy. The therapist is sensitive to someone's pain, and for this reason may find it difficult to charge.

When religion was dominant in our culture, people could approach their spiritual leader with their emotional problems, and would not have expected to pay. Therapy has largely replaced that place of spiritual healing, but this does not make therapists feel comfortable about charging.

There has long been a tradition in the medical profession that has been seen, in this country at least, as treatment for the sick without direct payment. Of course we do pay for our National Health Service, but for the last 50 years we have not passed money over to the doctor under that service. As psychoanalysis is the traditional form of psychological 'talking' treatment and the patient is usually referred by a doctor, there is an association in many people's minds of medical treatment with therapy. There are, therefore, expectations that therapeutic treatment should be free.

When the history of women was drawn into sharply defined lines of those who worked and those who did not, there was a tradition of women – largely from the middle classes – who were willing to listen to people's problems. This may have been a continuation of the wise-woman that has existed in communities. A number of well-known volunteer agencies recruited women in this way. The volunteers were usefully employing their time and their good will, without expecting or needing remuneration for their efforts. It is a very different story today.

Another factor is that many qualified therapists may have worked in the voluntary sector at some time during their training; I worked as a voluntary supervisor and trainer for the bereavement organisation CRUSE for a number of years. Previously, I had worked with a youth counselling agency. Working for organisations like these is both a valuable contribution to the people who need them and a worthwhile experience for therapists. Working for charities without payment becomes normalised, which adds a further layer of discomfort to asking for fees.

Therapy is likely to attract people who are genuinely concerned to help others, and this adds weight to the conflict of asking for fees. Given this background, it is no wonder that many therapists have difficulty with fees.

The reality is, however, that many people have to earn their living this way. Trainees will have spent many thousands of pounds on their training, their own therapy and supervision, and will have given a number of years of time and effort. Training is ongoing for qualified therapists. This means that there is always an output of earned income that goes into being a therapist.

There may be an unresolved personal difficulty for the therapist regarding money. This may be about power. Money does represent power in our society. Charging fees gives a therapist an aspect of her own power to reflect on. The therapist already has a powerful role just by being the therapist. A therapist may well have unresolved power issues, just like anyone else, and the currency of power – money – comes to the foreground when there are fees to be paid.

The power element for the client is also viewed from the other side. A therapist is a person who is perceived as 'doing something to someone else', namely the client. A client comes to a therapist for something that the therapist is believed to have. A client may feel uncomfortable about the whole issue of money.

If you want to set up in private practice, any difficulties you have surrounding the fees has to be addressed.

It is appropriate to consider your stage of experience before you think about the fees you will charge. It is useful to find out what other therapists charge who work in your area. One way is to contact some of the agencies included in the List of Resources (see pp. 203–24) and ask for a list of therapists in your area. There are directories held in some libraries. The therapists' fees may be stated with their details. If not, ringing some up and asking how long they have been qualified, what their experience is and how much they charge, may give you the information necessary. A note of caution here; there are therapists who would not reveal these details on the telephone, for a number of reasons.

There are therapists who work on a sliding scale. That is, they will see people who have financial difficulties and charge them a much lower fee. Some practitioners charge according to what a client earns. There are other therapists who do not operate in this way, and have a fixed fee. Those therapists may refer individuals to practitioners who work on a sliding scale, or to a voluntary agency where fees are waived. It is an arbitrary and a personal choice.

It is apparent that therapists charge more in some areas than in others. Fees in London vary considerably according to area.

Knowing how many clients you want to see each week is important, even if you take some time to achieve that number. Calculating how much money you need to pay your bills will also help you to know how much you need to charge in fees. Feeling resentful towards clients because you are not earning as much as you need is an inevitable consequence of not preparing before you begin your practice. It is therefore a therapist's responsibility to consider the whole question of fees.

Analysts and psychotherapists have traditionally given monthly invoices to their patients. I practise a different method. I ask that the fee is paid at the beginning of each session, and this is written into the contract. If there are any problems – forgotten chequebook, ill-feeling about the cost, etc. – then there is a session to deal with it. The therapist is not then left holding onto the resentment, dismay or any other feelings that could get in the way of the therapeutic relationship.

Having covered the points raised in this chapter, the therapist is ready to practise as a therapist!

FURTHER READING

BAC (1993) Information Sheet 6. *Counselling in Private Practice*, Obtainable from BAC.

BAC (April 1998) *Counselling Workloads*, with Information Sheet 9 *Guidelines for the Employment of Counsellors*, Obtainable from BAC, Rugby.

BAC *Guidelines for the Employment of Counsellors in Medical Settings*, Publication by Counselling in Medical Settings Division of the British Association for Counselling.

BAC Office Fact Sheet A3. Details of the policy on the wording that can be used regarding membership or accreditation of counsellors for advertising, on printed letterheads, cards, etc. Available from BAC.

Bell, E. (1996) *Counselling in Further and Higher Education*, Buckingham: Open University Press.

Bond, T. (1998) *Confidentiality: Counselling & the Law*, Available from BAC.

Bor, R., Miller, R., Latz, M. and Salt, H. (1998) *Counselling in Health Care Settings*, London and New York: Cassell.

France, R. and Robson, M. (1986) *Behaviour Therapy in Primary Care: A Practical Guide*, Beckenham, Kent: Croom Helm Ltd.

House, R. and Totton, N. (eds) (1997) *Implausible Professions*, Ross-on-Wye: PCCS.

Hudson-Allez, G. (1997) *Time-Limited Therapy in a General Practice Setting. How to Help Within Six Sessions*, London: Sage Publications.

Jobfile (Issued by the BAC under subscription, fortnightly).

O'Connell, B. (1998) *Solution-Focused Therapy*, London: Sage Publications.

Syme, G. (1994) *Counselling in Independent Practice*, Buckingham: Open University Press.

LIST OF RESOURCES

The following is a sample list of training centres. A few are regional, but most are based in London. For a comprehensive list, see the BAC training directory. The list of training centres and organisations has been extracted mainly from the BAC training directory (1999), and the UKCP Member Organisations list (1998). Every training centre, directory and journal are non-evaluated, and are not endorsed nor recommended by the author. They are listed as an indication of what is available.

Subscriptions for membership are given but the fees quoted may change after publication. There are varied ratings: individual rates, organisational rates, student/trainee concessions. There are frequently different ratings for paying by direct debit or by cheque. These details are not included. Generally, an individual rating is listed to give an idea of the costing.

PSYCHODYNAMIC AND PSYCHOANALYTIC

Birkbeck College University of London, Extra-Mural Studies, 26 Russell Square, London WC1B 5DQ. Tel. 020 7631 6626. For psychodynamic counselling.

The Lincoln Clinic and Institute for Psychotherapy, 25 Hillcroft Crescent, London W5 2SG. Tel. 020 8998 1949 (Training). For Child and Adult psychoanalytic psychotherapy.

The Guild of Psychotherapists, 47 Nelson Square, London SE1 0QA. Tel. 020 8540 4454. For psychoanalytic psychotherapy.

The Arbours Association, 6 Church Lane, London N8 7BU. Tel. 020 8340 0916. Fax 020 8314 5822. For psychoanalytic psychotherapy.

The British Psycho-Analytical Society, Mansfield House, 63 New Cavendish Street, London W1M 7RD. Tel. 020 7580 4952.

The Centre for Psychoanalytical Psychotherapy, 57 Cecile Park, Crouch End, London N8 9AY. Tel. 020 8340 2922.

Westminster Pastoral Foundation (WPF), 23 Kensington Square, London W8 5HN. Tel. 020 7937 6956. For psychodynamic counselling and psychotherapy.

The Association for Group and Individual Psychotherapy, 1 Fairbridge Road, London N19 3EW. Tel. 020 7272 7013. Fax 020 7272 6945. For psychoanalytical psychotherapy.

The Severnside Institute for Psychotherapy, 11 Orchard Street, Bristol BS1 5EH. Tel. and fax 01275 333266. For psychoanalytic psychotherapy.

The Centre for Attachment-based Psychoanalytic Psychotherapy, 12a Nassington Road, London NW3 2UD. Tel. 020 7794 4306.

University College London, Psychoanalysis Unit, Gower Street, London WC1E 6BT. Tel. 020 7380 7899.

British Association of Psychotherapists, 37 Mapesbury Road, London NW2 4HJ. Tel. 020 8452 9823. Fax 020 8452 5182. For psycho-analytic psychotherapy, adult, child and adolescent, Jungian analytical psychotherapy.

Centre for Freudian Analysis and Research, 76 Haverstock Hill, London NW3 2BE. Tel. 020 7267 3003. For Lacanian analysis.

Institute of Psychotherapy and Social Studies (IPSS), West Hill House, 6 Swains Lane, London N6 6QU. Tel. 020 7284 4762. For psycho-analytic psychotherapy.

The Tavistock Clinic & Portman NHS Trust, 120 Belsize Lane, London NW3 5BA. Tel. 020 7447 3722. For systemic, psychodynamic, and psychoanalytic psychotherapy. For training at the Portman Clinic: 8 Fitzjohns Avenue, London NW3 5NA. Tel. 020 7794 8262.

The University of Birmingham, School of Continuing Studies, Birmingham B15 2TT. Tel. 0121 414 5593.

The Manor House Centre for Psychotherapy and Counselling, 80 East End Road, London N3 2SY. Tel. 020 8371 0180. Fax 01708 620 858. For psychodynamic counselling and therapy.

Somerset Counselling Centre (Taunton), 38 Belvedere Road, Taunton TA1 1HD. Tel. 01823 337049. For Foundation Certificate in Coun-selling Skills, Diploma in Psychodynamic Counselling.

University of Sussex, Health Centre Building, Falmer, Brighton BN1 9RW. Counselling and Psychotherapy. Tel. 01273 678156. For Pre-Diploma in Counselling (Certificate of Attendance), Certificate in Psychodynamic Counselling, Diploma in Counselling.

The Northern Ireland Association for the Study of Psycho-Analysis, 75

Ballybentragh Road, Mucakamore, Co. Antrim, BT41 2HJ. Tel. 028 3264 8038. Fax 028 3249 1991.

The Scottish Association of Psychoanalytic Psychotherapists, 56 Albany Street, Edinburgh EH1 3QR. Tel. 0131 556 0924.

The Adlerian Society (of UK) & Institute for Individual Psychology, 77 Clissold Crescent, London N16 9AR. Tel. 020 7923 2472. For Adlerian approach.

INTEGRATIVE COURSES

The Minster Centre, 1–2 Drakes Courtyard, 291 Kilburn High Road, London NW6 7JR. Tel. 020 7372 4940.

Stockton Centre for Psychotherapy & Counselling, 77 Acklam Road, Thornaby on Tees, Cleveland TS17 7BD. Tel. 01642 649004.

Regent's College, School of Psychotherapy & Counselling, Inner Circle, Regent's Park, London NW1 4NS. Tel. 020 7487 7406. Also for existential, psychodynamic counselling and psychotherapy, and others.

Guildford College of Further Education & Higher Education, Stoke Park, Guildford GU1 1EZ. Tel. 01483 448500. For Diploma in Integrative Counselling, Diploma in Humanistic Counselling, Teacher Training for Counsellors.

Birmingham Counselling Centre, 62 Lightwoods Hill, Bearwood, Smethwick B67 5EB. Tel. 0121 429 1758. For Certificate in Humanistic and Integrative Counselling, also Certificate in Therapeutic Counselling, Certificate in Counselling Skills, Introduction to Counselling, Advanced Certificate in Therapeutic Counselling.

Mary Parker (Training), 66 Brixton Water Lane, London SW2 1QB. Tel. 020 7274 6531. For Integrating (Kohut) psychodynamic and humanistic approaches.

University of East London. BAC Accred. Department of Psychology, Romford Way, Stratford, London E15 4LZ. Tel. 020 8590 7000 (ext. 4502).

Newham College of Further Education, East Ham Campus, High Street South, East Ham, London E6 4ER. Tel. 020 8257 4000. Fax 020 8257 4307.

HUMANISTIC

Metanoia Institute, 13 North Common Road, Ealing, London W5 2QB. Tel. 020 8579 2505. Fax 020 8566 4349.

Physis, 12 North Common Road, London W5 2QB. Tel. 020 8567 0388.

City Literary Institute, Stukeley Street, Drury Lane, London WC2B 5LJ. Tel. 020 7242 1584.

The Open Centre, 188 Old Street, London EC1V 9FR. Tel. 020 8549 9583.

Spectrum, 7 Endymion Road, London N4 1EE. Tel. 020 8341 2277. Fax 020 8340 0426. Also Gestalt and integrative psychotherapy.

University College of Ripon & York St. John, Lord Mayor's Walk, York YO3 7EX. Tel. 01904 616675. Fax 01904 616749.

Roehampton Institute London, Senate House, Roehampton Lane, London SW15 5PU. Tel. 020 8392 3611. Also dramatherapy, psychological counselling, play therapy, dance movement therapy, music therapy, etc.

Stockton Centre for Psychotherapy & Counselling, 77 Acklam Road, Thornaby on Tees, Cleveland TS17 7BD. Tel. 01642 649004.

Centre for Counselling & Psychotherapy Education, Beauchamp Lodge, 2 Warwick Crescent, London W2 6NE. Tel. 020 7266 3006.

GESTALT

The Gestalt Psychotherapy Training Institute, 2 Bedford Street, London Road, Bristol BA1 6AF. Tel. 01225 482135.

The Gestalt Centre, First Floor, 62 Paul Street, London EC2A 4NA. Tel. 020 7613 4480.

Manchester Gestalt Centre, 7 Norman Road, Rusholme, Manchester M14 5LF. Tel. 0161 257 2202.

University of Strathclyde, Jordanhill Campus, Southbrae Drive, Glasgow G13 1PP. Tel. 0141 950 3359.

Gestalt Training Institute, 51 Lothian Road, Edinburgh EH1 2DJ. Tel. and fax 0131 228 3841.

PSYCHOSYNTHESIS

The Institute of Psychosynthesis, 65A Watford Way, Hendon, London NW4 3AQ. Tel. 020 8202 4525.

The Psychosynthesis & Education Trust, 92–94 Tooley Street, London Bridge, London SE1 2TH. Tel. 020 7403 2100.

Psychosynthesis UK, 4 Offham Terrace, Lewes BN7 2QP. Tel. and fax 01273 473113.

PERSON-CENTRED

Norwich Centre for Personal and Professional Development, 7 Earlham Road, Norwich NR2 3RA. Tel. 01603 617709. For counselling skills.

University of East Anglia, Centre for Counselling Studies, University Counselling Service, Norwich NR4 7TJ. Tel. 01603 592651.

Lewisham College, Breakspear's Building, Lewisham Way, London SE4 1UT. Tel. 020 8692 0358 (ext. 3088). Fax 020 8692 6258.

Person-Centred Counselling Services, Paragon House, 48 Seymour Grove, Old Trafford, Manchester M16 0LN. Tel. 0161 877 9877.

International Institute for Counselling and Professional Development, 45a New Street, The Barbican, Plymouth PL1 2ND. Tel. 01752 250056.

Sherwood Psychotherapy Training Institute, Thiskney House, 2 St James Terrace, Nottingham NG1 6FW. Tel. 0115 924 3994.

COGNITIVE AND COGNITIVE-BEHAVIOURAL PSYCHOTHERAPY

University of Derby, Mickleover Campus, Western Avenue, Derby DE22 5GX. Tel. 01332 622222 (ext. 2014).

Maudsley Hospital, Psychological Treatment Unit, Denmark Hill, London SE5. Tel. 0171 919 2815.

Goldsmiths College, University of London, New Cross, London SE14 6NW. Tel. 020 7919 7171.

Integrated Psychotherapy Training Section (IPTS) of the Department of Psychiatry and Psychology of the United Medical Schools of Guy's and St Thomas's Hospitals. Address for further information and application forms: Mark Dunn, IPTS, Munro Clinic, Guy's Hospital, London SE1 9RT. Tel. 020 7955 2906. Fax 020 7955 2983.

Institute of Psychiatry, Department of Psychology, De Crespigny Park, London SE5 8AF. Tel. 020 7919 3242.

TRANSACTIONAL ANALYSIS

The Manchester Institute for Psychotherapy, Lifestream House, 454 Barlow Moor Road, Chorlton, Manchester M21 1BQ. Tel. 0161 862 9456.

Institute of Transactional Analysis, BM Box 4104, London WC1 3XX.

Thanet Centre for Therapeutic Studies (TCPS), 63 Victoria Road, Sutton Coldfield B72 1SN. Tel. 0121 354 4042. For Certificate/Diploma in Humanistic Counselling (Transactional Analysis Core approach).

Transactional Analysis Training in Birmingham & South Yorks, 54 Bennetthorpe, Doncaster DN2 6AD. Tel. 01302 761 915. For Introductory Courses (Certificate of Attendance). Rolling Programme leading to Preparation for Clinical TA Examination.

Yorkshire Training Centre, 27 Clare Road, Halifax HX1 2JP. Tel. 01422 366356. For Introductory TA course. Ongoing TA training.

Lancaster Therapy Centre, 49 Westbourne Road, Lancester LA1 5DX. Tel. 01524 39443.

FAMILY THERAPY

Institute of Family Therapy, Training Department, 24–32 Stephenson Way, London NW1 2HX. Tel. 020 7391 9150. Fax 020 7391 9169.

Prudence Skynner Family Therapy Clinic, Springfield University Hospital, 61 Glenburnie Road, London SW17 7DJ. Tel. 020 8682 6195.

The Association for Family Therapy, Chris Frederick, 12 Mabledon Close, Heald Green, Cheadle, Cheshire SK8 3DB. Tel. and fax 0161 493 9012.

Marlborough Family Service, 38 Marlborough Place, London, NW8 0PJ. Tel. 020 7624 8605. A learning video/computer pack called Family Therapy Basics is available.

COUPLE THERAPY

London Marriage Guidance Council, 76a New Cavendish Street, Harley Street, London W1M 7LB. Tel. 020 7637 1318.

Tavistock Marital Studies Institute, Tavistock Centre, 120 Belsize Lane, London NW3 5BA. Tel. 020 7435 7111 (ext. 2484).

Institute of Psychiatry, Maudsley Hospital, Couple Therapy Clinics, Denmark Hill, London SE5 8AZ. Tel. 020 7919 2371.

Crawley College, College Road, Crawley RH10 1NR. Tel. 01293 442345. For Certificate in Family Therapy (working with couples and families).

ART THERAPY

The Institute of Arts in Therapy and Education, Terpsichore, 70 Cranwich Road, London N16 5JD. Tel. 020 7704 2534.

Person-Centred Art Therapy Centre, 17 Cranbourne Gardens, London NW11 0HN. Tel. 020 8455 8570.

EXISTENTIAL

School of Psychotherapy & Counselling, Regent's College, Inner Circle, Regent's Park, London NW1 4NS. Tel. 020 7487 7406. Fax 020 7487 7446.

INTER-CULTURAL PSYCHOTHERAPY

NAFSIYAT. Inter-Cultural Therapy Centre, 278 Seven Sisters Road, Finsbury Park, London N4 2HY. Tel. 020 7263 4130. Fax 020 7561 1870.

PSYCHODRAMA

Northern School of Psychodrama, 2 Palatine Road, Withington, Manchester M20 3JA. Tel. 0161 427 3307.

Jesmond Centre for Psychodrama & Counselling, 94 St George's Terrace, Jesmond, Newcastle upon Tyne NE2 2DL. Tel. 0191 281 6243.

COUNSELLING SKILLS

Richmond Fellowship Training & Consultancy Services, 8 Addison Road, Kensington, London W14 8DL. Tel. 020 7603 6373. Also Post-traumatic stress counselling.

The Manor House Centre for Psychotherapy and Counselling, 80 East End Road, London N3 2SY. Tel. 020 8371 0180. Fax 01708 620858.

Counselling South West, PO Box 1848, Glastonbury BA6 9YG. Tel. 01458 834744. For Certificate in Counselling Skills. Also Certificate and Diploma in Therapeutic Counselling, Counselling Supervision, Diploma in Counselling Psychology.

Bristol University, Department for Continuing Education, 8–10 Berkeley Square, Clifton, Bristol BS8 1HH. Tel. 0117 928 7166. Many short courses. Also, Diploma/MSc in Counselling at Work and Diploma in Counselling in Primary Care.

Sandwell College, Department of Teacher Education & Counselling, Smethwick Campus, Crocketts Lane, Smethwick B66 3BU. Tel. 0121 556 6000. For Certificate in Counselling Skills, Introduction to Counselling, Certificate in Counselling Theory, Diploma in Counselling.

Solihull College, Student Counselling Service, Blossomfield Road, Solihull B91 1SB. Tel. 0121 678 7000. For Introduction to Counselling and Interpersonal Skills, Certificate in Counselling Skills (Coventry University), also Diploma in Person-centred Counselling (Warwick University).

Sutton Coldfield College, Lichfield Road, Sutton Coldfield B74 2NW. Tel. 0121 355 5671. Fax 0121 355 0799. For certificates in Basic Counselling Skills, Counselling, Counselling Skills, Counselling Theory. Diploma in Therapeutic Counselling. Diploma in Counselling.

Trowbridge College, School of Community Studies, College Road, Trowbridge BA14 0ES. Tel. 01225 766241. For Introduction to Counselling Skills, Combined Certificate in Counselling Skills and Therapeutic Counselling, Diploma in Counselling.

Barnsley College, Old Mill Lane Site, Church Street, Barnsley S70 2AX. Tel. 01226 730191 (ext. 340). Fax 01226 298514. For Introduction to Counselling Skills, Certificates in Counselling Skills, Counselling Theory. Diploma in Counselling.

Bradford & Ilkley Community College, School of Teaching & Community Studies, Great Horton Road, Bradford BD7 1AY. Tel. 01274 753118/753204. Fax 01274 753198. For RSA Counselling Skills in the Development of Learning. Diploma in Counselling and Human Relations.

Doncaster College, Faculty of Client Services, Waterdale, Doncaster DN1 3EX. Tel. 01302 553741. For Foundation Course in Counselling Skills, Certificates in Counselling Skills, Counselling Theory. Introduction to Counselling in the Workplace.

Harrogate College, Hornbeam Park, Hookstone Road, Harrogate HG2 8QT. Tel. 01423 879466.

Pembrokeshire College, Haverfordwest SA61 1SZ. For Introduction and Certificate in Counselling Skills and Diploma in Counselling. Tel. 01437 765247.

HUMAN SEXUALITY/PSYCHOSEXUAL

Albany Trust, 280 Balham High Road, London SW17 7AL. Tel. 020 8767 1827.

Relate. Head of Psychosexual Therapy, Relate, Herbert Gray College, Little Church Street, Rugby CV21 3AP. Tel. 01788 573241.

St George's Hospital Medical School (University of London), Human Sexuality Unit, Springfield Hospital, Glenburnie Road, London SW17 7DJ. Tel. 020 8682 6778.

London Marriage Guidance Council, 76a New Cavendish Street, Harley Street, London W1M 7LB. Tel. 020 7637 1318.

Institute of Family Therapy, 24–32 Stephenson Way, London NW1 2HX. Tel. 020 7391 9150. For family and couple therapy.

Institute of Psychiatry, Maudsley Hospital, Couple Therapy Clinics, Denmark Hill, London SE5 8AZ. Tel. 020 7919 2371.

The Whittington Hospital, School of Counselling and Psychotherapy, St Mary's Wing, Highgate Hill, London N19 5NF. Tel. 020 7288 3074.

Relationship and Sexual Problems Therapy. IPTS at Guy's Hospital, ALGBP-UK. PO Box 7534, London NW1 0ZA.

GROUP TRAINING

The Institute of Group Analysis, 1 Daleham Gardens, London NW3 5BY. Tel. 020 7431 2693. Fax 020 7431 7246. For group analytic psychotherapy.

Group Analysis North/Institute of Group Analysis, 78 Manchester Road, Swinton, Manchester M27 5FG. Tel. 0161 728 1633.

Association for Group & Individual Psychotherapy (AGIP), 1 Fairbridge Road, London N19 3EW. Tel. 020 7272 7013. Fax 020 7272 6945.

Groupwork Consultation & Training, Meridian House, Royal Hill, Greenwich, London SE10 8RT. Tel. 01705 750030.

Human Potential Research Group, School of Educational Studies, University of Surrey, Guildford GU2 5XH. Tel. 01483 300800. For group facilitation.

TRAINING IN SUPERVISION

International Institute for Counselling & Professional Development, 45a New Street, The Barbican, Plymouth PL1 2ND. Tel. 01752 250056. For Diploma in Supervision/Training/Professional Counselling/ School Counselling.

Centre for Counselling and Psychotherapy Education, Beauchamp Lodge, 2 Warwick Crescent, London W2 6NE. Tel. 020 7266 3006.

Manchester University, Centre for Educational Needs, Faculty of Education, Manchester M13 9PL. Tel. 0161 275 3307.

PERSONAL CONSTRUCT PSYCHOLOGY

David Winter, Psychology Department, Barnet Healthcare NHS Trust, Napsbury Hospital, Nr St Albans, Hertfordshire AL2 1AA. Tel. 0800 731 6859.

Counselling & Psychotherapy Services, Coudray House, Herriard, Basingstoke RG25 2PN. Foundation course in Personal Construct Psychology. Tel. 01256 381787.

STRESS MANAGEMENT

Centre for Stress Management, 156 Westcombe Hill, London SE3 7DH. Tel. 020 8293 4114. Fax 020 8293 1441.

Salford College, Wardley Campus, Mardale Avenue, Swinton, Manchester M27 3QP. Tel. 0161 886 5556.

Great Yarmouth College of Further Education, Great Yarmouth NR31 0ED. Tel. 01493 655261.

Rugby College of Further Education, Lower Hillmorton Road, Rugby CV21 3QS. Tel. 01788 338800. Fax 01788 338575.

BEREAVEMENT TRAINING

CRUSE, Cruse House, 126 Sheen Road, Richmond TW9 1UR. Tel. 020 8940 4818. Fax 020 8940 7638.

Gold Training and Counselling Services, 79 Ellis Road, Old Coulsdon CR5 1BP. Tel. 01737 553258. For Diploma in Bereavement Training.

Counselling Training Services at Keele University, 48 Sidmouth Avenue, Stafford ST17 0HF. Tel. 01785 664080. For Loss, Bereavement and Change. Introduction to Counselling, Counselling Skills.

University of Keele, Department of Applied Social Studies, Newcastle under Lyme ST5 5BG. Tel. 01782 621111 (ext. 8035). For Certificate in Bereavement Counselling. Certificate, Diploma, MA in Counselling. Diploma in Counselling in Primary Care.

The Compassionate Friends, c/o Gill Hodder, 60 Denmark Street, Bristol BS1 5DQ. Tel. 0117 929 2778.

TELEPHONE HELPLINE SKILLS TRAINING

Broadcasting Support Services, Union House, Shepherds Bush Green, Ealing, London W12 8UA. Tel. 020 8735 5042. Beginners and advanced skills. Stress management for telephone work.

AIDS, HIV; DISABILITY; CANCER; ALCOHOL/DRUGS

Central School of Counselling & Therapy, 80 Paul Street, London EC2A 4NE. Tel. 020 7613 3660. Fax 020 7739 6754. All of the above.
Cancer BACUP (British Association of Cancer United Patients), 3 Bath Place, Rivington Street, London EC2A 3JR. Tel. 020 7696 9003.
Cancer Research Campaign Psychological Medicine Group, Stanley House, Christie Hospital, NHS Trust, Wilmslow Road, Withington, Manchester M20 4BX. Tel. 0161 446 3681.

THE ELDERLY

Age Concern, Bath and N.E. Somerset, Mobile Counselling Services, 2 Hetling Court, Bath BA1 1SH. Tel. 01225 484510.

HYPNO-PSYCHOTHERAPY

British Association for Autogenic Training and Therapy, 6 Avenue Road, Malvern WR14 3AG. Tel. 01684 576657.
Centre Training School for Hypnotherapy and Psychotherapy, 145 Chapel Lane, Longton, Preston PR4 5NA. Tel. 01772 617663.
The National Register of Hypnotherapists and Psychotherapists, 12 Cross Street, Nelson BB9 7EN. Tel. 01282 699378.

JOURNALS

An address and telephone number is given for information about each journal. Many public libraries, colleges and university libraries should hold copies of these journals and others.

Counselling. The journal of the British Association for Counselling. Publishes varied and comprehensive material: counselling activities and concerns, articles, practice dilemmas, research, training resources, book reviews, classified advertisements, etc. Available free to members quarterly. Annual subscription for non-members is £31 per annum. Single issues are available for £8.50. An index by subject of articles since 1990 is available from BAC for £1. Photocopies of back articles are available for £2.50 per item. Apply to BAC, 1 Regent Place, Rugby, Warwickshire CV21 2PJ. Tel. (office) 01788 550899, (information) 01788 578328.

International Journal of Psychotherapy. The official journal of The European Association for Psychotherapy (EAP). The journal publishes articles which make connections or comparisons between different themes relevant to psychotherapy – for example, between psychotherapy and its social, scientific, political, cultural and religious contexts; between clinical practice and its wider setting; or any significant connections or comparisons that facilitate its development, differentiation and inclusiveness. Available from Carfax Publishing Ltd, c/o Taylor & Francis, Rankine Road, Basingstoke, Hampshire RG24 8PR. Fax 01256 330245. Published three times a year. Subscription rates £44.00 for individuals.

European Journal of Psychotherapy, Counselling and Health. A new journal (April 1998) intended to examine appropriate and inappropriate developments of European thinking world-wide. One of the journal's purposes is to address the fact that so many well-intentioned professionals – doctors, nurses or others – involved in activities supplementary to medicine, are providing various forms of individual and group therapy with little training, and sometimes with supervisors whose training is similarly limited. The attempt is towards a wide range of theoretical orientations. Available from Routledge Ltd, c/o Taylor & Francis, Rankine Road, Basingstoke, Hampshire RG24 8PR. Fax 01256 330245. Cost £30, individual rates.

Self & Society. A journal of Humanistic Psychology. Published by the Association for Humanistic Psychology in Britain (AHP(B)). *Self & Society* publishes articles in the field of humanistic psychology, particularly those concerning issues of personal development. Articles, reports, letters, book reviews, advertising, etc. Available from AHP(B), BM Box 3582, London WC1N 3XX. Tel. 0345 078506. Produced bi-monthly. Cost £30 (trainee member £23).

Counselling News. Available from 80 Paul Street, London EC2A 4NE. Tel. 020 7613 3666. Fax 020 7739 6706/6754. Cost £28. Published six times a year.

The Therapist. Journal of the European Therapy Studies Institute. Costs £45 to join ETSI (The European Therapy Studies Institute) and receive *The Therapist* (£40, by standing order). Back copies £8 per copy. Available from ETSI, Henry House, 189 Heene Road, Worthing, West Sussex BN11 4NN.

British Gestalt Journal. Publication of the Gestalt Psychotherapy Training Institute in the UK. Published twice a year. Articles, research, discussion papers, clinical reports, reviews of books and videos, letters and commentaries. Published material relates to the theory and practice of the Gestalt approach to psychotherapy and counselling, organisational consulting, education, professional and personal development and to other fields of application in medicine, the arts and social sciences. Costs £11 per copy; £22 per year, per volume (plus 10 per cent p.&p.). Address for all correspondence: British Gestalt Journal, PO Box 2994, London N5 1UG. Tel. 020 7359 3000.

British Journal of Psychotherapy. The journal is sponsored by a majority of the analytically oriented psychotherapy organisations. The Lincoln Clinic and Institute for Psychotherapy, The London Centre for Psychotherapy, The Guild of Psychotherapists, The Arbours Association, The Centre for Psychoanalytical Psychotherapy, The Institute for Psychotherapy and Counselling (WPF), The Association for Group and Individual Psychotherapy, The Severnside Institute for Psychotherapy, and the Centre for Attachment-based Psychoanalytic Psychotherapy. The emphasis is on clinically oriented papers which concern the practice of analytical psychotherapy, or that have theoretical implications, or which concern the application of psychotherapeutic practice and theory to institutions, society and other settings. Published quarterly. Available from Artesian Books, 18 Artesian Road, London W2 5AR. Tel. 020 7229 2855. Costs £27. For individuals.

Transformations. The newsletter of psychotherapists and counsellors for social responsibility, written to open up a range of social and professional issues to a wider readership. It aims to do this by bringing new perspectives to bear on old debates and by establishing new debates around old prejudices. Published by PCSR, 26 Eaton Rise, London W5 2ER, twice a year. Costs £25 (£15 trainees).

Sexual and Marital Therapy. Journal of the British Association for Sexual and Marital Therapy. *Sexual and Marital Therapy* is an international refereed journal for everyone professionally concerned with sexual and relationship function. Its readers include academics and researchers, clinicians, therapists and counsellors. The results of original research, subject reviews, accounts of therapeutic and counselling practice, case studies, short communications and book reviews all feature in the journal. Available from Hon. Secretary, British Association for Sexual and Marital Therapy, PO Box 13686, London SW20 9ZH. Email BASMT@BASMT.demon.co.uk Back numbers, offprints available. Four issues per year. Personal rate costs £106.

BASMT Bulletin. Members of the British Association for Sexual and Marital Therapy are sent a copy of the *Bulletin* twice yearly.

The Family Journal. The Official Journal of the International Association of Marriage and Family Counselors. Advances the theory, research and practice of counselling with couples and families from a family systems perspective. It is an American-based quarterly. Available from Sage Publications, 6 Bonhill Street, London EC2A 4PU. Introductory rate for individuals £39 for one year, four issues per year, one issue free; £62 for two years, two issues free. From 1999 access to this journal will also be electronically, see their website: www.sagepub.co.uk/elect.html

British Journal of Guidance & Counselling. The journal is concerned to promote development in the field by providing a forum for debate between academics, trainers and practitioners on topical and/or controversial issues relating to the theory and practice of guidance and counselling. Empirical studies are reported. Published four times a year. Cost £66. Back numbers and offprints. Available from Carfax Publishing Ltd., PO Box 25, Abingdon, Oxfordshire OX14 3UE. Tel. 01235 401000.

Illness, Crisis & Loss. New quarterly journal, exploring all aspects of grief, death and loss. Each issue covers new ideas, book reviews, peer-reviewed articles, psychosocial and ethical issues associated with life-threatening illnesses, traumatic human crises and grief and loss. Available from Sage Publications, 6 Bonhill Street, London EC2A 4PU. Tel. 020 7374 0645. Fax 020 7374 8741. Costs £33.

Dialogue. New journal for trainee counsellors and psychotherapists. Information on training, job opportunities, legal and financial issues, ethical debates, etc. Available from Dialogue Ltd, FREEPOST SEA 3961, Richmond TW10 7BR. Tel. and fax 020 8296 9127. Costs £18 for six issues.

Behavioural & Cognitive Psychotherapy. Quarterly journal published by Cambridge University Press. Aimed at disseminating research and information about the applications of behavioural and cognitive psychotherapies. Available from BABCP, PO Box 9, Accrington BB5 2GD. Tel. 01254 875277. Membership and journal £30 (direct debit) or £33 by cheque. Concessions £16.

The Journal of Analytical Psychology. Covers a broad spectrum of recent information related to Jungian psychology. Looks at clinical practice, theoretical contributions, research, current controversies in practice and theory, historical and cultural perspectives, and features an extensive review of books and journals by leading figures. Address: Blackwell Publishers, 108 Cowley Road, Oxford OX4 1JF. Tel. 01865 244083. Individual rates. £53.

Psychodynamic Counselling. Explores the relevance of psychodynamic ideas to different occupational settings. It emphasises setting and application, as well as theory and technique. Issues consist of editorial, articles, short papers and book reviews. Four issues per volume. Subscription rates (individual) £34. Published by Routledge.

The Counselling Psychologist. Journal of Counselling Psychology of the APA. Published six times a year. Topics of interest to counselling psychologists. Individuals £51. Available from Sage Publications, 6 Bonhill Street, London EC2A 4PU.

Journal for Specialists in Group Work. American based. Directed towards the interests of educators and counsellors concerned with productive implementation of group counselling and group processes in educational, industrial and community settings. Costs £31. Available from Sage, London.

Psychoanalytic Studies. A new journal primarily for people actively involved in the field of study and aims to provide a focus and outlet for academic and scholarly writings of this kind. Published by Carfax. Individual rate £44. Can be found on Home Page at http://www. carfax.co.uk/pst-ad.htm

DIRECTORIES

The Training in Counselling & Psychotherapy Directory. BAC. Available through libraries, training institutions and direct from BAC. A comprehensive listing of courses in the UK, by geographic area, from 'tasters' to PhD level and more advanced and specialised training for counsellors. Cost £9 (members), £9.50 (non-members). Tel. 01788 550899.

Counselling & Psychotherapy Resources Directory. BAC. For

counsellors/psychotherapists supervisors and trainers listed on a local area basis and trainers within four regions. £20 for members, £25 for non-members. The BAC will provide a photocopy of one area free of charge; £1 per area thereafter.

The British Confederation of Psychotherapists. 1998 Register of Psychotherapists. Containing the names of 1,200 psychotherapists under the headings 'practitioners trained to work with adults' and 'practitioners trained to work with children'. Available from The BCP, 37 Mapesbury Road, London NW2 4HJ. Tel. 020 8830 5173. Costs £20.

The National Register, The UKCP Directory of Member Organisations. Available from UKCP, 167–169 Great Portland Street, London W1N 5FB. Tel. 020 7436 3002. Costs £35.

ORGANISATIONS FOR MEMBERSHIP AND ACCREDITING

Association of Child Psychotherapists, 120 West Heath Road, London NW3 7TU. Tel. 020 8458 1609. A non-training organisation. The ACP accredits other training courses.

IPC. This is a professional psychotherapy membership of the Institute of Psychotherapy and Counselling. All members of IPC, both trainee and graduate, are subject to the Institute's Code of Ethics. The members of IPC can be registered as psychotherapists in the Psychoanalytical section of the UKCP through being a graduate of a training centre, such as the Westminster Pastoral Foundation. Address of IPC: Unit 607, The Chandlery, 50 Westminster Bridge Road, London SE1 7QY. Tel. 020 7721 7660.

AHPP. The Association of Humanistic Psychology Practitioners is a humanistic psychotherapy accrediting body recognised by the United Kingdom Council for Psychotherapy. AHPP membership is open to humanistic practitioners with a wide range of related disciplines. All members are required to adhere to the AHPP Codes of Ethics and Related Procedures. Membership provides a Directory of members and a bi-monthly journal. A therapy referral service is offered to members. Address: Box BCM AHPP, London WC1N 3XX. Tel. 0345 660326.

BAC. British Association for Counselling, founded in 1977. The BAC is the largest counselling organisation and counselling representative in this country. The Association has seven divisions representing work settings and special interest groups. There are autonomous local groups in different parts of the country which are affiliated to BAC.

A quarterly journal for members is provided. The BAC publishes a growing number of books and leaflets intended for the public and the profession. It participates in the development of National Vocational Qualifications, and responds to and promotes activities in the counselling arena.

There is an accreditation scheme for individual counsellors, trainers, counsellor training courses and supervisors. A course needs to complete a minimum of 400 hours of teaching to acquire accreditation. An individual needs to complete 450 hours of client work over three years. Acceptance of the Codes of Ethics and Practice and being subject to the Complaints Procedure is a condition of membership. Address: 1 Regent's Place, Rugby, CV21 2PJ. Tel. 01788 578328.

UKRC. United Kingdom Registered Independent Counsellor. Offered by The British Association for Counselling to counsellors who are already accredited by the BAC.

UKCP. The United Kingdom Council of Psychotherapy was formed in 1990 when delegates to the United Kingdom Standing Conference for Psychotherapy voted to form a voluntary Register of Psychotherapists. Meetings were held with Members of Parliament and the Department of Health. First moves were made towards forming a European Psychotherapy Association. In 1992–3 the UKCP became a Council and in 1994 co-operated with the Department of Health on a survey of registered psychotherapists.

The UKCP is the umbrella organisation for 78 member organisations, promoting and maintaining the profession of psychotherapy. The requirement for registration is through membership of a UKCP member organisation, or through training with a UKCP recognised training course.

There are 11 diverse psychotherapeutic approaches listed under sections of the UKCP, amongst which are Humanistic Integrative Psychotherapy, Analytical Psychology, Behavioural and Cognitive Psychotherapy, Experiential Constructivist Therapists, Hypno-Psychotherapy, Psychoanalytic and Psychodynamic Psychotherapy, and Psychoanalytically Based Therapy with Children sections. There are also Institutional Members and Special Members. Address: 167–169 Great Portland Street, London W1N 5FB. Tel. 020 7436 3002.

BCP. The British Confederation of Psychotherapists is an umbrella for member organisations. All the member organisations are psychoanalytic psychotherapy, analytical psychology or psychoanalytic in nature. Seven of the member organisations provide training in either psychoanalytic psychotherapy, analytical psychology (Jungian) or psychoanalysis.

Most of the member organisations require applicants to have a degree or qualification in the field of medicine, psychology, social work, or equivalent, and some experience in the field of mental health. All training courses are for a minimum period of four years and require candidates to undertake personal analysis or therapy with an approved analyst or therapist for a minimum of three times a week for the duration of training. Candidates are also required to have extensive supervised clinical experience with two approved supervisors and to attend seminars covering theory and technique. Address: The BCP, 37 Mapesbury Road, London NW2 4HJ. Tel. 020 8830 5173.

BAP. British Association of Psychotherapists. Founded in the 1940s. A professional body that trains and qualifies adult, adolescent and child analytic psychotherapists to a high level of competence. All trainees must be in individual psychotherapy with an approved training therapist for a minimum of three times a week; training patients must be seen three times weekly and the work with each patient is supervised weekly by a separate supervising therapist.

The Association specialises in individual analytic psychotherapy based on the original work of Freud and Jung and the development of their ideas by other clinicians such as Klein, Winnicott, Fairbairn and Fordham. There are very strong links with the Institute of Psycho-analysis and the Society of Analytical Psychology. The BAP provides an assessment and clinical service, and refers patients to their members. The Association is organised on a regional basis. There is a low-cost treatment scheme available. Address: 37 Mapesbury Road, London NW2 4HJ. Tel. 020 8452 9823.

IPN. Independent Practitioner Network. Founded in 1994 in response to dissatisfaction with the power and dominance of the large counselling and psychotherapy organisations. Association with IPN is open to anyone, but membership requires that a practitioner be a member of a cell group consisting of a minimum of five other practitioners who support each other's professional work. These member groups must have established ongoing links with two other similar groups. Co-supervision, self and peer assessment, accreditation and complaints procedures are dealt with democratically. Address: Sue Pot, 4 Macaulay Avenue, Hereford HR4 0JJ. Tel. 01432 357203.

AGIP. Association for Group and Individual Psychotherapy. Address: 1 Fairbridge Road, London N19 3EW. Tel. 020 7272 7013.

BABCP. British Association for Behavioural and Cognitive Psycho-therapies. Membership includes a quarterly academic journal

Behavioural & Cognitive Psychotherapy. A newsletter, information regarding regional and special interest groups and automatic membership of the European Association of Behavioural and Cognitive Therapies (EABCT) facilitate the formation of geographical and interest groups in order to provide a local and special interest service to members.

Accreditation as a psychotherapist for registration with the Behavioural & Cognitive Psychotherapy Section of the UKCP is available to members who fulfil their criteria. Current subscriptions: £33, concessions at £16. Address: PO Box 9, Accrington, Lancashire BB5 2GD. Tel. 01254 875277.

IGA. The Institute of Group Analysis. Provides clinical training in group analytic psychotherapy. Based on the methods of S.H. Foulkes, it combines psychoanalytic insights with an understanding of social and interpersonal factors. It also draws on a range of contemporary approaches: systems theory, developmental psychology and social psychology. Offers training, seminars, clinical referral service, organisational consultancy service, scientific programmes, experiential and seminar groups. Member of UKCP, also has numerous European and International affiliations. Address: 1 Daleham Gardens, London NW3 5BY. Tel. 020 7431 2693. Email iga@igaLondon.org.uk

LCP. London Centre for Psychotherapy. A professional association for about two hundred practising psychotherapists, it runs a membership course and holds public events and professional activities. Member of UKCP and BCP. Address: 32 Leighton Road, London NW5 2QE. Tel. 020 7482 2002/2282.

BPS. The British Psychological Society was founded in 1901. It is both a learned society and a professional association which has maintained a Register of Chartered Psychologists since 1987. The BPS has a clear Code of Ethics. Membership is restricted to university graduates whose main subject is psychology. Thousands who graduate qualify for membership, but only a very small number develop a career as psychologists, and it is they who form the membership of the Society. There are approximately 8,000 chartered psychologists.

The BPS has six divisions: Educational and Child, Clinical, Occupational, Criminological and Legal, Counselling Psychology and the Scottish Division of Educational and Child Psychology. Membership of a division confers chartered status, and is proof that a recognised training has been completed and specialist knowledge in that area has been tested by examination. *The Psychologist* is the BPS members' journal. A *Directory of Chartered Psychologists* is published and is available from public libraries or from the BPS direct. Address: BPS, St Andrews House, 48 Princess Road East, Leicester LE1 7DR. Tel. 0116 254 9568.

AFT. The Association for Family Therapy and Systemic Practice in the UK. This is a national association with the aims of promoting the scientific study, practice, research and teaching of family therapy. The Association has regions and branches nation-wide which bring together people from all professional disciplines who are concerned with the care or treatment of families. Many branches offer a varied programme of workshops and courses for practitioners, including non-members, at different levels of interest and experience. It publishes *Journal of Family Therapy*, and a news magazine of family therapy and systemic practice, *Context*. Fee for joining AFT (which includes the journal and magazine), £45. Address: Administrator, 12 Mabledon Close, Heald Greeen, Cheadle, Cheshire SK8 3DB. Tel. 0161 493 9012.

EAP. The European Association for Psychotherapy. Formed in 1990. It is supported by the World Council for Psychotherapy. The EAP represents about 180 organisations from 28 European countries, with more than 50,000 psychotherapists. Membership is open to organisations, umbrella associations and individual psychotherapists. The EAP has acquired a European Certificate that will be the basis of mutual recognition of psychotherapists in Europe. The principles of the EAP, and of the official journal, *International Journal of Psychotherapy*, are laid down in the EAP's Strasbourg Declaration. This Association is concerned with the wider debate about the future of psychotherapy within the European psychotherapy profession and its relations world-wide. Address: Prof. Dr Alfred Pritz, Rosenbursenstrasse 8/3/7. A-1010 Vienna, Austria. Tel. +43 1 513 17 29.

Association for Lesbian, Gay and Bisexual Psychologies. Membership is open to heterosexual as well as homosexual and bisexual individuals with an interest in psychology and counselling. Address: ALGBP-UK, PO Box 7534, London NW1 0ZA.

British Association for Sexual and Marital Therapy (BASMT). Its members have opted to change the title to 'Sexual and Relationship Therapy' from the year 2000. Publishes a bulletin twice yearly, and its official journal four times a year. Holds conferences. Has a code of ethics and practice and a complaints procedure. Address: PO Box 13686, London SW20 9ZH. Email info@basmt.org.uk

Association of Accredited Psychospiritual Psychotherapists. Accrediting body. Contact Kathie Hilliard, 21 Silverston Way, Stanmore, Middlesex HA7 4HS. Tel. 020 8954 2504.

Centre for Transpersonal Psychology. An accrediting organisation and member of the UKCP. Address: 86A Marylebone High Street, London W1M 3DE. Tel. 020 7935 7350.

British Psychodrama Association, Heather Cottage, Rosneath, Helensburgh, Argyll Bute G84 0RF. Tel. 01436 831838.

AWARDING BODIES THAT VALIDATE COURSES

Associated Examining Board, Stag Hill House, Guildford, Surrey. Tel. 01483 506506.

Association for Rational Emotive Behavioural Therapy, 49 Wood Lane, Harbourne, Birmingham B17 9AY. Tel. 0121 427 7292.

British Psychological Society, St Andrews House, 48 Princess Road East, Leicester LE1 7DR. Tel. 0116 254 9568.

British Accreditation Council, Suite 401, 27 Marylebone Road, London NW1 5JS. Tel. 020 7487 4643.

Counselling & Psychotherapy Central Awarding Body. Tel. 01458 835333.

City & Guilds of London Institute, 1 Giltspur Street, London EC1A 9DD. Tel. 020 7294 2468.

Northern Examinations & Assessment Board, Devas Street, Manchester M15 6EX. Tel. 0161 953 1180.

Royal Society of Arts, Progress House, Westwood Way, Coventry CV4 8JQ. Tel. 024 7647 0033.

The Scottish Qualifications Authority, Ironmills Road, Dalkeith, Midlothian EH22 1LE. Tel. 0131 663 6601.

Welsh Joint Education Committee, 245 Western Avenue, Cardiff CF5 2YX. Tel. 029 2026 5000.

BOOKSHOPS THAT SPECIALISE IN COUNSELLING AND PSYCHOTHERAPY

Compendium Bookshop, 234 Camden High Street, London NW1 8QS. Tel. 020 7485 8944.

H. Karnac Books Ltd, 58 Gloucester Road, London SW7 4QY. Tel. 020 7584 3303. Also at 118 Finchley Road, London NW3 5HT. Tel. 020 7431 1075.

Rathbone Books, 76 Haverstock Hill, London NW3 2BE. Tel. 020 7267 2848.

Anglo-American Book Company, Crown Buildings, Bancyfelin, Carmarthen SA33 5ND. Tel. 01267 211880. www.anglo-american. co.uk

GLOSSARY

CATHARSIS

A releasing of tension, anxiety and other emotions through expression.

CONJOINT THERAPY

Two therapists working with a couple.

COUNTERTRANSFERENCE

These are all the feelings, thoughts, attitudes, beliefs and fantasies that the therapist has for the client. They are important to therapeutic work. They may be projections from the client that the therapist feels. They may be the therapist's own difficult feelings towards the client. They are worked through in supervision so that they can aid the therapeutic process when understood.

DYADIC RELATIONSHIP

A relationship of two people.

ENMESHMENT

Where relationships are so close that people cannot tell the difference between their own feelings and those of the person they are enmeshed with. Differences are not easily tolerated or are mistrusted and discouraged.

EXPERIENTIAL LEARNING

A form of heightened experience in learning. To learn by having an immediate and felt experience. In many counselling and some psychotherapy training courses, experiential learning is carried out in a group. The group members conduct the session themselves and have the opportunity to practise the skills and interventions with each other that they have been learning on the course.

FANTASY

An unconscious image that Melanie Klein described, and a term referred to frequently in couple therapy. The couple may be seen as living a shared fantasy in the form of an unspoken but feared catastrophe. Both partners act as if it were really going to happen.

GROUP DYNAMICS

The process that takes place within the group, and the changes that develop the group, are the dynamics. It is a process that emphasises movement. In psychodynamic therapy the dynamic refers to the unconscious processes that take place between people.

INDIVIDUATE

According to Jung, it is the process of becoming a separate person, an individual. It is the realisation that one is oneself. To do this, the person has to know that they are different from others in the ways that they feel, think, speak or behave. If someone tries to please others by being and doing what they believe others want they have not individuated.

NEURO-LINGUISTIC PROGRAMMING

Neuro-linguistic programming (NLP) was developed in the mid-1970s. The name reflects the synthesis of the fields that were integrated to form NLP: 'neuro' from neurology (how the brain processes the five senses); 'linguistic' (how thinking is structured by language); 'programming' – from cybernetics and mathematics (how behaviour can be structured and sequenced for learning). The methodology is on replicating particular behaviours, called modelling. Used particularly in business and in other areas.

NEUTRAL APPROACH

In psychodynamic therapy the therapist maintains a stance that fosters the transference process so that the client has the chance to work through his transferential problems. The therapist intends to be neither withholding nor indulgent. Neutral refers to the middle ground, not to indifference.

OFF-LOADING

The client ventilates his feelings to the therapist. If an individual can express the feelings as well as the thoughts (off-load), he is likely to feel lighter, as if he has unburdened himself.

PHENOMENOLOGY

An individual's relationship to events. How the individual perceives, experiences and reacts to events. The therapist observes the client's phenomenology to help her understand the client.

PIRKE AVOT

'The Sayings of the Fathers'. A tractate of the Mishnah (earliest part of Jewish law known as the Talmud), dealing with ethical teachings and sayings in praise of the study of the law.

PROCESS

The 'process' in therapy is that which takes place over time in the therapeutic alliance, or working relationship. The changes and transformations that happen. The slow evolutionary development that make a difference to the client's life.

PSYCHIC PAIN

This is emotional wounding or injury that the client has suffered from childhood. The term differentiates it from physical pain.

TRANSFERENCE

The client or patient experiences the therapist in a way that he experienced aspects of one or both of his parents. He may also experience the therapist as another significant person from his early childhood: a grandparent, sibling or teacher, for example. Transference refers to the feelings, thoughts, perceptions, fantasies and behaviour of the client towards the therapist. The transference can be negative or positive. With the therapist's help, the client has the opportunity to work on those reactions that belong to his past.

UNCONDITIONAL POSITIVE REGARD

The therapist must relate positively and warmly to the client without any preconceptions, assumptions or judgements being made. Not to attach any conditions to relating to the other person – the conditions that many people felt in their childhood (e.g. 'I will only love you if you do/behave/are . . . the way I want you to be').

APPENDIX 1

SAMPLE CONTRACT BETWEEN
THERAPIST AND CLIENT

AGREEMENT BETWEEN (client's name) ....

(address and phone number) ....

....

and (therapist's name and qualifications) ....

The process of therapy is to help us make sense of our inner world and our interaction with the world around us. At times this will involve exploring difficult and painful issues. Taking care of basic practical details at the beginning can help us create a structure and a safe place where we can work therapeutically.

The following points will help to outline the therapeutic work:

Sessions are usually weekly on a given day and time, and last for 50 minutes.

Your day is .... and your time is ....

Cancellations. If for any reason you are unable to attend a session, and I am available, you will be charged for that session. This includes days off for sickness, and holidays, apart from the ones agreed between us (8 weeks per year). I would ask you to advise me of any intended absences as much in advance as possible.

Payment. Is made at the beginning of the session.

Confidentiality. To create and maintain safety and privacy within the therapeutic relationship, confidentiality is essential. To fulfil my professional commitment, it is necessary for me to monitor and evaluate my work with clients. This involves regular consultancy with another professional where my work is discussed, whilst protecting your identity. I do not disclose any details of my work to any other outside agencies. The exception to this would be if a client was in danger of harming her/himself or others, or seemed unable to take responsibility for her/his actions. In this situation I would always attempt to get the client's agreement first.

Commitment and endings. The process of therapy can sometimes feel slow moving and may need a particular commitment from you to stay with it at these times. The length of time in therapy varies for each person and this is decided and reviewed between us. Ending therapy is an important part of the process and adequate time needs to be allowed for it.

The therapist is (an accredited member of . . . .) and abides by their code of ethics and practice.

(Both client and therapist sign and date the Agreement. Each keeps a copy.)

APPENDIX 2

SAMPLE CONTRACT BETWEEN SUPERVISOR AND SUPERVISEE

Agreement between . . . .

(Supervisee) . . . .

Address . . . .

Telephone number . . . .

And (supervisor's name and qualifications) . . . .

. . . .

. . . .

. . . .

Establishing a clear supervision contract at the start is a good way to ensure that the expectations and needs of both supervisor and supervisee are met. It is suggested that we review from time to time as the relationship and the nature of the work changes.

The following points will help to clarify some of these expectations and needs.

Duration of supervision. The session is 50 minutes unless otherwise agreed.

Regularity of sessions ....

Fees £ .... per session, payable at the beginning of the session.

Cancellations. If for any reason you are unable to attend a session, and I am available, you will be charged for that session. This includes holidays other than those agreed between us for Xmas, Easter and Summer. I will, however, try to rearrange a session if I have the space to do that. I would ask you to advise me of any intended absences as much in advance as possible.

Confidentiality. I abide by the BAC code of ethics in protecting the confidentiality of your clients. I have regular consultation to monitor my own professional standards. I would discuss with you what breach of confidentiality would be relevant if I thought that a client was unable to take responsibility for their actions and was in danger of harming themselves, you or others. I would also discuss any potential breach of confidentiality or unethical practice if I believed that a client was being harmed, and my evaluation of the situation was not accepted.

Accountability. I offer a professional, supportive consultancy. The supervisee is ultimately accountable to their clients.

Supervision management: record keeping, preparation for supervision, functions of supervision, taping, etc., to be discussed in the assessment session.

I have read and understand the above, and agree to work with the supervisor.

.... date ....

APPENDIX 3

Questions to understand why you want to train

Why do you want to be a counsellor or psychotherapist?:

- You may be in a job where you feel that counselling skills would enhance your work.
- It may be that you have had some counselling or psychotherapy yourself, and found the experience so valuable, or the therapist or counsellor so helpful, that you want to do the same for someone else.
- You may be the kind of person to whom others are always bringing their problems.
- You believe that a training would offer you discipline and boundaries, as well as theory and structure.
- You may like helping or caring for others and are interested in their stories.
- You may want to find out more about yourself.
- You are fascinated by human behaviour.
- It may be that you want to train for a different career, and consider that you would make a good counsellor or psychotherapist.
- You may not recognise your own needs, vicariously helping others who are needy.

What appeals to you about therapy work?
What other reasons might there be?

How do you learn?

Are you anxious about asking questions? Explore where this comes from.

In what way and in which circumstances do you learn best:

- Being shown
- Being told
- Doing it yourself
- Feeling safe to ask and make mistakes
- With some humour or lightness
- Changes of presentation that are creative and stimulating
- Through association
- Taking in and digesting over time
- Through repetition or practice
- Through experiences
- Through an empathic relationship
- With support and encouragement from others
- Feeling relaxed and open
- Watching others
- Speaking about it to others.

Questions about the course

What is the selection criterion?
Is the course accredited? And by whom?
What is the tutorial structure?
Is there support and guidance given about essay writing?
Is the setting conducive to learning?
What are the aims and objectives of the course?
What are you expected to learn and how will the material be taught?
What will you be equipped to do at the end of the training?
What is the theoretical approach?
What are the different levels of training?
What are the procedures for paying fees? Is there a contract to pay?
Will fees will be increased during the training?
What do the fees cover and what do they not cover?
What is the balance of theory, reading, writing, skills practice, discussion and reflection?
What period of time is given for each component?.
How many people are accepted on the course? – and whether this changes?

Are there are any other changes that could occur?

What are the roles and expectations of the tutors, supervisors and any other educative providers?

What supervision and other support is provided?

What is not provided?

Is there an experiential group?

What support is offered for trainees in the group?

Does the course have its own list of practitioners to choose from?

How frequently will you be required to be in therapy?

Is there a personal development element in the training?

Are there extra weekends or days that are mandatory?

Is there a library?

What is the responsibility of the trainees?

What is the responsibility of the course organisers?

How are assessments conducted?

What is the procedure for continuing on to the next level of training?

What is the procedure for trainee placements – does the trainee have to find their own clients?

Are previous trainees willing to be contacted by prospective trainees?

Do trainees evaluate the course, and if so, are the changes put into effect?

What questions does the potential trainee have?

Questions for self-reflection before applying for a course

Do you enjoy studying?

What are your anxieties and expectations about going on a course?

How do you feel about writing essays?

How do you feel about sharing personal feelings in a group?

Are you anxious in large groups, small groups, or both?

Do you dominate, shrink or behave in particular ways in groups?

Can you manage your time constructively, for studying and other parts of your life?

Are you able to accept and make use of others' constructive criticisms?

Can you give constructive criticism to others?

Can you give and accept support from others?

INDEX

accreditation 141; Association of Humanistic Psychology Practitioners 145–46; British Association for Behavioural and Cognitive Psychotherapies 144–46; British Association for Counselling 146–50; list of organisations for 218–23

Adler, Alfred, individual psychology 42–3

'adult, the', ego state 62

advertising, private practice 196

advice, danger of giving 19

age, personal qualities of therapists 83

Age Concern 186; training centre 213

aggression, young children 44

AHPP see Association of Humanistic Psychology Practitioners

AIDS 13; counselling/therapy, list of training centres 213

alcohol dependency counselling/ therapy, training centre 213

analysands 16

analytical psychology 41–2

anger, therapist dealing with 88–9

anti-Semitism 38

anxieties, holding of 88

archaic images, Jung on 41

archetypes, Jung's theory of 41–2, 43

art therapy, list of training centres 209

Assagioli, Roberto, psychosynthesis 57

assertiveness, and intercultural therapy 175

assertiveness training 65; feminist movement 81

assessment: for entry to certificate course 111–12; progress during training 120; skills of 115–16, see also supervision

Associated Examining Board 140

Association of Accredited Psychospiritual Psychotherapists 222

Association of Child Psychotherapists 218

Association of Child Research 44

Association for Counselling at Work (ACW) 185

Association for Family Therapy and Systemic Practice in UK (AFT) 168, 222

Association for Group and Individual Psychotherapy (AGIP) 220

Association of Humanistic Psychology Practitioners (AHPP) 145–46, 218

Association for Lesbian, Gay and Bisexual Psychologies 222

Association for Pastoral Care and Counselling (PCC) 185

Association for Student Counselling (ASC) 185

awarding bodies, list of 223

awareness, and Gestalt therapy 57

BABCP see British Association for